A GLIMPSE OF HEAVEN

CATHOLIC CHURCHES OF ENGLAND AND WALES

A GLIMPSE OF HEAVEN

CATHOLIC CHURCHES
OF ENGLAND AND WALES

CHRISTOPHER MARTIN
PHOTOGRAPHS BY ALEX RAMSAY

CATHOLIC BISHOPS' CONFERENCE
OF ENGLAND AND WALES

ENGLISH HERITAGE

First published in 2006 by English Heritage, Isambard House, Kemble Drive, Swindon SN2 2GZ
www.english-heritage.org.uk

10 9 8 7 6 5 4 3 2 1

English Heritage is the Government's statutory adviser on all aspects of the historic environment.

ISBN-10: 1 85074 970 1
ISBN-13: 978 185074 970 7
Product code: 51083

British Library Cataloguing in Publication Data
A CIP catalogue record for this book is available from the British Library.

**This book is a collaboration between the Patrimony Committee of the Catholic Bishops'
Conference of England and Wales and English Heritage. The Patrimony Committee would like to
thank The Scorpion Trust, The Oakmoor Trust, The Stanley Foundation and Mr and Mrs John
McDonnell for their generous support, which enabled the commissioning of Alex Ramsay's
outstanding photographs.**

Concept by Sophie Andreae
Brought to press by Adèle Campbell
Designed by Simon Borrough
Indexed by Susan Vaughan
Printed in Singapore by Craft Print

Excerpt from *An Arundel Tomb* from *Collected Poems* by Philip Larkin. Copyright © 1988, 2003 by the Estate of
Philip Larkin. Reprinted by permission of Farrar, Straus and Giroux, LLC, and by permission of Faber and
Faber Ltd in the UK.

Frontispiece: Medieval Virgin and Child: A W N Pugin's gift to St Chad's Cathedral, Birmingham.

Contents

Author's Acknowledgements

Last year Alex Ramsay and I started on our two separate odysseys to research and record some of the best Catholic churches in England and Wales. We had little idea of the richness of what we would see or the generous amount of time that would be given to us by the people for whose help we asked. Apart from wanting to talk to someone who knew about each church, appointments were necessary as well as desirable. Many churches are locked up for most of the time. In some cases strong-minded ladies, fearing that Father would be subjected to time-wasting nonsense, put up resistance; 'No man cometh unto Father but by me' said one daunting notice on the desk of a guardian secretary. One priest said no, he didn't have time to talk to us and would we make absolutely sure we turned out the lights when we left? But overwhelmingly, people saw the point of the project and were anxious to share their knowledge and enthusiasm. The journey taken by myself and Felicity my wife, who assisted me throughout with planning and research and through whose Catholic eyes I as an Anglican was helped to see much I might have missed, was a long one. It was of human as well as architectural interest. Priests, deacons, gardeners, caretakers, monks, nuns, sacristans, two Lords, several laymen and a lay brother, dedicated local historians, a bishop and two abbots showed us around churches, cathedrals and monasteries. One or two priests, I think, were suspicious that the 'heritage' aspect of their church, given too much publicity, would inhibit their ability to do what they liked with their own churches. Their principal mission was religious not conservationist and they did not want to be prevented from sticking up posters announcing the next parish pilgrimage to Lourdes over the pulpit when they wanted to. Nonetheless they extended their help. Some priests were awesomely knowledgeable and enthusiastic about the history and architecture of their churches and nearly all were patient and generous with their time. They are too numerous to name but to them all we are very grateful. We are also grateful to the local historians and authors of all the church and cathedral guides which I have ruthlessly plundered. There were, however, nothing like enough of them. Fabulous buildings – some with a Grade I listing – offer little or nothing to the visitor to help explain their particular history, their architecture and their often amazing contents. It is easy to visit many of these places and to miss an unacknowledged masterpiece of an altar, reredos, window, screen, carving or painting.

I am also grateful to all those true experts on the subject who helped. Particularly I would mention Abbot Geoffrey Scott of Douai who cast a knowledgeable and generous eye over the text as did Michael Hodgetts whose knowledge of Catholic history, particularly in the English midlands, is legendary. Also Kenneth Powell, the writer and authority on all things architectural, and Peter Howell who has written about Catholic churches with insight, knowledge and humour. No one could undertake a book like this without constant reference to Denis Evinson's *Catholic Churches of London*, an incomparable guide, and Bryan Little's *Catholic Churches Since 1623* – a magisterial survey of the subject up to the early 1960s.

Lastly my great thanks for much good advice from Sarah Brown, Elain Harwood and others at English Heritage as well as Andrew Derrick, formerly of English Heritage, who not only endeavoured to steer me away from error but supplied much priceless information, Tricia Brooking whose firm grasp of geography and planning laid an indispensable foundation for our journeys and whose sharp eye and infinite capacity for taking pains in the revision, checking and production of the final text was invaluable, to the Bishops' Conference and all the Secretaries of the Diocesan Historic Churches Committees for their support and to Bishop Thomas McMahon, Chairman of the Patrimony Committee. Lastly I am more than grateful to Sophie Andreae, Vice-Chairman of the Patrimony Committee, who devised, encouraged and, with unwilting strength of purpose, saw the project through.

Preface

The Reformation that convulsed England in the reign of King Henry VIII appropriated for Protestantism the ancient churches of England and Wales. In the reign of Henry's daughter Elizabeth (1558-1603), in which the Church of England became irrevocably established, England's Catholics faced stark choices. They could conform, participating in the new reformed liturgy that took place in their old parish church made unfamiliar by the removal of traditional furnishings and images, or face crippling financial penalties and even imprisonment. Many Catholics continued to observe the Catholic Mass in clandestine services in private homes. Only in 1791 did Catholic worship and church building become legal once more. Notwithstanding, churches remained modest and unassuming for many years to come. Only in the relative seclusion of the private estates of the wealthy did Catholic devotion find serious architectural expression.

From the 1840s onwards, the situation was transformed. The Catholic populations of England and Wales grew dramatically and increasing confidence and growing prosperity encouraged church building on an ambitious scale. The restoration of the Episcopal hierarchy in 1850 was an important watershed. Even so, the funds to pay for new churches were amassed in the face of great hardship, many poor worshippers contributing pennies they could ill afford. Some of their new buildings would surpass those of the Established Church for the grace of their architecture and splendour of their furnishings and decoration, captured here in Alex Ramsay's glorious photographs. Their sheer variety will come as a surprise to many.

Nonetheless, Catholic churches remain under-valued. Of over 3,000 churches and chapels, only 625 – just 18% – are 'listed'. English Heritage's recent work in partnership with Catholic dioceses has demonstrated that many more deserve recognition for their contribution to our historic environment, and thus ought to benefit from public funding and tax relief towards the cost of their repair and restoration. In the 21st century these churches face new challenges as, in common with many other denominations, the Catholic Church in England and Wales is experiencing diminishing and ageing congregations and declining clergy numbers. Despite these difficulties, author Christopher Martin has found Catholic clergy and congregations to be in remarkably good heart, continuing to cherish the buildings they have inherited from their parents and grandparents and holding them in trust for their children and grandchildren. His appreciative prose will bring to life the architectural, historical and human stories behind these wonderful structures for readers far beyond the Catholic community itself. English Heritage is delighted to be joining the Catholic Church in publishing this celebration of over one hundred of its finest buildings.

Sir Neil Cossons.
Chairman, English Heritage

Foreword

I have always been susceptible to the beauty of art and architecture. Particularly I suppose, but by no means exclusively, by the architecture of sacred spaces. However, I do not consider myself an architectural expert which is why this book, intended for the non specialist reader, is such a revelation. Its aim is to bring both to Catholics and to a wider public some indication of the richness and variety of Catholic churches in England and Wales. Many of our historic churches and chapels are not as well known as they should be, even amongst Catholics.

The Catholic heritage in this country is in many ways a hidden heritage, under-sung and under-appreciated. I am therefore enormously grateful to Bishop Thomas McMahon of Brentwood and the Patrimony Committee of the Bishops' Conference of England and Wales for embarking on this project and for bringing together the team that has made this book happen and for involving English Heritage as publishers. Many of the churches illustrated in this book have not been professionally photographed before. I would particularly like to express my gratitude to The Scorpion Trust, The Oakmoor Trust, The Stanley Foundation and to John and Susan MacDonnell for their very generous sponsorship of Alex Ramsay's superb photography. I would like also to thank Christopher Martin for his immense hard work on the text and Sophie Andreae for managing the project from its inception.

My own love of architecture began when I was a teenager and at school in Bath. I was captivated by Bath stone – its translucent and rather vulnerable quality – and by the perfect contours of the Royal Crescent, and the grandeur of the Roman Baths. It was not just the elegance of the spaces, forms and significant details created by the architect which intrigued and excited me, it was the material that made this possible – the stone, iron, wood and slate; as well as the elements against which these forms were juxtaposed – earth, sky and water.

Then aged 19 and in Rome, the first time I walked up the Via della Conciliazione and was almost literally embraced by Bernini's Colonnade, before emerging into the magnificence of Bramante, Michelangelo with the great front of St. Peter's towering above me, I experienced my first real sense of being surrounded by remarkable and abundant genius. I would have to say that if Rome cannot move you to admire the imagination, the ambition, the inspiration of architectural creativity then quite possibly nothing can. Now, at Westminster, in contrast to the classical splendours of Rome, I can rejoice in the serene beauty of Bentley's Cathedral. As the architect Norman Shaw said, Westminster Cathedral is 'beyond all doubt the finest church that has been built for centuries. Superb in its scale and character and full of the most devouring interest, it is impossible to over-rate the magnificence of the design'.

If we believe that God created the world then architecture must be one path by which we discover Truth, Goodness – and yes, why not, God Himself. Spaces are as important as buildings so architecture has its own particular and very important part to play in creating space for meeting, a space for humanity, a space for the sacred. Architecture has a noble purpose: which is about meeting and community, about our humanity, and in some circumstances about raising the human heart and mind to the Creator of all things, Who is God. I believe that good architecture can be a bridge to religious experience in its search to uncover natural beauty and truth.

This book looks at the history of Catholic church building in England and Wales since the Reformation. It tells some extraordinary stories about the people involved in re-establishing the Catholic tradition on these shores and their architectural achievements following years of persecution. It is also a testimony to the renewed interest and sense of pride in its heritage which the Catholic community has developed in recent years. It is vital for our sense of identity that buildings such as those illustrated in this book be carefully and competently managed. I am happy that through the work of the diocesan Historic Churches Committees within the Ecclesiastical Exemption we can publicly display our determination to accomplish this. History apart, these buildings are first and foremost places of prayer and of reflection in this busy world. Again, I warmly commend this fine book.

His Eminence Cardinal Cormac Murphy-O'Connor

Introduction

For over two hundred years, from the accession of Queen Elizabeth I in 1558 to 1791, Catholic worship in Britain was illegal. The building of Catholic churches was also illegal and, apart from a few years under James II, Catholics who practised their faith faced legal sanctions. In the 17th century they might suffer torture and death. They also faced – and would continue to face – the hostility of the mob. Two hundred years of repression reduced the Catholic population to a few thousand but it still hung on. Parts of the north had active congregations, other parts of the country had no Catholics at all. What happened after the Catholic Relief Act of 1791 was extraordinary. The great revival that followed, slowly at first then as a torrent of conversions and expansion, was a phenomenon of the age. It brought with it a huge programme of church building – in the villages, in the expanding industrial cities and later in the suburbs – to accommodate the old Catholic families, those who converted and the thousands of immigrants, mostly Catholic Irish, who poured into the cities of England during the 19th century. Many were unremarkable as architecture but served, and continue to serve, their communities. But many were splendid and the best were magnificent. They equalled, and sometimes surpassed, anything being built in their time. In their ambition they echoed the 15th-century Pope Nicholas V: 'But if the authority of the Holy See were visibly displayed in majestic buildings…seemingly planted by the hand of God himself, belief would grow and strengthen like a tradition from one generation to another, and all the world would accept it'. Over the years many Roman Catholics have taken the point. In 1910 Amy Elizabeth Imrie, a nun who was heiress to the White Star shipping line, gave a church designed to bring the majesty of Rome to a desperately poor neighbourhood of Liverpool. She furnished St Mary of the Angels sumptuously, with rich Italian furnishings and artefacts as well as glittering stained glass. Like many such churches given by pious benefactors, it would give the impoverished working man and his family 'a glimpse of heaven'.

Our Catholic churches are not only structures of different quality and architectural style but buildings that reflect the politics and drama of their times. They tell us about their architects and patrons, the priests and princes of the church as well as the people who worshipped in them. It is a remarkable and, oddly, unknown story. This book attempts to bring a too-often ignored, misunderstood and sometimes threatened part of our architectural history to a wider, and not exclusively Catholic, audience.

Catholic churches are a part of the 'heritage' that until quite recently was little known and mostly disregarded. Many people thought of them as 'Victorian', and the term was not meant as a compliment. The Catholic architectural heritage is not, of course, all Victorian. It includes all those medieval churches, abbeys and cathedrals that were lost to it at the Reformation. It includes distinguished buildings of the 18th century, erected when intolerance of Catholics was beginning to weaken. And much later, in the 20th century, Catholics, like Anglicans, adopted the styles, materials and technologies of the modern age. But the very zest with which Catholics embraced radical changes in design and liturgy led to a weakening of appreciation of what had gone before.

Augustus Welby Northmore Pugin (1812–52), a convert to Catholicism, directed his polemics against the crudities and horrors of the industrial age. He pointed backwards to an idealised, lost medieval society of craftsmen, beauty and virtue. Churches should be built in a medieval style. Pugin campaigned to bring back to churches the things that had been thrown out of them after the Reformation when communities were instructed in Henry VIII's reign to strip their churches of Romish ornament. They were then told to put them back by Queen Mary. Queen Elizabeth I enforced a further clear out. Windows, altars, vestments, plate, candlesticks, roods and screens were lost, sold, hidden or burnt. Resigned acceptance marked this change in people's prayer and worship but it was not a time when the opinion of the people was either very articulate or much sought. Eamon Duffy, author of *The Stripping of the Altars*, remarks that people resigned themselves to the will of the monarch and the great ones who ran their nation. They grew weary of change and settled for the new order which did, after all, have continuity with the past. There was the sombre authority and splendour of Thomas Cranmer's Book of Common Prayer and the King James Bible to echo through their denuded churches and their lives. The Roman Catholic Church that had been a supporting pillar of the constitution now dropped out of the political conversation, except as a demonised and dangerous source of treason and treachery. The triumph of the Puritans in the English Civil War led to churches becoming yet more austere and unaccommodating to decoration and ornament.

Tolerance waxed and waned and under the Stuart kings some substantial Catholic places of worship were built. There were Catholic chapels for Catholic embassies and these were available for worship to all. The Spanish ambassador laid the foundation stone in 1623 for a chapel at St James's Palace, built for the Spanish Infanta, who was thought to be

Henry VIII's break with Rome spelt the end of medieval Roman Catholicism in Britain. In this 19th-century window in the church of Our Lady and English Martyrs, Cambridge, St John Fisher refuses to take the oath declaring the king to be head of the church.

Two stained-glass windows in St Mary's Derby vividly show the fate of the English Martyrs. Nicholas Garlick and Ralph Sherwin were Derbyshire Martyrs.

going to marry Charles I, to hear Mass. It was designed by Inigo Jones. The planned marriage fell through, but the chapel was available when Henrietta Maria, the French Catholic princess, did marry Charles I. The Queen had Inigo Jones build her another chapel at Somerset House in the 1630s; a large and ambitious building, served by the Queen's Capuchin priests, and again open to all. Papal legates reappeared in London, an Englishman was proposed as cardinal and the recusancy laws seemed to be in abeyance. The young Puritan poet John Milton was speaking of Rome when he wrote in *Lycidas* 'the grim wolf with privy paw daily devours apace and nothing said'. The Somerset House chapel was sacked during the Civil War.

Charles II died in 1685 after receiving the last rites of the Roman Church. James II employed Christopher Wren, together with Antonio Verrio and Grinling Gibbons, to work on a spectacular chapel for the Palace at Whitehall, and both the king and his Italian-born Catholic queen, Mary of Modena, went there openly and ceremonially to hear Mass. Astonished Londoners could witness the Catholic faith in all its Roman splendour at the heart of court life. The chapel was destroyed by fire in 1698 – ten years after James II had fled to France.

If the Stuart kings were sympathetic, most of the people and the authorities were not. How did the stubborn Catholic faithful manage at a level less exalted than royalty? The pressure to conform was fearsome. It is not surprising that most men and women, under penalty of large fines, attended the new Anglican services in the now bare churches. 'Church papists' would go on to hear Mass in secret later, elsewhere.

The forbidden rituals took place unobtrusively. The great Catholic families continued to worship and provide places of worship for their dependants and servants in their own houses. Other Catholics went to private houses or barns. But though worship was still conducted secretly the services, the premises and the furnishings were sometimes elaborate. In 1605 Jesuit missionaries felt able to lead a Corpus Christi procession around the great garden at Fremland in Essex with 'solemnity and music' as well as saying Mass. As architectural historian Michael Hodgetts comments, 'Anything less hole and corner would be hard to imagine'.

The Jesuit order had been founded in 1534 and they had hardly made an entry to the English scene until after the Reformation. But in the 1580s Jesuits were sent over from the English mission at St Omer. They saw themselves as soldiers of the Counter-Reformation with a fervent loyalty to the pope, who had declared the queen a heretic in 1570 and absolved her subjects of any loyalty towards her. Some Jesuit priests, like St Edmund Campion, were martyred but in 1621 there were 211 Jesuit priests and by 1636 there were 374 in England. An idea of how successfully they could draw a large congregation is given by a tragic event of 1623. Vespers were being conducted by the Jesuits in a garret of the French embassy in Blackfriars when the floor collapsed and two priests and 61 members of the large congregation were killed.

According to disgruntled Puritans, Wolverhampton in 1654 was 'swarming with papists' with 'many of inferior rank…drawn to popery'. Evidence of the continuing vitality of the old ways can be seen in the records of Carlton Hall in Yorkshire where the accounts for 1660 and 1668 reveal that among the 'things for the chapell' purchased were '…12 yards of pinke coloured floored tabbye at 3s a yard for making a vestment…a cannopye to hang over the Aulter with carveing …picture frame and doores'. The chapel at Harvington in 1696 contained 12 vestments including '1 Crimson plushe vestment and Antipendium with silver lace' much 'Linning for the Alter' and among the Plate were '2 Chalices and pattens, …one little box for oyles, and a pixe, one pax'. The services which used these items were not unambitious. Tenebrae was sometimes celebrated on the appropriate day and polyphony was sung.

Some public chapels were built during the three-year reign of James II. There was one in Wigan in Catholic Lancashire, two in London and one behind the White Hart Inn in Newcastle. James II helped pay for a 'proper' Catholic chapel in Birmingham. As the terrors aroused by Titus Oates and the Popish Plot abated in the 1680s, Catholics generally felt more confident about worshipping openly. They began to organise, and the country was divided into four Vicariates, or Districts. The Bishops who held sees *in partibus infidelium* were the beginning of the new ecclesiastical structure for England and Wales. (From the time of the Reformation, Catholic bishops were not allowed to take the name of a see in this country and were therefore ordained bishop 'in the land of unbelievers', a custom that remained until the Restoration of the Hierarchy in 1850.)

The Birmingham chapel was destroyed by the mob in 1688 when the king fled after the Glorious Revolution. This was an event marked, as Michael Hodgetts has said, by 'arson, looting and priest-hunting and by the destruction…of the new Catholic chapels'. In the years around 1688 about a third of Catholics lived and worked in the towns and cities which were becoming more and more the centres of gravity for Catholicism. Franciscans built a friary in Edgbaston, Birmingham, where they served the community for almost a hundred years. Elsewhere, congregations of the middle, yeoman and working classes built chapels with their own money and without looking to a patron for help. A Mass-house was built in Wolverhampton in 1723 at a cost of £1,069 2s 2½d and Catholics went there quite openly. When this was reported to the local magistrate, he declined to act.

These urban congregations were not the prime target for fines. The laws against recusancy were aimed at the landed gentry. The interconnected Catholic families – Welds, Arundells, Eyres, Stonors, Petres and others – paid the fines for themselves and their Catholic villagers and waited for better times. The fines were extracted with varying degrees of severity; much depended on which county the recusant lived in, and quite often the law enforcers were relatives or friends of the family. Often the amount said to be owed was set generously low. As a result some families faced crippling burdens while others, thanks to nepotism, administrative incompetence and bribery, paid almost nothing. Even the Double Land Tax exacted in the 1690s after the wars with France was ameliorated by inflation and, besides, rents were satisfactorily rising. Even if they were excluded from public life they could afford to cut a dash in the fashionable world. Pragmatic Catholic aristocrats were more than prepared to seek a *modus vivendi* with the Court and Establishment.

But if the ferocity of repression slackened, disapproval radiating down from the court was still a powerful disincentive in class-structured Britain. In the Age of Reason and Enlightenment, Roman Catholicism might seem to be the very embodiment of obscurantism and reaction. Nonetheless the tide was turning. The Grand Tour was introducing Protestant aristocrats not just to the glories of the ancient world but to the undeniably impressive architectural and artistic achievements of Rome.

For all that, there was only one considerable English Catholic architect at the time and he never designed a Catholic building. James Gibbs (1682–1754) had studied for the priesthood in Rome but was so impressed by the Baroque wonders he saw there that he abandoned a clerical career and became an architect. In England he assiduously courted the great landed patrons and helped them plan and build the estates by which they are remembered, including the Harley-Cavendish Estate in Marylebone. By the time he died Gibbs had built two masterpieces in London, St Mary-Le-Strand and St Martin in the Fields, for the Anglicans. He designed the Senate House in Cambridge but his greatest achievement was the Radcliffe Camera at Oxford. It is spectacularly round, grand and self-assured. Here, at least, was something of the secular Baroque Counter-Reformation in England. As architectural historian Robert Furneaux-Jordan put it, 'If Wren hob-nobbed with the church and crown, Vanbrugh with the Whig lords, then James Gibbs did much the same with the High Tories and with Jacobites in the dark

Order, light and an almost Nonconformist simplicity: pews at the 18th-century St Mary's Chapel, Lulworth.

panelled rooms of old Catholic houses'. Not all the rooms of the Catholic aristocracy were dark panelled. The houses and chapels built by the Welds at Lulworth and the Arundells at Wardour in the late 18th century were magnificent. The lesser gentry too could now consider it safe enough to move their illegal chapels downstairs from the attic.

There was a more relaxed spirit in the towns as well. Preston was famously Catholic with a long association with the Jesuits. It had, according to Bishop Petre in 1773, 1,000 communicants ('In Liverpool by the Irish Sea there are 1500'). In 1761 (the same year that Pope Clement XIV suppressed the Society of Jesus) a big new Catholic chapel was opened – James Boswell commented on its size. In 1778 the First Catholic Relief Act allowed bishops and priests to perform their religious duties without fear of prosecution, Catholics could own and inherit property and educate their children as Catholics. This relaxation provoked the Gordon Riots in 1780, when the mob burned and looted Catholic premises in London, Bath and Bristol. Despite the public hostility the Catholic Relief Act of 1791 allowed Catholics to build churches, under licence – as long as they did not have bells or steeples (a ban that remained legally in place until 1926).

The dangerous possibility of restoring the Catholic Stuarts to the throne vanished once Bonnie Prince Charlie had died in unglamorous exile in 1788. A year later the French Revolution drove thousands of French priests, bishops and monks to England for safety. They were welcomed. French Roman Catholics were no longer considered as traitorous Jacobites but as anti-Jacobins. Some of them stayed and colleges of exiled English scholars and religious were repatriated. The college at Douai moved to Ushaw and Ware, the Jesuit school to Stonyhurst, and Benedictine monks came to Ampleforth and Downside. Benedictine nuns from Cambrai went to Stanbrook, via Evesham. Seminaries were established in all the Districts. The chapels they would build were confident and, in some cases, splendid.

In contrast, most of the chapels built in the towns for ordinary use were modest. The new churches were usually small, self-effacing (for fear of the mob) and looking less like Counter-Reformation Rome than the Nonconformist meeting houses being built by Baptists, Quakers and Calvinists at the same time. Some, however, were ambitious and had opulent furnishings; Lord Petre gave £100 and Thomas Weld £30 towards an altarpiece with Corinthian columns and pilasters for a church in Oxford in 1793. This was the church where John Henry Newman would first go to Mass as a Catholic in 1845.

The return of medieval sumptuousness: A W N Pugin designed these angels for St Giles, Cheadle.

After the First Catholic Relief Act the Catholic gentry would meet to press for further concessions. Bishop Hay, Vicar Apostolic of the Lowlands, attempted to join one such meeting at the Thatched House Tavern in London. 'We don't want bishops here', he was told. These things were better handled by the aristocracy. But for all that, power was drifting away from the traditional, wealthy patrons to the bishops and priests.

John Milner was a formidable champion of the authority of the church against the power of the grandees – and the government. He became in time the first bishop of Birmingham and he took an uncompromising line against the government's wish to have a say in such matters as the appointment of bishops. Milner had a large congregation when he was a priest in Winchester and built a large church there in the Neo-Gothic style of which he was an advocate. He did not think much of the prevailing meeting-house look and throughout his career he continued to push for the Gothic cause. He gave money for Oscott, the seminary near Birmingham and eventually took it over. Oscott's prestige was immense. Historian Lord Acton called it 'the centre of the world'. (He added, with the grandeur appropriate to a Regius Professor at Cambridge, 'apart from Pekin'.) It would become the first power-base of A W N Pugin in his fanatical campaign for a 'pointed' or Gothic style of church architecture.

On the other hand the Benedictine Bishop Peter Augustine Baines, who succeeded Milner in the Western District, was a fervent believer in Classical architecture. He agreed with Pope Nicholas V that to 'create solid and stable convictions in the minds of the uncultured masses, there must be something that appeals to the eye'. New, majestic churches would do that. Baines knew Rome well. He had lived there, enchanted by the Classical buildings and monuments of the Eternal City, and when he was appointed to the Western District he bought Palladian Prior Park outside Bath (which was converted into Prior Park Roman Catholic College in 1829–34). But Baines never got to build the Classical chapel he planned above and behind the house, which would have indicated to the town below that Roman Catholicism was back in Britain and in robust mood. He wrote to Oscott recommending (vainly) the merits of Classical architecture to the President and remarking that 'It was quite impossible that Gothic would look good there'.

Another Benedictine with an interest in church building, Bishop William Ullathorne, wanted a Catholic cathedral in Bristol. Ullathorne was the son of a Yorkshire grocer who had gone to sea before realising his vocation. He had served in Australia and done much to ameliorate the lot of the convicts there. The site at Bristol was sloping and prone to crumble.

With his seaman's eye Ullathorne looked at the problem practically and recommended that the structure should be constructed of light wooden struts so that the building would not slide down the slope under its own weight. The cathedral was opened satisfactorily in 1848.

Ullathorne was one of a number of powerful churchmen who laid the plans for the restoration of the Episcopal Hierarchy. The Catholic Church in England and Wales was presided over by four Vicars-Apostolic with missionary bishops directly responsible to the Holy See – a system of church government that had existed since James II. There was no proper structure of parishes or priests and the system could not begin to deal with the challenges that the church was facing in fast-growing industrial cities. The Catholic Hierarchy was re-established in 1850.

The hierarchy consisted of twelve bishops and an archbishop. Cardinal Wiseman's Pastoral *From Out the Flaminian Gate* provocatively stated that now he 'would govern and continue to govern…with the islands annexed, as administrator and with ordinary jurisdiction'. There was a row. The Prime Minister spoke of 'papal aggression'. Guy Fawkes' night was celebrated with particular relish that year but the Catholic Church was back at the heart of British life and running its own affairs once more. For Ullathorne and a whole new generation of energetic bishops, building churches and church schools would now be a priority.

Like Ullathorne and Baines, Cardinal Wiseman wanted to move from gloomy, unambitious chapels to a real church architecture. The emphasis now lay less on style than on how successfully to accommodate enormous congregations of urban poor who lived in the 'labyrinths of lanes and courts, and alleys and slums'. The Cardinal wrote about '…nests of ignorance, vice, depravity and crime, as well as squalor, wretchedness and disease in which swarms a huge and almost countless population that is in great measure, at least nominally, Catholic'.

A W N Pugin's comment on the desperate state of the poor was that 'Catholic England was merry England, at least for the humbler classes'. Mark Girouard commented, 'As a formula for dealing with discontent among the lower classes and yet retaining the upper classes in a condescending role, Pugin's brand of Christian paternalism met with a responsive audience'. John Talbot, 16th earl of Shrewsbury, was the most generous benefactor among the Catholic aristocracy; Pugin enlarged and decorated Alton Towers for him. Wiseman would visit ('I intend to quarter myself on some of the nobility and gentry…as can sufficiently appreciate the honour'). With the Earl's backing Pugin had built churches all over the Catholic north and midlands. His church for Shrewsbury in the mining and textile town of Cheadle in Staffordshire was meant to be a triumphant expression of 'English' rather than 'Roman' Catholicism, but with Wiseman and the hierarchy now in charge the Catholic Church in England and Wales became more 'Roman'. Shrewsbury's benefactions were seen as a means of keeping control over a church that was moving into the hands of a professional clergy – no longer to be regarded as chaplains to the Catholic nobility – who owed their loyalty to Rome rather than merry England. Pugin and the Earl of Shrewsbury died in 1852, two years after the Restoration of the Hierarchy.

Pugin had received fewer and fewer commissions towards the end of his life but the Gothic he championed would be the abiding influence on church architecture – Anglican as well as Catholic – for the rest of the Victorian age. As Mark Girouard wrote, 'To take to Gothic was like taking the pledge: one never touched another style again'. There were points of resistance, at Brompton and Birmingham Oratories for instance, and by the turn of the century Gothic might seem more or less played out. Again, there would be exceptions. Sir Giles Gilbert Scott's great Gothic nave at Downside would not be completed till the late 1920s (and his towering Anglican cathedral in Liverpool was not finished until 1978). But the 13th-century Gothic favoured by Pugin, already the subject of

Byzantine gold: mosaic and
marble in the Lady Chapel of
Westminster Cathedral, London.

The Lady Chapel of Liverpool's Metropolitan Cathedral of Christ the King: windows by Margaret Traherne, Madonna & Child by Robert Brumby.

infinite, even wearisome, variations of interpretation, was further subverted by the Arts and Crafts movement and a perfunctory but stubborn revival of Romanesque and Byzantine architecture. The most important Catholic commission of the 19th century went to John Francis Bentley for a Byzantine cathedral at Westminster.

As the 20th century progressed the suburbs rather than the city centres became the focus of church building. A few architects, such as F X Velarde in the north, might suggest new ways of designing them. (In the 1930s and 50s Velarde played with, and elaborated on, unusual forms in a sort of Spanish Romanesque style.) But Catholics in Britain paid even less attention to the avant-garde church architecture that was being designed and argued about on the continent than did the other Christian denominations. After the Second World War, as post-war austerity very slowly relaxed, new social expectations emerged and there were new ideas about the liturgy. The Second Vatican Council (1961–5) was interpreted as demanding the vigorous re-ordering of churches with the innovatory positioning of new altars and the removal of anything that might get in the way of the new, vernacular liturgy. A whole new generation of churches was commissioned by churchmen and designed by architects firmly committed to the Modern Movement which, though it arrived late in Britain, flourished when it did. These generated technical and structural problems as well as aesthetic debate. Some laity and clergy felt that the old ways of expressing and reaching towards the transcendent through architecture, ceremony, furnishings and decoration should not be lightly abandoned. Nor were the re-orderings of existing churches always carried out with sensitivity or skill. Catholic writer and architectural savant James Lees-Milne wrote in 1977 '…bishops and priests adopted a policy of aggressive iconoclasm. They set about despoiling the churches themselves…they turned upon the church treasures …which contributed to the beauty of the buildings and helped sustain religious faith'. However, the spirit of the 1960s and 70s carried nearly all before it. Old churches were transformed and new churches like those at Twickenham and Woodthorpe, new cathedrals like Liverpool and Clifton, a new monastery church like Worth, were built in variations of the Modernist style – which became almost as much a matter of faith to its adherents as Gothic had been to its.

The boom in church building is over. There are fewer young men seeking ordination. Some communities and congregations have declined, shifted or been dispersed. Consequently there are architectural masterpieces left stranded and ill-attended because of the new demographics as much as any general decline in faith. But debate over how a church should be built, or furnished and decorated, continues. It is an extraordinary irony that the last important Catholic building to be erected in England – Brentwood Cathedral in Essex in 1988 – turned its back on Modernism and was built from traditional materials and designed, amid much controversy, in a meticulous and scholarly Classical style.

If there is a question mark over how to build churches in the present day there is also another, more pressing one. What is to happen to the best of the churches that the Catholic Church already has in its care? Some of the ambitious and elaborate buildings of a century or so ago (and much more recently) have developed leaking roofs, dry rot and damp. Vandalism and neglect threaten many buildings. The Catholic Diocesan Historic Churches Committees, English Heritage and Cadw, as well as the priests and parishioners of innumerable churches all over the country, ponder the challenge of how to conserve a magnificent inheritance. It should be a challenge not just for Catholics and committees, but for us all.

Christopher Martin
Bwlch-y-llys 2006

1 Before and After the Reformation:
Survivors and Successors

There are only a handful of churches that are used for Roman Catholic worship today that were built before the Reformation. There are few survivors from those built during the years after it when Catholic worship was forbidden. Of course, the Christian architecture of the Middle Ages was Catholic; the great medieval cathedrals and parish churches are now in the hands of the Church of England – re-branded, so to speak, and largely depleted during Cromwell's Commonwealth of any of their original furnishings or decoration that might smack of Rome. Those places of worship that did survive in Catholic hands owed this to their inaccessibility or the stubborn courage of some landed Catholic families who combined a heroic attachment to their faith with sufficient funds to pay the fines that were imposed on them and their dependants. These were powerful families that had been at the heart of the nation's affairs. Henry VIII reigned for decades as a loyal, even zealous, Catholic but after the break with Rome the great men of the court who refused to follow him (and their descendants) were exiled to the political wilderness for over two hundred years.

The chapels at Stonor and East Hendred had been founded in the early Middle Ages and are still in use. They were consistently used during the recusant years – even if it was sometimes thought prudent to retreat for Mass to a well-concealed space under the roof of the house. The Fitzalan Chapel at Arundel maintained some continuity and is still a place where members of the Norfolk family are commemorated when they die – in services of remembrance as well as in monuments. At Ely Place in London the tradition of worship in the old bishop's palace was broken but re-established in the late 19th century when it was reclaimed for Rome. At Walsingham, a different sort of tradition was revived. The medieval pilgrimage that seemed to have been destroyed by Henry VIII's legislation was triumphantly re-instituted in the last century. Once again it exercises a grip on the national Catholic imagination. Rotherwas, near Hereford, which maintained Catholic observances through thick and thin is no longer used for services. Having survived centuries of official and informal persecution it lost the family who built it and its congregation. English Heritage has seen that it does not lose its character or atmosphere.

Canons of the College of Arundel: medieval carvings in the Fitzalan Chapel where Catholic worship was maintained throughout the years of persecution.

During the late 18th and the early 19th centuries the wealthy Catholic families felt that better times had arrived. The Catholic Relief Act of 1778 permitted the Catholic clergy to hold services in private chapels without fear of the law, but this was rather ahead of public opinion; two years after the 1778 Act the Gordon Riots erupted in response to the liberalising legislation. Cautious Catholics ensured the look of their first chapels did not betray their Roman Catholic allegiance. Wardour Castle's chapel in Wiltshire is magnificently self-assured inside but is well screened from the public eye, while at Lulworth the Welds built a chapel with a fabulous interior and an exterior tactfully designed to look like a mausoleum.

The Catholic Relief Act of 1791 extended toleration. Catholics could start schools and seminaries, and build churches – provided that the doors were kept unlocked during services. The church at Everingham in Yorkshire was built later, in 1836, after the Catholic Emancipation Act of 1829 (which allowed Catholics into public life) had given a further lift to Catholic morale. Despite its remote location the church still hid its interior splendours behind non-committal, blank walls. But aristocratic Catholic self-confidence was re-asserting itself. In 1816 the Eyres had commissioned a Catholic architect to design a brooding masterpiece of a church at Hassop in the Derbyshire hills about which there is nothing self-effacing at all.

Monsignor Ronald Knox paid tribute at Lulworth in 1955, not just to the aristocrats but also to the lesser gentry who 'when the faith had dwindled to almost nothing; and was only kept alive where a handful of country squires still practised in secret the medieval rites of long ago'. Catholicism was no less indebted to middle- and working-class Catholics. In some parts of the country they numbered thousands and they too stuck resolutely by their religion. Of their places of worship little remains.

Classical confidence: massive gilded capitals triumphantly support the roof of St Mary and St Everilda, Everingham, Yorkshire.

St Amand's Chapel, East Hendred, Berkshire (*c.*1256)

The village of East Hendred is quiet now, but was a major thoroughfare in the Middle Ages and a well-used route for pilgrims, some of whom would pause and go into the chapel of St Amand to hear Mass before continuing on their way. Pope Alexander IV gave permission for Sir John de Turberville to build the chapel in 1256. It forms a wing of the home of the Eyston family – descendants of the Turbervilles. It was used for Catholic worship throughout the 300 years of persecution and was a centre of recusant activity.

Edward VI's commissioners destroyed the medieval altar in about 1548. The chapel had a gallery and that in turn became a secret chapel where Mass could be celebrated. It had its own access to the house where there was – above a false plaster ceiling – a hiding hole for a priest.

A centre for recusants: St Amand's Chapel attached to the house which had a priest's secret hiding-hole.

The actual chapel was for a time disguised, and used, as a log store. Mass was celebrated there again with a new, wooden altar in 1687, when the enthusiasm for persecuting Catholics was abating under James II, and the chapel was refitted with some confidence. The following year it was once again vandalised by supporters of the Protestant William of Orange who dragged off an old vestment to a Guy Fawkes' bonfire in Oxford.

Today the chapel is restored but its sense of history has not been compromised. It is of modest size, with white walls (three of them original) punctuated by Gothic windows, and a tile roof. Inside there is a new (1860) stone altar against the east wall with a reredos in carved wood. Above it is Victorian stained glass, framed by some original tracery. There are also windows which are partly painted in the Flemish style, benches thought to date from the late 18th century and the gallery is restored to its proper use. Remarkably it is possible to see, when the daylight falls in a helpful way, traces of medieval wall paintings on the plaster walls. The chapel contains St Thomas More's drinking vessel.

It was, and is, a private chapel, outside the jurisdiction of the parish. Mass is celebrated, and the public welcomed, every Friday morning.

St Etheldreda's Chapel, Ely Place, London EC1 (c.1300)

Just north of High Holborn, discreetly sheltered among the business properties of Hatton Garden, is one of the oldest Catholic places of worship in Britain. It originated as the 'new chapel' of the Bishop of Ely, John de Kirby (1286–90) and it remained the private chapel of the immensely wealthy bishops of Ely whose London palace, long since demolished, once stood here. Saint Etheldreda was the abbess of two nunneries on the Isle of Ely in the 7th century and her shrine was in Ely Cathedral. The chapel passed to Protestant and sometimes secular hands after the Reformation although it was briefly used for Catholic worship by the Spanish Embassy

Statues of the English Martyrs by May Blakemore stand between the windows in the south wall of St Etheldreda's. Some martyrs would have passed St Etheldreda's on their way to Tyburn.

The carved oak coat-of-arms of Charles I above the entrance to the chapel: 'Returned to the Old Faith'.

in the early 17th century. In the early 19th century it became home to a London Welsh congregation. In 1873 it was bought for the Rosminian order.

St Etheldreda's is built on two storeys with the chapel over an undercroft, a common arrangement for palace chapels. Upstairs the bishop could attend to his worship; in the Middle Ages the locals might worship in the undercroft, or use the space for more day-to-day activities. In the Second World War it was used as an air-raid shelter. The large roof is supported by 19th-century columns. There are Stations of the Cross by Charles Blakeman on the walls, designed to blend in with the rough-cast nature of the walls. A flight of stone stairs leads up, past a finely carved oak coat-of-arms of Charles I, to the chapel – 'Returned' as a sign near the door puts it 'to the Old Faith'. The chapel has seen many changes since its return to the Catholic faith. It was restored by George Whelan after its purchase from the Welsh in 1874. Sir Giles Gilbert Scott worked on it again in 1935. It was badly damaged by bombing in 1942 then restored again after the war by J H Greenwood. The tracery of what is a largely medieval east window was unblocked in 1874 and in 1952 Joseph Nuttgens, the Catholic stained-glass artist, was commissioned to design new glass for it. His response to this huge commission was a blazing Christ in Majesty, which is probably his masterpiece. The chapel itself is sombre but Nuttgens's vision of Christ, the Dove and God the Father surrounded by angels, the evangelists, Mary, Joseph and St Etheldreda herself, all depicted in burning reds, fills the east wall – the glass wonderfully interpenetrating the complicated tracery of the window's edge. The altar is low and simple and the view of the window is unimpeded. There is more good glass along the south and north walls including scenes from the Old and New Testaments designed by Charles Whelan. Between them stand resin and fibre-glass statues of English martyrs by May Blakemore. Saint Etheldreda's was on the route from Bridewell prison to Tyburn and, though mostly hidden behind a jumble of medieval buildings, would have been passed by many of the Catholic martyrs on their way to execution. They are commemorated in the colossal west window – said to be the largest area of stained glass in London. It was erected in 1964 and designed by Charles Blakeman. At the bottom of the window stand five martyrs holding palms under the shadow of the Tyburn gallows. Above the gallows a redemptive cross emerges bearing the figure of Christ.

Stonor Chapel, Stonor Park, Henley-on-Thames, Oxfordshire (c.1350)

Stonor Park lies among the Chiltern hills, home to the Stonor family since about 1100. In the Middle Ages the Stonors were rich, powerful and close to the centre of political power in England. They paid a heavy price when they remained true to their faith after the Reformation. Many family members are buried in or next to the chapel, where Mass has been celebrated without a break since 1349.

The flint-and-stone chapel is connected to the east wing of the family house, near to a pagan stone circle. It is thought to date from the late 13th century and was built on an even older foundation. The chapel is first mentioned in 1331 and was enlarged in 1339. It has an unusual-looking brick tower which was one of the earliest uses of brick in southern England. The chapel was Gothicised in 1797 and given its current vaulted roof. Two doors with ogee hoods flank the altar which is made of antique marble from Egypt. Monsignor Gilbey – a priest much in favour with the Catholic aristocracy in the last century – gave the cross on the white marble tabernacle which stands on the altar. The altar itself remains unreordered, firmly in its traditional position against the east wall.

Stonor Chapel (above): beyond a 'Strawberry Hill' Gothic arch are grim, war-time Stations of the Cross carved from Red Cross boxes.

A peaceful pastoral scene now but once a centre of heroic Catholic resistance: the old flint chapel anchored to the later Stonor house.

The chapel was redecorated in 1959 with advice from family friends – writer and cartoonist Osbert Lancaster and the artist John Piper who lived nearby. The pink, grey and white colour scheme reflects its own time as well as the 18th-century it was intended to evoke. The result is a light, even cheerful, hall that belies the heroic history of the chapel's owners. The Stonors paid ferocious fines and suffered savage confiscations during the penal period, paying up for their tenants as well as themselves. Close relatives were executed and banished and in 1577 Dame Cecily Stonor was fined the present-day equivalent of £50,000. She was also imprisoned for her part in harbouring the Jesuit Father Edmund Campion at Stonor, where he had his secret printing press. He was arrested nearby and executed in London in 1581. You can still see the discreetly hidden space beneath the roof of the house where Campion and other priests were concealed. Despite the dangers, Dame Cecily continued to shelter priests.

Indeed, none of the Stonors wavered. John Talbot Stonor (1678–1756) became Bishop of Thespae (*in partibus infidelium*). Monsignor Christopher Stonor (1716–1756) was Chaplain to the Young Pretender, Bonnie Prince Charlie, which can have done little to recommend the family to the authorities. Edmund Stonor (1832–1912) was Archbishop of Trebizond. After the Catholic Relief Act of 1791 the family set about a continuing process of reviving the chapel. Francis Eginton (1737–1805) was commissioned to design the stained-glass windows in 1797. The east window shows 'Salvator Mundi' after a painting by Carlo Dolci at Burghley House. A gallery and Gothick altar rails were added at much the same time. The windows on the south side are of Saints Augustine, Jerome and Bede. The baroque statues were put in place by the 6th Baron Camoys in the 1960s; at the same time Will Carter carved memorial tablets in black slate to Dame Edith Sitwell (who was a friend and benefactor to the chapel) and to the 6th Baron. In the ante-chapel are Stations of the Cross carved out of wooden Red Cross boxes by Jozef Janas, a Polish prisoner of war, during the Second World War. These were given to Stonor by another family friend, the novelist Graham Greene.

The chapel is private but the public are welcomed to Mass on Sundays. House and chapel are open to the public during the summer.

The Slipper Chapel, Walsingham, Houghton St Giles, Norfolk (c.1360)

The Slipper Chapel was one of several chapels that catered for pilgrims on their way to the Shrine of Our Lady of Walsingham, one of the great medieval shrines of Christendom. The shrine was, and still is, venerated because the Virgin Mary was said to have appeared in 1061 to a pious and aristocratic woman. She asked that a replica of the house in Nazareth, the scene of the Annunciation, should be built in Norfolk. With the miraculous assistance of angels this was duly carried out. In time the Slipper Chapel became a focus of pilgrimage in its own right, but was also the place where traditionally pilgrims might remove their shoes – their slippers – before walking the last, penitential mile to the Walsingham shrine.

For four centuries pilgrims, among them princes and kings, came to Walsingham to worship, but in 1538 Henry VIII destroyed the shrine and the chapel was abandoned. A local farmer used it as a barn and he was only occasionally bothered by Catholic visitors asking if they could see it. The general dereliction that followed the Reformation only ended when the chapel was bought by a High Church Anglican who later converted to Catholicism. Charlotte Boyd had been dismayed by its condition and fought to re-establish it as a place of pilgrimage. She was among those who first made a restored pilgrimage from King's Lynn to the chapel in 1897. The idea of a restored pilgrimage slowly caught on and, in 1934, Cardinal Bourne led a multitude of

In the Slipper Chapel, the 1954 statue of Our Lady of Walsingham stands beneath a blue and gold spirelet. It replaced one burnt on the orders of Henry VIII.

pilgrims to what had been re-established as the Shrine of Our Lady of Walsingham and which has now become the Roman Catholic National Shrine.

The Slipper Chapel is made of stone and flint and was thoroughly and faithfully restored in 1904 by architect and Catholic convert Thomas Garner (1839–1906), a former pupil of George Gilbert Scott. It was finally reopened for worship in 1934, the year of the great pilgrimage. The current furnishings were installed in around 1934 by Miss Lillian Dagless who was advised by Monsignor Squirrel. They were responsible for the altar and reredos above which is a fine east window by Geoffrey Webb (1954). Adjoining is a chapel of the Holy Ghost.

The Slipper Chapel is dominated by a large statue of Mary, carved in 1954. The original statue was taken from the Priory to Chelsea on the instructions of Henry VIII and burnt. Her replacement, based on the Virgin portrayed in a 15th-century seal of Walsingham Priory, wears a Saxon crown. The statue has a Gothic pedestal and above is a spirelet in gold and blue that indicates Mary's status as Queen of Heaven. When Pope John Paul II celebrated Mass at Wembley stadium in 1982 the statue was placed on the altar at his request.

The Slipper Chapel, a centre of pilgrimage for kings, princes and the people. During penal times it was used as a barn.

Fitzalan Chapel, Arundel Castle, West Sussex (c.1380)

Richard, 4th Earl of Arundel, founded a collegiate church in 1380 and at the Reformation Henry VIII sold the eastern half – what had been the chancel and the Lady Chapel on the north – to the family. The western half, the nave, became and remains the Anglican parish church. A brick wall once divided the two places of worship but in more ecumenical times a glass partition has been put in through which it is possible to peer from one denomination's space into the other. It is an odd arrangement. You must go through the Arundel Castle grounds to enter the Fitzalan Chapel, which is comparable in splendour to Westminster Hall and to the royal chantry chapels of Canterbury and Westminster.

Catholic services have been held at the chapel on an irregular basis since its foundation, in the great, radiant space that is lit by clear Perpendicular Gothic windows and framed by a mighty wooden vault. It was famous for its music and in the 15th and early 16th centuries the carved ribs and beams echoed to polyphony.

The chapel went through hard times after the Reformation. Neglect and damage inflicted during the Civil War in 1643 led to the eventual destruction of the original medieval vault in 1782, though fortunately the bosses were preserved and used again when the vault was reconstructed in 1886. Much restoration was carried out in the 19th century under the supervision of various dukes of Norfolk and architects such as

The Perpendicular east window of the Fitzalan Chapel bathes the monuments and tombs of a great Catholic family in light.

C A Buckler (1824–1905) who was the principal hand behind the almost total reconstruction of the actual castle in the medieval style. Buckler showed exemplary respect for the fabric of the chapel, restored the roof and designed the window which fills the east wall.

The famous glories of this chapel, however, are the family monuments and tombs. They range in period from Gothic and Renaissance to Victorian and form one of the most remarkable collections of their kind in Britain. They give witness to the power and piety of one of Britain's great Catholic families and, though they are undoubtedly expressions of ducal prestige, the details of faces, hair, hands, armour and clothing are affectingly human. The monuments go back to Thomas Fitzalan, the 5th Earl who died in 1415, and his wife. Family members are buried here to this day.

Detail of the effigy of Thomas, 5th Earl of Arundel, carved in about 1430.

In the chapel is a remarkable marble chantry with Gothic tracery and its own altar. The effigies of William the 9th Earl (d. 1487) and his countess lie here and the quality of the carving is exceptional, with traces of the original colour still surviving.

The abundance of marble and alabaster tomb-chests, with their sometimes grim but always human-looking effigies as well as carved griffins, faithful dogs, angels bearing cushions and many Latin epitaphs, inspired Philip Larkin to write one of his most famous poems, *An Arundel Tomb:*

> Side by side, their faces blurred,
> The earl and countess lie in stone,
> Their proper habits vaguely shown
> As jointed armour, stiffened pleat,
> And that faint hint of the absurd –
> The little dogs under their feet.

Medieval Rotherwas Chapel with its idiosyncratic Victorian spire stands isolated among Herefordshire fields.

Rotherwas Chapel, Chapel Road, Dinedor, Hereford (14th century)

The chapel lies to the south of the city of Hereford, in an area of industrial estates and new development. But the chapel is oddly isolated, approached through green, flat meadows. Because its immediate surroundings are so depopulated there is no longer a congregation and the chapel is now in the care of English Heritage. But for centuries, during the fiercest years of suppression, it was used for worship; not as a parish church but as the private chapel of a significant local Catholic family, the Bodenhams.

Only a farm and some gaunt outbuildings survive as reminders of Rotherwas House where the family lived (it was demolished in 1926) but the solitary medieval chapel remains, its 18th-century tower crowned by what Nikolaus Pevsner calls 'a weird Victorian spire'. The nave is 14th century and most of the structure is 14th and 16th century: the roof bears the date 1589. The religious fervour of the family seems to have waxed and waned over the centuries but there was a revival of Catholic enthusiasm in the mid-19th century which inspired the much more richly designed and decorated sanctuary. These Victorian additions were put into place by Edward Welby Pugin (1834–75) during the restoration of the chapel in 1868 and the apse was added later by his brother Peter Paul, who was also responsible for the furnishings.

Even though it is no longer a place of worship the chapel does not feel secular or drained of atmosphere. The roof has queen posts supporting hammer-beams and from the stairs toward the tower there are odd perspectives down the nave through the beams. Some of the windows are 16th century and in the south transept there is a Victorian window that tells vividly how the chapel was brought back to the Catholic faith.

Sir Roger Bodenham (born 1583) was a Protestant married to a recusant Catholic. He was afflicted by leprosy and his doctor, a Welshman, recommended a visit to the miraculous shrine of Our Lady at Holywell in North Wales (see page 55). After bathing there he emerged entirely cured, and in gratitude he became a Catholic himself and re-established the family chapel as Catholic.

The Bodenhams would go on to have excellent connections with other important Catholic families, including the Welds of Lulworth Castle (see page 35) and by marriage to Mrs Fitzherbert, the Catholic wife of the Prince Regent. But before that, they had not escaped pressures to conform and in 1645 had been visited by bailiffs who came with musketeers to 'seize their belongings for the state'.

After the family home was demolished Catholic worship was continued in the chapel by soldiers stationed in Hereford and munitions workers employed nearby during two world wars. Underground, all around the chapel, are sealed up tunnels where the explosives they manufactured were stored. The last Catholic service was held in the chapel in the 1940s.

The chapel is 1½ miles south-east of Hereford on the B4399, left into Chapel Road. It is kept permanently locked. The key is available from the local filling-station.

The impressive beams of the
16th-century roof at Rotherwas.

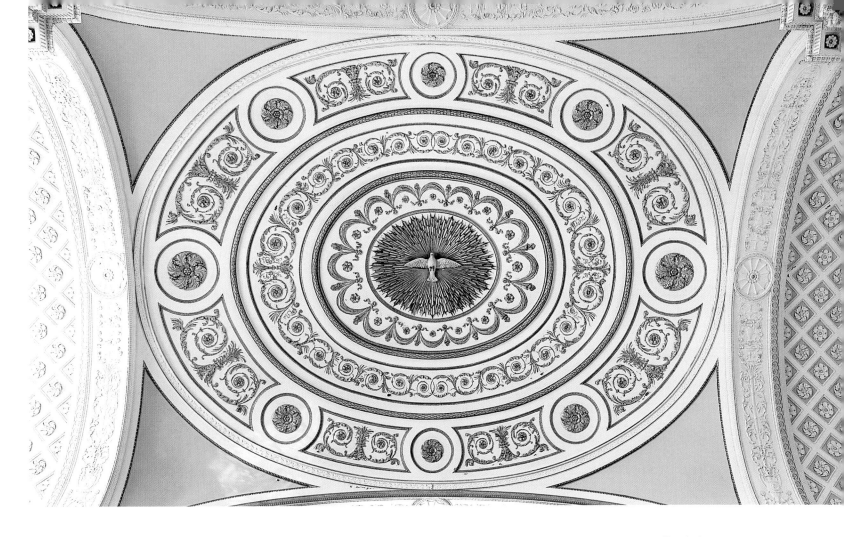

Wardour Castle Chapel, Tisbury, Wiltshire (1776)

The Arundells, a very rich and very old Catholic family indeed, had stayed true to the faith despite imprisonment and persecution over the penal centuries. When Bishop Charles Walmesley OSB, Vicar Apostolic of the Western District, stated that the laws circumscribing Catholic worship 'may almost be considered as not existing', Henry the 8th Baron Arundell decided the coast was clear enough to build a chapel which would be a confident expression of his family's beliefs. He chose one of the foremost Palladian architects of the day, James Paine (1717–89), to build a new house as well as the chapel, not far from the ruins of medieval Wardour Castle. Paine designed a Classical house with a long, almost unadorned front, with the chapel hidden inside one of the wings. Architect John Soane extended Paine's chapel between 1789 and 1790. The magnificent interior they designed would have held its own with anything being built at the time in London – or in the city which inspired it, Rome.

The house became a girls' public school and is now divided into apartments, but little has changed in the chapel. It is entered through an unspectacular, stoned-floored chamber which gives little indication of the grandeur that lies beyond.

The chapel is rectangular with Corinthian pilasters sliding up the walls to high windows. These cast light on a frieze, cornice and a very fine, high, shallow vault. There is much exuberant plasterwork. Bishop Walmesley celebrated the opening of the chapel in 1776 with ecclesiastical ceremony 'more magnificent than any seen by Catholics since the Reformation' (a claim made at many such openings). Arundell was advised in architectural matters by a Jesuit Father in Rome called John Thorpe, who wanted the interior decoration to

be put into the hands of Giacomo Quarenghi in Rome. Quarenghi was much in demand by wealthy English patrons, as well as by aristocratic Russians making their mark on St Petersburg, and was difficult to pin down, but he delivered some at least of what was asked of him.

Father Thorpe made sure that Quarenghi supervised the building of the marble altar in a Roman workshop. He also obtained the altar-piece painted by Giuseppe Cades (1750–99), though the altar was not to remain long in position. When John Soane took over he lengthened the chapel by expanding the sanctuary. It has a gently curving east wall flanked by Composite columns. There are elegant transepts with galleries supported on marble columns which have wrought-iron balustrades. Most striking is the ceiling which has an extraordinary series of shallow, coloured plaster domes and ellipses that seem to melt into one another. Where there might have been windows on the nave walls there are large paintings that strengthen the impression of being in a Roman church. One came from Notre Dame in Paris, rescued from the French Revolution, and another is hopefully ascribed to Rubens. Father Thorpe got hold of the beautiful relief of the Virgin and Child, carved by P E Monnot in 1703; it had been plundered from the private chapel of the Jesuit Superior General in Rome during the suppression of the Jesuit Order in 1773.

In 1780 the Gordon Riots erupted and, fearing a visit from the incensed and drunken Bristol mob, Lord Arundell sought protection for his home and chapel from the authorities. This he received, but for some time after it was thought prudent to maintain a keeper of the peace at all services, and a notice was posted warning any who might come 'ill-intentioned' to the chapel of the legal consequences of any disturbance.

Opposite: Wardour Castle Chapel: 'More magnificent than any seen by Catholics since the Reformation'.

Left: P E Monnot's superb relief of the Virgin and Child, once plundered from the Jesuits in Rome.

St Mary's Chapel, Lulworth Castle, Wareham, Dorset (1786)

Lulworth Castle lies a mile or so inland from Lulworth Cove and some of the most beautiful coastline in southern England. It remains the property of an ancient Catholic family, the Welds. The old castle, built early in the 17th century for Thomas Howard, 3rd Earl Bindon, was gutted by fire in 1929, and within a few yards of its much visited ruin is St Mary's, the first free-standing Roman Catholic chapel to be built in England since the Reformation. It is also one of the most attractive in Britain. It was built for Thomas Weld and its designer was a little-known London architect called John Tasker (c. 1738–1816). Tasker worked mainly for Catholic patrons and he had redecorated the castle interior before working on the chapel.

Things were still uncertain enough then for even a powerful landowner like Weld to be wary, and he sought permission from his monarch before he proceeded with the chapel. Happily the family was on good terms with George III, who visited Lulworth during a stay in Weymouth. The king counselled caution:

Garden temple or mausoleum? Thomas Weld still thought it prudent to disguise the purpose of his chapel at Lulworth Castle.

Large, clear Georgian windows light the interior of St Mary's Chapel at Lulworth which seems to celebrate more tolerant times. The organ dates from 1785.

build it by all means, he advised, but don't make it look too much like a church – perhaps more like a mausoleum? Thus emboldened, work began. Some of the stone was brought over from Portland by sea via Lulworth Cove. The builders were the Bastard brothers of Blandford (who had rebuilt that town in a Classical manner after Blandford's own Great Fire in 1731). A magnificent marble altar with six candlesticks was acquired in Rome and much admired by Pope Pius VI before it was transported to Dorset. An elegant organ by Richard Seede of Bristol was installed in 1785.

A year after the consecration in 1788 the king was invited to inspect the chapel. Once the monarch had entered, 15 Weld children sang 'God Save the King'. 'I think the King's seeing the chapel in that publick manner' wrote Thomas Weld 'might be a kind of sanction to it'.

The chapel is about as unlike a mausoleum as can be imagined. It is rotunda in form and looks, if anything, more like a very large garden temple. With its graceful proportions and restrained lightness of touch it celebrates an approaching age of tolerance; visible proof that the spirit of the European Enlightenment had reached these remote acres of Dorset. As Pevsner comments, it is 'wonderfully serene'.

The overall effect of clarity and light in the interior is achieved by the large, clear Georgian windows flanked by Classical columns and pilasters. There are four apses – three of which have galleries supported by Tuscan columns. Such was the chapel's prestige that the first bishop to hold a Catholic see in the United States of North America was consecrated at Lulworth in 1790. On his return to America, Bishop Carroll of Baltimore designed his new cathedral there (1805–18), albeit on a vaster scale, to be like the chapel at Lulworth Castle.

In 1865 Edward Weld commissioned Joseph Hansom (1803–82) to bring the chapel into line with the then current ecclesiastical fashion. Hansom went for a quite different, Byzantine look and added a mural above the altar which showed Edward Weld as Edward the Confessor and his wife as Saint Helena holding the True Cross. This style subsequently fell out of fashion and in 1951 architect H S Goodhart-Rendel, a Catholic convert, was commissioned by Sir Joseph Weld to restore the chapel in the spirit in which it had been founded. The altar was returned to its original position and the mural removed. The chapel was re-consecrated in a service in 1953 with a sermon by Monsignor Ronald Knox, in which he dwelt upon the immense debt owed by English Catholics to the gentry who had done so much to keep the faith alive in the dark years.

The chapel has been repainted more recently in cheerful tones. The domed roof (based it is said upon the Pantheon in London) was painted like a blue sky, with clouds, in the 1980s. The galleries now have an exhibition space which shows delicately crafted and woven copes and plate. One cope belonged to a Thomas Weld who was ordained after the death of his wife and who later became a cardinal. He caused some surprise in Rome when he walked round the city with his grandchildren under his ceremonial umbrella and drove them around in his carriage. Below the chapel is a crypt where lie the earthly remains of several generations of Welds. It is as near to being a mausoleum as St Mary's Chapel gets but even here it is not uncheerful.

Built to look like a conservatory, Llanarth's chapel is seen here across the lawns from the big house.

St Margaret and St Michael, Llanarth,
Raglan, Monmouthshire (1790)

In the late 18th century even Wales was beginning to have a more relaxed attitude towards Roman Catholics. Nonetheless it was still thought imprudent to draw attention to Catholic places of worship. So, although St Margaret and St Michael is well off the beaten track, approached along a winding, private drive through the countryside, the chapel was built to look like a conservatory. Not a very convincing conservatory – the windows are too small – but still an indication of the need that even substantial Welsh Catholic families felt to give their chapels a low profile. In this case there is no record of a hostile mob ever coming up the drive and a priest was installed without causing civil commotion.

It is one of the oldest Catholic churches in Wales and was built for the Joneses, an ancient Catholic family, a few yards to the north of their grand Classical house, Llanarth Court. The Joneses changed their name to Herbert in the 19th century. The house and chapel were bequeathed to the Catholic church by Mrs Fflorence Roche; the chapel initially given to the Benedictines is now run by the parish. The house is now a private residential nursing home. The chapel stands unobtrusively between the house and the stable

Detail of a window of St John at Llanarth, with a Welsh-looking dragon in a chalice. The glass came from the Rhineland or Flanders.

The view from the apse to the gallery echoes the appearance of a Nonconformist chapel.

block and has changed little in appearance. An apse was added in about 1930 and a cross was added to make the building look a bit more church-like. It is Georgian in style with a simple interior reminiscent of a Nonconformist chapel. There is a gallery and there are important, and attractive, round-headed windows. The relatively new apse is framed by two white Doric columns, made the more striking by their contrast with the purple paint applied to the walls in a recent redecoration. The old altar, altar rails and reredos were removed in the 1960s re-ordering, no-one knows whither. But the windows of the apse (1939) remain, designed in the Arts and Crafts manner by artist and nun Margaret Rope. They show St Bernard and St Francis and were put there as memorials to members of the family – most touchingly to Elydyr Herbert who was killed in action in 1917. Another memorial remembers Sir John Arthur Herbert (d. 1945) who left this quiet corner of Wales to become Governor of Bengal.

Even finer windows line the south wall. There are five and they were erected in the late 19th century but are much older: the glass is 16th and 17th century, and came either from the Rhineland or Flanders. The Salvator Mundi, St John the Evangelist and St James windows are of *c.* 1520 and come from Cologne. The Circumcision is mid-16th century. Particularly splendid is the window with the expressive portrait of a wistful-looking St James of Compostela with pilgrim staff and cockle-shell. There is also some 17th-century Swiss or German grisaille glass. These windows are a relatively rare survival in a Catholic context of what was a growing antiquarian (and more usually Anglican) interest in Gothic stained glass, brought to England in the years immediately after the Napoleonic wars. The gallery is supported on Doric columns and is accessible from a stately, winding stairway that leads up from the stone-flagged entrance hall.

All Saints, Hassop, Bakewell, Derbyshire (1816)

An early 19th-century print hangs on the presbytery wall at Hassop. It is an artist's impression of the church standing alone on the bare Derbyshire hillside with only an occasional tree around it and a stream running beside it. It could be a temple on a mountain in ancient Greece – the very image of the Sublime. The church now stands austere and formidable, next to, but sheltered from, the main road from Chesterfield to Buxton.

Four immense Doric columns guard the entrance, supporting a portico that juts out from the main church. The frieze is unadorned; the cornice is punctured by one round window. Four Doric pilasters embrace the east wall. It is said the projecting eaves and the jutting portico were adapted from the design of Inigo Jones's St Paul's, Covent Garden. The impact achieved is unforgettable.

Money for the building was given by the Eyre family, who were connected with just about every important Catholic family in the north and could trace their roots back to the Norman Conquest. Thomas Eyre, who later styled himself the 7th Earl of Newburgh, commissioned Joseph Ireland (1780–1841) to design All Saints. Ireland was himself of an old Catholic family and took many Catholic commissions. In this case he declined to take a fee, though the records say that he spent 152 days away from London during ten separate visits to Hassop. He took as an apprentice-assistant a young Catholic to whom he was

Classical Greece in the Derbyshire moors: the stern west front at Hassop.

related, Joseph John Scoles (1798–1863), who was to become one of the most celebrated English Catholic architects of the 19th century. All Saints was built of local stone and timber that was brought, by a specially purchased horse and cart, from Chapel-en-le-Frith. The church cost over £2,400.

After the stern exterior it is something of a relief to find an interior that has charm as well as grandeur. It is rectangular and Classical in the manner of some London churches. Doric pilasters complement the walls (now painted pink) that lead up to the coffered ceiling. In the gallery there is a fine chamber organ and the arms of the Eyre family are mounted on the gallery balustrade. The glass in the windows is exceptional and so are the statues of St Peter and St Paul, one on either side of the altar. St Peter, unusually, looks away from the altar.

The original altar, a frenzy of carved Italian marble, has an important painting of the Crucifixion by Ludovico Carracci hanging above it. The 8th Earl of Newburgh, who had succeeded his brother the 7th Earl in 1833, is buried under the altar. He died from gout and was reported as being 'so extremely kind and condescending in manner that individuals have exclaimed that in his company they forgot his rank and title'.

Despite paying for this substantial church, the Eyres were less enthusiastic about financing its mission; there are records of desperate priests trying to extract money from the Eyres, the diocese and other sources. The correspondence also reveals that disputes over the aesthetics of church restoration are not new. In 1877 the Bishop of Nottingham wrote discouragingly to a Canon Nickolds about his plans to paint the ceiling: 'I have heard a blue and gold ceiling much reprobated by an experienced architect…and also concerning the use of imitation marbling…I have never heard of any Repair and Improvement Fund at Hassop'.

St Mary and St Everilda, Everingham, Yorkshire (1836)

There is something of Brideshead about this chapel with its breath-taking interior. It dates from 1836 – seven years after the Catholic Emancipation Act removed the last legal constraints on the building of Roman Catholic chapels and churches. Its founder was William Constable-Maxwell who came from an old Scottish Catholic family, the Herries. The 9th Lord Herries was sentenced to death for his part in the Jacobite Rising of 1715 (he evaded execution and died in Rome '…faithful to the Pretender's cause'). Constable-Maxwell's granddaughter Gwendolyn married the 15th Duke of Norfolk, a prolific church builder himself, in 1904.

Everingham Hall stands in flat parkland next to a traditionally Catholic village. St Everilda, a 7th-century Saxon princess, came from Everingham. The house originally had its own chapel but William determined to build a new one as, somewhat inconveniently, worshipping villagers had to enter the existing one through his house. He looked to Rome for inspiration and commissioned a Roman architect, Agostino Giorgoli, whose designs were drawn up and executed by John Harper, a Catholic architect from York. The new chapel was originally attached to the house but the connecting wing was pulled down when the house was restored. So the chapel stands massively, and not altogether promisingly, by itself in the grounds.

Little relieves its blank, almost windowless walls apart from iron railings that screen some family memorials. Beyond the massive doors, however, is a vast, sombre basilica which is one of the most powerful evocations of the ancient world in Britain. There are giant Corinthian columns with massive, gilded capitals which thrust triumphantly up to bear the weight of a great, heavily coffered, barrel-vaulted roof. Only a small amount of natural light penetrates the interior from the small, high windows, and dimly visible in the niches halfway up the walls of this august space are dramatic statues, carved in the Baroque style, of the twelve apostles. Above them are solemn reliefs of the life of Christ, carved by Luigi Bozzoni of Carrara who came over from Rome in 1838 and took a studio in London to work on the project.

The altar, with six tall candlesticks, closes the view with Baroque flourish. It was constructed by Roman marble-cutter Giuseppe Leonardi, from marble and polished porphyry. Apparently work was worryingly slow. Constable-Maxwell was sent this intelligence from Rome: '…he (Leonardi) is slowly advancing with your altar…he gave me to understand that with a little money on account he would be able to proceed with greater ease and faster'. Above the altar, between two gilded pilasters and topped by a carved golden hood, is a painting of the crucifixion. Two flanking niches contain theatrically posed statues – one of which is of St Everilda.

Baroque statue of St James the Great at St Mary and St Everilda.

North of the sanctuary is a large side chapel which has well-preserved encaustic tiles and many intriguing reliquaries on the altar – though no relics. There are some romantically faded wall paintings. At the west end of the nave is another extraordinary piece of polychrome marble, the font, which is supported on legs with ormolu claws and which has an intertwined bronze serpent as its central column. Above it, on a gallery standing on thin iron columns, is an organ by Charles Allen of London, little altered.

Constable-Maxwell longed to go to Rome and eventually did so. There, to his great joy, he met the pope. (His daughters were less lucky: one of his letters home complains that some 'very pushy French Sisters of Charity' got in the way.) But the chapel was not entirely the product of its patron's ultramontane passion for Rome. Local craftsmen J R Willoughby of York, William Crabtree and S Marshall of Hull were the mason, plasterer and wood carvers. The servants of the Hall chipped in as well, contributing plate and two silver flagons for wine and water.

The chapel was consecrated on July 9th, St Everilda's feast day, in 1839. The occasion had '...something well-calculated to awaken the inattentive, and to shed over the mind of the Protestant, and even of the irreligious, a feeling of mingled reverence and awe' according to a local report. In 1982 the Everingham estate, including the chapel, was sold. The purchaser leased the chapel to the diocese and Mass continued to be said there until 2004 when it was closed for worship because of its remote location.

Uncommunicative of the splendour within, the non-committal exterior of St Everilda.

Giorgoli's and John Harper's powerful evocation of the ancient world for Yorkshire's East Riding: St Everilda's coffered ceiling, columns, High Baroque altar and sanctuary.

2 After Emancipation:
New Churches for a 'New People'

The first Catholic Relief Act of 1778 was passed because the government wanted to recruit Catholic Scottish Highlanders to fight the American colonists. Some concession to Catholics generally seemed to be necessary and Bishop Hay, Vicar Apostolic of the Lowlands, was asked what concessions he thought might be appropriate. The Catholic gentry rather resented this clerical intrusion into the affairs of a church that they considered their responsibility. Told of this, Bishop Challoner famously prophesied the passing of aristocratic power over church affairs. 'There will be a new people', he said. John Henry Newman in his famous 'Second Spring' sermon at Oscott in 1852 spoke of the early years of the century when 'there was no longer the Catholic church in the country…a few adherents of the Old Religion, moving silently and sorrowfully about, as memorials to what had been… as ghosts flitting to and fro'. Newman's description hardly did justice to the self-assured Catholic gentry happily attending balls and building big houses. It also ignored the emergence of Catholic professionals, tradesmen and skilled workers. They would be the 'New People' and the inheritors. The shift from the country house chapel to chapels in the towns, supported by their own congregations, marked the end of an era.

The Catholic Relief Act of 1791 led to the building of thousands of Catholic churches. Their patrons built, not just for themselves and their families, but for the community. They may originally have been expressions of family piety and pride but the local congregations would eventually take ownership of them. The architectural style and furnishing might reflect the taste of a commissioning patron or priest or bishop but these churches became shared, with different levels of society worshipping and contributing to all facets of their life.

Most parishes or missions were unambitious. In most cases there was very little money. The unassuming character of their buildings had another cause too. The great tradition of the Catholic liturgy had been broken. Decades of worship in barns and private rooms had left their mark on Catholic expectations. The first chapels looked like

Unrestrained colour and drama of the Holy Trinity carved above the High Altar at St Charles Borromeo, Hull.

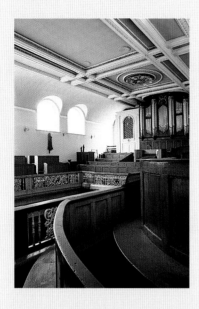

Our Lady of the Assumption, Warwick Street, Soho, London.

Nonconformist chapels and not just for reasons of caution. The first services held in them were simple. As in Nonconformist services, there was much emphasis on the sermon and little on ceremony.

Like the Anglicans, Catholics were often expected to pay pew rents to attend church. This led to a great debate within the church. It was felt that the urban poor – fast becoming the single greatest part of the Catholic community – should not be excluded from the services of the church. Some wealthier churches charged nothing for the early Mass but enforced a charge at the later, more fashionable, times of worship. As the century progressed the custom of charging died out, the interiors of the churches became richer and more lavish and the altar, rather than the sermon, took on a greater significance. Splendour and pageantry returned to Catholic worship.

The dedication ceremonies of the new, grander churches were complicated and long. The proceedings sometimes lasted days and could involve hundreds of clergy. They were not there just to watch. The dedication involved such intricate rituals as laying diagonal stripes of ash across the nave and transept. Relics were guarded overnight. The Greek alphabet was honoured. The pungent smell of scented oil rose from where it had been poured over the Mensa of the High Altar. To the working-class congregations these ceremonies marked something wonderful – the coming of a sacred space into the midst of impoverished lives.

Most of the first wave of Catholic churches was swept away as the industrial revolution and the mass immigration of Irish Catholics into the cities of Britain created a need for much bigger churches that could accommodate the explosion in Catholic numbers and devotion.

Our Lady of the Assumption, Warwick Street, London W1 (1730, 1789–90)

It is easy to miss this large brick church which was deliberately designed to avoid attention. It was gutted by a drunken mob during the Gordon Riots in 1780 and the contents looted. Pews, balustrades and the organ were broken up and together with the altarpiece dragged out and burnt in the street. The restored building was reconsecrated – after prominent Catholics had raised a public subscription – in 1789. The architect was Joseph Bonomi (1739–1808). He was born in Italy and came to England where he became a fashionable designer of country houses. For reasons of defence then still assumed to be necessary for the church he designed no windows at street level (although two were added later). There is a steep and purposely twisting stairway that leads up into the church. Inside, apart from the east end, Our Lady of the Assumption resembles a grand Nonconformist chapel of the same period with galleries on three sides and has a used, urban look to it. It is the only London church built on the original site it occupied during penal times that has survived and is still in use. Nearby Golden Square housed the Portuguese and then the Bavarian embassies where this church had its origins.

In the 19th century Soho was a very smart address and the congregations reflected this. Mrs Fitzherbert was a regular worshipper. Cardinal Wiseman lived in what had been the embassy and John Henry Newman was taken as a boy to church here by his father. The music was excellent. Many Italian opera stars came and sang here. As the century progressed the very simplicity of the church began to seem at odds with a growing feeling that the church should express a more confident look. In 1875 there were plans to build an entirely new church in the shell of the old one. Architect John Francis Bentley (1839–1902) was given the job. Happily, funds for the ambitious new basilica that he planned were never forthcoming but his more modest alterations to the church were made.

The walls of the church are brick (so discoloured in 1950 that the priest 'had it dyed red'). The steps from the street lead into the west end of the church below the steeply sloping gallery which continues along the north and south sides. This gallery is supported on iron columns with acanthus capitals and has patterned iron railings. In the gallery is a large, much restored and venerable organ. The wooden pews are said to be the 18th-century originals. Below the gallery is the font, thought to date from 1788 and moved to this position in recent years.

There is a large relief of the Assumption (1853) high on the east wall over the sacristy door (which has a spy-hole). It was carved by J E Carew,

Once sacked by the mob: the deliberately unassertive walls of the Soho church.

John Francis Bentley's Byzantine-looking apse transformed the church's meeting-house appearance. To its left is the relief of the Assumption by J E Carew.

a 19th-century Classical sculptor of considerable fame in his time. This large feature was once positioned over the main altar but was moved in 1875 when Bentley reconstructed the sanctuary and utterly transformed the east end of the church. Steps lead up to a mosaic floor divided from the church by railings presented in 1908 by the 15th Duke of Norfolk, a parishioner. (His residence, Norfolk House, was within the parish boundaries. It was reported by impressed contemporaries that he would sometimes sit, during services, among the poor people from the Poland Street workhouse.) Above the altar and tabernacle, the vaulted apse of 1876–7 is covered in Byzantine-style mosaics, the best of which, high in the semidome, were designed by Bentley. They illustrate the Coronation of the Virgin and were executed after his death.

Bentley also designed the mosaics at the front of the Lady Altar and Shrine of Our Lady Immaculate to the right of the sanctuary. It was the first time he had shown the human figure in a mosaic form and the images represent the Adoration of the Magi. The large statue of the Virgin Mary was brought from France in 1875. It attracted much devotion and generated many votive silver hearts. Bentley disliked them but failed to get rid of them. In 1960 a Regency-style reredos was put in to frame the Virgin. The sides of the new reredos display some of the silver hearts.

In the baptistery there is a memorial to a distinguished parishioner with connections going back to the old embassy church – the Crown Prince Regent of Bavaria (1869–95), '…Head of the Royal Households of Stuart, Wittelsbach, Tudor and Plantagenet…'.

During the Second World War the church escaped serious damage; the walls that had been thickened to keep out the rioters were also able to absorb enemy bomb blast.

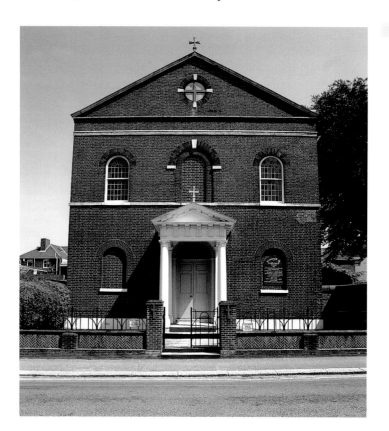

More confident, more church-like: the west front of St Thomas of Canterbury.

St Thomas of Canterbury, Pyle Street, Newport, Isle of Wight (1791)

This beautiful church has been in continuous use since it was built in 1791. It has a claim to be the oldest Catholic church built since the Catholic Relief Act of 1791 and is remarkably unchanged. The exterior has strong red brick walls, clear round-headed windows and a confidently projecting Doric columned porch. It is not as self-effacing as was usually thought prudent at the time and stands on a busy road just off the centre of town.

A broad and attractive lawn divides the church from the presbytery which was also built in brick. The church itself is light and gracefully proportioned. Galleries on three walls contain the original 18th-century benches, now painted white. The modern balustrades that front the galleries are wooden and were carved in the style of the age in which the church was built.

The galleries are supported by elegant, green, fluted columns which have recently gilded Ionic capitals. Daylight pours in through the large upper windows on to the simple altar which stands in front of a coved recess – unadorned except for a crucifix and a projecting canopy. Two chapels stand to either side of the sanctuary. Green wooden doors screen off the confessional space. The pews have been arranged to face each other in the manner of a college chapel. The font is of carved marble and stands just below a memorial tablet to the church's founder and benefactor, Mrs Elizabeth Heneage. This tablet is the oldest monumental tablet in a Catholic parish church in Britain; it speaks of her '…munificence in erecting sacred edifices'.

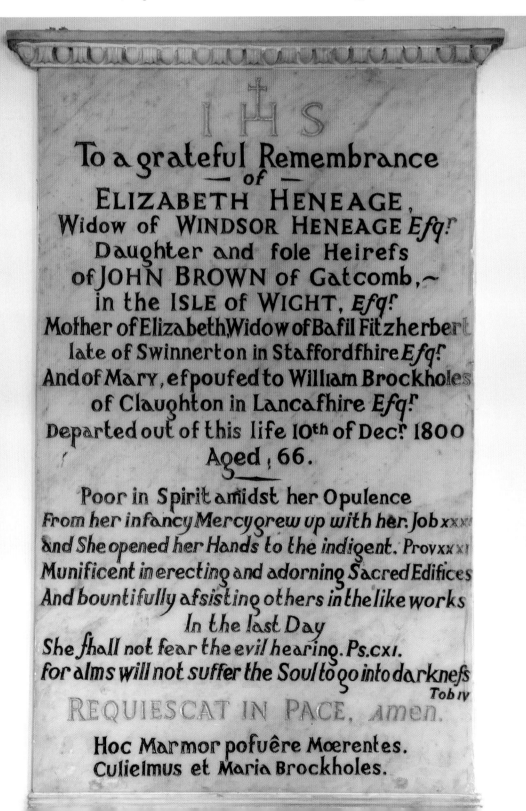

IHS

To a grateful Remembrance
— of —
ELIZABETH HENEAGE,
Widow of WINDSOR HENEAGE Efq.ʳ
Daughter and fole Heirefs
of JOHN BROWN of Gatcomb,~
in the ISLE of WIGHT, Efq.ʳ
Mother of Elizabeth, Widow of Bafil Fitzherbert
late of Swinnerton in Staffordfhire Efq.ʳ
And of Mary, efpoufed to William Brockholes
of Claughton in Lancafhire Efq.ʳ
Departed out of this life 10th of Dec.ʳ 1800
Aged, 66.

Poor in Spirit amidst her Opulence
From her infancy Mercy grew up with her. Job xxx
And She opened her Hands to the indigent. Prov xxxi
Munificent in erecting and adorning Sacred Edifices
And bountifully afsisting others in the like works
In the last Day
She fhall not fear the evil hearing. Ps.cxi.
for alms will not suffer the Soul to go into darknefs
Tob iv
REQUIESCAT IN PACE, Amen.

Hoc Marmor pofuêre Mœrentes.
Culielmus et Maria Brockholes.

At St Thomas of Canterbury a marble slab commemorates Elizabeth Heneage, a generous benefactor to Catholic churches. She sent catechisms to American Catholics after the War of Independence.

St Mary and St John, Pleasington, Blackburn, Lancashire (1816–19)

Standing in the middle of a large flat cemetery, Pleasington 'Priory' looks both impressive and odd. This is a robust example of the Gothic Revival, built before the ferocious debates about which particular form of Gothic was most appropriate for Catholic worship had been ignited. Pleasington combines genuine architectural gravitas with elements of intriguing curiosity. Pevsner called it 'astonishing'.

It was paid for (£23,000) by John Francis Butler, a local landowner from a long-standing Catholic family as a thank-offering. Built in a kind of free-style 'Gothick', the church has a Perpendicular silhouette. The west front has a large rose window. Below this window are three carved heads; the central head is generally thought to be a portrait bust of the patron Francis Butler (though some have claimed that the bust is that of George, Prince Regent and indeed the letters G and R are inscribed on the stone to left and right of the head).

There is more idiosyncratic carving around the Romanesque-style portal. Dog-tooth carving and carved heads, presumably of biblical figures, intermittently encircle the portal in a 12th-century fashion. The sculptor has carved a decorated niche to himself to the left and above the west door. It bears the inscription 'THOMAS OWEN SCULPTOR'. The niche is empty but a serious, even scowling, figure which may be Thomas Owen, stands to the right of it. There are heads carved to the left and right which may be Owen and his wife. Further to the right, Owen carved a niche for the architect inscribed 'JOHANNES PALMER ARCHITECTUS'. The unsmiling heads of the architect's wife and son are carved on either side of the hoodmould.

John Palmer was a Manchester-based architect with a reputation as an antiquarian. Evidence of his fascination with the past is his inclusion of the 'eye of providence' on the west front of Pleasington. The eye looks unwinkingly from a flaming pyramid, a not uncommon detail on Catholic churches of the time.

Pleasington owes much of its character to the sturdy and original contributions of Thomas Owen but Palmer's interior is light and tall. There is good stained glass. The columns are slender and there is Early English dog-tooth carving on the arcades. The sanctuary is framed by a very high arch, and was re-ordered by Gerald Murphy.

Pleasington's west front – a rose window and some idiosyncratic carvings.

Spirit of place: head carved by Thomas Owen. Is it the church's founder or George IV?

St Mary, Standishgate, Wigan, Lancashire (1818)

St Mary's is graceful and, inside at least, elegant. Outside it presents a sturdy, early Gothic Revival face to Standishgate, built in the Perpendicular style. It is battlemented and there are dramatic pinnacles which flank a bell tower. The architect is unknown.

The interior is wonderful. Very tall and very slender pillars, painted partly in blue and gold and partly banded, rise up – en passant supporting considerable, raked side galleries – to a ribbed and plastered ceiling of the sort to be seen in many Regency Gothic churches of the time. At the east end the steepled Victorian canopy of the throne, on which the monstrance could be displayed during Benediction, breaks into the front of a perfectly proportioned five-light window. Below the window there is a relief of the Annunciation and lining the sanctuary walls are reliefs of Old Testament figures and saints. They were installed as late as 1904 and though they were made from an unpromising sounding prototype of fibreglass they look at home in their grand setting. Parish folklore has it that the venerable face of Abraham as well as those of Judah, David, Ruth and others were based on members of the congregation. There is an elaborate, highly carved reredos painted in reds and gold and below the altar are unusual marble steps encrusted with crushed shells.

Set among the floor tiles is a brass tablet to the first parish priest at St Mary's. He was Father Charles Middlehurst (1818–47) who was '…struck down by a malignant fever caught in his unremitting attention to the sick during a time of God's awful visitation'. There is another memorial tablet, much grander, on the wall of the side chapel dedicated to the Greenhaulgh family who put up most of the money for the church. There are rich side altars, plaster with inlaid tiles, to the Virgin Mary and to St Anthony. The elaborately carved marble font is original and stands in its original position. The Stations of the Cross are not original. More parish folklore says that they are probably the work of nuns, so like nuns do the figures appear. A hundred yards or so down the road from St Mary's is St John's, a church that looks and feels very different.

St Mary's: the columns of the graceful and beautifully lit gallery.

The Holy Spirit in the form of a carved dove hovers above J J Scoles's masterful tempietto and the tabernacle at St John's.

St John, Powell Street, Standishgate, Wigan, Lancashire (1819)

During penal times Lancashire was the most steadfastly Catholic county in England and Wigan was a very Catholic town. The Jesuits ran a school here in the time of James II and acted as missionaries to the town. They were highly successful; 1331 people were confirmed in 1687 alone. Wigan was embroiled in the Jacobite rebellion of 1715 and in 1745 the Young Pretender paused for the night here as he advanced, and did so again as he retreated. The Protestant Bishop of Chester said the Wigan Catholics were 'stubborn and contemptuous recusants'. St John's, like St Mary's, has its origins in those heroic times.

The congregation of St John's was founded in 1723. By 1817 the old Jesuit chapel of St John had about 3,000 'customers', as its worshippers were discreetly called (the chapel had purported to be a shop). A great meeting was held and it resolved that changing times demanded a new, more spacious church; 1,400 people signed a resolution demanding that immediate steps be taken to raise the necessary funds. The new St John's church was opened in 1819 at a cost of £9,000. The architect is unknown.

That exalted mood of confidence was well expressed by the actual church. It is a huge, spacious, Classical building; big enough to seat a multitude. Though there is an attractive Ionic colonnade-porch to the front, the exterior is austere. It is the vast interior space that spectacularly reflects the hopes of the new age. This has an enormous, unsupported ceiling and a massive west gallery approached by two curved and graceful stairways. The gallery holds the organ and is curved, like the stairways, with an ornate balustrade. The Corinthian capitals on the great columns under the gallery are also on a colossal scale and elaborately carved and gilded, as are the pilasters under the jutting entablature that encircles the nave.

The congregation looks from generously spaced benches towards the dramatic east end. The apse is

decorated in elaborate plasterwork and lined by
Corinthian half-columns. All of this is only a
backdrop to the altar itself, but not just the altar:
the amazing sanctuary was reworked in 1834–5
by Joseph John Scoles (1798–1863) who had
already been employed by the Jesuits in
Lancashire. Here he designed a truly Roman and
magnificently confident golden tempietto resting
on eight pillars that enclose the tabernacle.
Framed by the columns is a large crucifix,
enshrined with figures of the Virgin Mary and
St John. Much of this is marble, marbled wood
and rich gilt.

In 1933 the Jesuits withdrew from St John's.
In 1950 the need for redecoration after the war
prompted the parish to hold a bazaar in the
Parochial Hall. It raised £3,000. Most of the
redecoration that followed can still be seen.

The fine stone cross outside the church was
given by the Catholic Walmesley family and just
a short walk away from St John's is St Mary's, built in a spirit of competition. There continued to be some
unchristian rivalry between the two Catholic congregations which went back to their Jesuit and 'secular'
foundations. This has now been happily resolved by the recent necessity of appointing one priest to serve
both churches.

The unwavering confidence of
Wigan's Catholics expressed in
St John's substantial gallery with
its chunky balustrade and huge
columns.

St Patrick, Park Place,
Liverpool (1821–7)

The massive church stands on the main road, east
of the city centre, in working-class Toxteth. This
was provocative – as far as the local Irish Orange
community was concerned. The church attracted
Protestant invective and was frequently attacked.
Outside on the west wall is a statue of St Patrick
with arm outstretched and gesturing. It was a gift
from sugar refiner Joseph Brancker and had, until
1827, adorned the St Patrick Insurance Company
of Dublin. It so enraged anti-Catholics that they
would make spasmodic attempts to pull it down.
There is an inscription on the west wall which
reads: 'Built by public subscription under the

Nicaise de Keyser's painting of
the Crucifixion dominates
St Patrick's.

The Crucifixion, brought to
St Patrick's from a church in
Manchester, has darkened
over the years.

express stipulation that the whole of the GROUND FLOOR should forever remain FREE for the accommodation of all'. This was not an attempt to ingratiate the church with the neighbours: it was drawing attention to the fact that pew rents would not be charged – not on the ground floor at any rate. Below the inscription there is a memorial to the Catholic priests who died during the typhus epidemic that swept through the city slums in 1847. Their graves are nearby.

The church looks like a bulky Classical Nonconformist chapel and was mostly paid for by the subscriptions of its impoverished congregation. Though there was some leadership from the better-off Catholic laity, no single great patron came forward to supplement 'the pennies of the poor'. For all that, St Patrick's lacks nothing in grandeur. The architect was John Slater, a Liverpool man, who was a joiner as well as an architect. He gave the building two tiers of windows, two impressively grand porches (no longer in use, but containing staircases to the galleries) with powerful Doric columns and a square, white bell-cote.

The interior is bright, broad and spacious with galleries on three sides that are supported by cast-iron columns painted white. Above is a light, segmental ceiling. What catches the attention is the gigantic painting above the altar of the Crucifixion by Nicaise de Keyser of Antwerp (*c.* 1834). To add to its impact the painting is framed by two white columns with gilded Corinthian capitals. The scale of the ensemble makes it all look as if it might have been designed with a cathedral in mind and indeed the painting did come from another church, in Manchester, that had been damaged by fire. The painting has darkened with the years. On either side of *The Crucifixion* are commanding stone figures in niches, high on the east wall and above the height of the galleries, of St Matthew and St Mark.

There are photographs of how the High Altar and reredos (1867, by J F Bentley) once looked. Both were removed many years ago. There were steps leading up to a raised sanctuary with a curving altar rail that existed until the more recent re-ordering of the 1970s destroyed the sanctuary – an act of extraordinary cultural confidence. Left of the altar is a chapel to St Joseph. The chapel has kept its very fine marble relief of the Holy Family with Jesus holding a saw while Joseph looks encouragingly on.

A large Victorian painting of the *Baptism of Christ*, by an unknown artist, hangs at the rear of the church where the space under the west gallery has been partitioned off to make a large parish meeting room. Up some steep stone stairs the gallery has original box pews intended for those better-off members of the congregation who did pay pew rents. Dominating it all is the organ with a magnificently panelled and gilded case.

St Charles Borromeo, Jarratt Street, Hull, Humberside (1828 and 1894)

This church has one of the most opulent and dramatic interiors of any 19th-century church in England – a fantastical Roman church, with a heavy touch of the Austrian rococo.

The city's first Catholic chapel since the Reformation was burnt down in 1780 when the Gordon Riots rippled up as far north as Hull. Not long after a French priest, an aristocrat on the run from the Revolution, came to Hull and commissioned a new one. When he went home it was thought too modest for a city whose fortunes were expanding with the growth of the whaling industry and the newly installed docks. A new church was designed by a local architect called John Earle who had contributed much to the look of the prospering city. But soon his church too was criticised; it was thought to be a bit barn-like and dull, like just another Nonconformist chapel. Money was sought and the versatile Catholic architect J J Scoles (1798–1863)

Opposite: The burnished
magnificence of St Charles
Borromeo: the north-west corner.

The astonishingly flamboyant central set-piece of the Trinity above the High Altar at St Charles Borromeo.

was brought in. He widened and altered the church externally and internally. Later, in 1894, architects Smith, Broderick and Lowther made more, substantial changes.

The façade received a new porch, with Corinthian columns, a dentillated pediment and a frieze inscribed 'DOMUS DEI'. Above that is a papal coat of arms. On either side of the door there are niches with statues of St Charles Borromeo and St Margaret Clitherow, the York martyr. The church was now much more explicitly Catholic and grand but the façade gives no indication of what lies within.

The nave windows are very high up and the aisles and nave are dark, but light bursts through the lantern of the colourfully decorated dome above the High Altar. It shines on an astonishing polychromatic representation of the Trinity. Large, brightly painted, sculpted figures of God the Father, Christ in Glory and the Holy Spirit rise theatrically above a tumultuous explosion of billowing white clouds.

It owes its inspiration not just to the Italian Baroque but also to the belated inspiration of the Austrian rococo. This was the work of an Austrian craftsman called Heinrich Immenkamp who was living in Hull. Above the High Altar he added a painted scene of the Last Judgement. One figure among those being weighed in the balance was recognisable as the then parish priest and he is shown selected for heaven. Another figure is being sent in the opposite direction. He looks, according to parish legend at least, very like a neighbour who had been disagreeable and disputatious in his dealings with the church; a neighbour from hell, as it were.

This amazing central set piece is flanked by colossal, fluted Ionic demi-columns supporting an elaborate frieze. The altar itself is made from carved marble and shows scenes from the life of St Charles Borromeo, who was Bishop of Milan. On either side there is another great *coup de théâtre*: in ornately carved niches a row of highly coloured, almost life-size and weirdly realistic statues of saints and martyrs stand gesturing towards the congregation in rhetorical attitudes.

There is a Lady Chapel with its own extravagantly decorated and coffered dome above a contemporary statue of the Virgin and Child. Light gently diffuses through the cupola on to an Infant Jesus represented, unusually and touchingly, as laughing.

The confessionals, appropriate to the scale of such a place, are large, polished and commodious. The organ, which came from a local Anglican church, sits majestically on a very solid gallery. The pulpit is of carved wood with paintings of British saints. At the back of the church there is a war memorial. In eloquent counterpoint to all the burnished magnificence around it is a simple wooden cross taken from the grave of an unknown soldier in France.

St Winefride, Well Street, Holywell, Clwyd (1832–3)

St Winefride's is neo-Classical, red brick and, until a later enlargement, was quite small. It was one of the earliest church designs of J J Scoles (1798–1863). The road that sweeps past the church leads down the hill to the shrine from which the church derives its name and Holywell its fame.

St Winefride was a 7th-century aristocrat who attracted the attentions of a Prince Caradoc. She resisted his advances and, enraged, he cut off her head. Her uncle, St Beuno, was passing, saw what had happened and prayed that she might be healed. Her head was restored and she became a nun; Prince Caradoc, meanwhile, was swallowed up by the earth. Where the saint's head had hit the ground a spring gushed forth. It became known for its miraculous powers of healing and has been a place of pilgrimage, even in the years after the Reformation, ever since. The well chapel built over the spring is late Perpendicular dating from the early 16th century, much restored and now Anglican. The Catholic church at Holywell administers the well and there are services there daily during the pilgrimage season from Pentecost to September.

In the transept of the Catholic church there is a very large, white and imperious stone statue of St Winifride by M Blanchart of Ghent, carved in 1881. Otherwise, the church is not dominated by its associations with its famous patron saint. It is a large, rectangular, civilised space that has recently been redecorated. Round-topped windows with stained motifs in the centre of clear glass panels, some depicting the miracle and the pilgrimage, light the nave. The Stations of the Cross are large, colourful reliefs, crowned by substantial gold pediments. They are subtitled in Welsh and English. There is a gallery above the narthex and at the east end the sanctuary is simplicity itself – an altar, a rood and a tabernacle. More dramatic are the transepts which were built when the church was extended in 1909–12. These irregularly shaped spaces contain the statue of St Winefride and an elaborate altar to Our Lady.

The splendidly over-the-top Catholic banners painted by Frederick Rolfe, or Baron Corvo as he liked to be called, during his famously stormy time at Holywell are kept in an exhibition room near the well itself.

Classical sobriety; the west front of St Winefride.

Pope Gregory the Great with English slaves ('*non angli sed angeli*') in Rome: detail from a processional banner painted by Frederick Rolfe ('Baron Corvo').

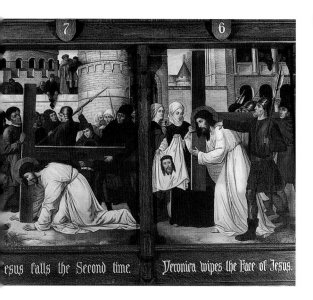

Jesus falls the Second time.   Veronica wipes the Face of Jesus.

Large Victorian Stations of the Cross contrast with the simplicity of the church's plain interior.

The 'stuck-on' Gothic stone west front of St Anthony of the Desert facing the Scotland Road.

St Anthony of the Desert, Scotland Road, Liverpool (1832–3).

St Anthony's was founded by Father Gerardot, a French émigré priest, and was the mother church of St Patrick, Park Place (see pages 51–2). Both churches were built at the edge of the town. St Anthony's was built when Liverpool was rapidly expanding northwards. Not far from the railway, the canal and the docks and once surrounded by slum housing, the church served a huge number of working-class Roman Catholics. Today the slums have been cleared and a much diminished population lives in small, modern housing estates. But the size, history and design of this church remain as a witness to those epic days of expansion and squalor, disease and devotion.

John Broadbent (1803–42), a Liverpool architect and a former pupil of the Gothic Revival pioneer Thomas Rickman, won the commission to design St Anthony's in a competition set by the church building committee. They stipulated that everyone in a large congregation of about 750 should have an unrestricted view of the High Altar. Broadbent designed a lofty, Gothic, battlemented church with a huge, apparently unsupported roof with no pillars to get in the way of the view. There are no side galleries which would have required view-obstructing columns. The clear interior is lit by tall, almost clear glass lancet windows that add to the feeling of spaciousness. The ceiling is darker, panelled and flat. The total impact is sensational. When the church was officially opened there was, a reproachful witness reported, much pushing and shoving to gain admittance. Those who did get in heard a Mass by Haydn and enjoyed the unrestricted view of Bishop Baines of the Western District preaching a sermon that lasted almost two hours.

The High Victorian Stations of the Cross are very large and elaborate, in contrast with the plain, almost featureless structure of the church. As if in further compensation, the east end is divided into three huge Gothic niches, each containing a window and an altar. All the altars have ambitious carved stone reredoses. All were designed by Broadbent and the most spectacular is the High Altar in the middle. This is of carved and painted stone and the usual theme of rejoicing angels is muted to a more abstract, architectural look. Next to the altars there are niches which contain large statues of saints. None, as it happens, is of St Anthony of the Desert.

The narthex under the west gallery has been separated from the nave by a glass screen. The area behind it has become a setting for a collection of statuary from the local Catholic churches that are now closed or have been demolished. A good, modern statue, of St Anthony accompanied by a wild boar, was commissioned to make up for his omission in the church.

Some steep, balustraded stairs lead to the west gallery where there are original pews and an elegant, classical organ. On either side of it are broad, carved panel reliefs of the Nativity and the Epiphany. They are said to be 17th century and Spanish or Portuguese in origin.

One of the most spectacular features of St Anthony's is the brick-vaulted crypt, now accessible as part of the new Heritage Centre. The crypt runs under the whole length of the church and is the oldest place of Catholic burial in the city. In the darkness, under the High Altar, lies the church's founding priest – Father Gerardot – and many of the priests who succeeded him.

The façade of the church is distinctive: stone, Gothic and 'stuck on' a fairly plain box. There are over a hundred individual carved heads above the windows and doors, based apparently on parishioners, to draw a second glance from motorists caught in the traffic along the Scotland Road.

St Bartholomew, Warrington Road, Rainhill, Lancashire (1836–40)

The sandstone walls have darkened over the years almost to black and the severe temple-like church stands sternly above, and among, the tombs of the family who founded it. They were not Catholic aristocrats. The founder was Bartholomew Bretherton who had made his fortune from the stagecoach business he owned that linked Liverpool with other English cities. Rainhill was the scene of the 1829 locomotive trials organised by the Liverpool and Manchester Railway and won by George Stephenson's 'Rocket'. Bretherton, observing the way the wind was blowing for the coaching business, sold up and bought railway stock. He also bought land and property in Rainhill, including Rainhill Hall where he lived. Next to it he built a Catholic church. Pevsner was to call it 'the noblest Catholic church in south Lancashire'.

The architect Bretherton chose was Joshua Dawson of Preston, but the real brains behind the project is said to have been an artist in stained glass – a Mr Carter, also of Preston. Bretherton sent Dawson off to Rome to study the churches there and when he returned work commenced. Two years later its profile, 'in the form of an Ionic temple, similar to that which is still to be seen on the banks of the Tiber', according to Dawson, loomed over the road to Warrington. It was opened with much religious ceremony and a big party at the Hall. Among those present were many rich Catholics who would themselves go on to build, or help to build, Catholic churches all over the very Catholic county. At St Bartholomew's the blackened walls have pilasters but no visible windows. The portico is massive and Ionic; the more elaborate campanile was added in 1849. If the church looks forbidding from the road the contrast inside is startling.

It is a basilica, barely lit by small windows above the entablature. This subtle illumination is nowadays augmented by a vigorous electric lighting system that blazes on to the rich colours that have been applied to the detail of the complex moulding. It was not always so. Bretherton's church was quite austere – the interior originally had stone-coloured walls and grey columns. It did not remain that way for long. Carter's original painting was overprinted in 1855. But it was Frederick Annesley

Built for a stagecoach operator, the blazing polychromatic interior of St Bartholomew: one of Lancashire's most extraordinary churches.

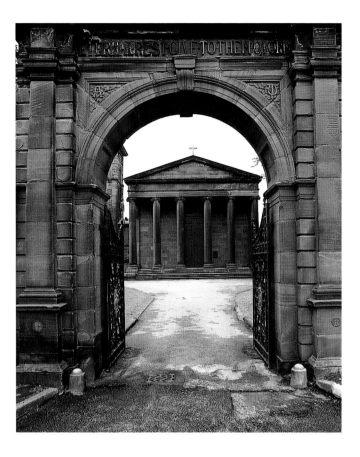

The west fronts at St Bartholomew, Rainhill (above) and St Francis Xavier, Hereford (below) echo Greece and Rome.

Stapleton-Bretherton (there had been some complicated marriage arrangements with the local Catholic squirearchy) who in 1886 was responsible for instituting a more ornate decoration in the church. He inspired the finely painted Latin inscriptions that were once highly prominent all around the church. The arch above the sanctuary bore the text *'Terribilis est locus iste: hic domus Dei est et porta coeli: et vocabitur aula Dei'*: 'How terrible is this place. This is the house of God and the gate of Heaven and it shall be called the Court of God'. The texts are now obscured. Undeterred, perhaps spurred on by their message, a major and highly contentious restoration and re-ordering took place in 1984 and after. The result is the brightly coloured architectural vision that irritated objectors but provides an undoubted *coup de théâtre* for visitors and congregation alike.

Corinthian columns (marbled with gold capitals) support a coffered barrel vault (blue and royal blue). The frieze is generously decorated (gold and blue). The sanctuary has vivid paintings of St Bartholomew, St Peter and St Paul, with fluted pilasters between them. On the apsidal dome above the sanctuary is a painting of the Ascension – set in a sea of stars. The altar, lowered during the re-ordering, is of Sienese marble but worked by local craftsman.

The Lady Chapel was dedicated to the husband of Bartholomew Bretherton's daughter in 1845 and displays his coat of arms.

St Francis Xavier, Broad Street, Hereford (1838)

This remarkable church was based on the Treasury of the Athenians at Delphi – an unusual source of inspiration for a building in the centre of an English county town. It is only a stone's throw away from the medieval cathedral and its two giant, yellow, Doric, stuccoed columns and pediment rise purposefully and intriguingly above Hereford's grandest street. It was one of the last churches to be built in the Greek Revival style, was much restored in 1889 and fell on hard times in the 1980s. It is something of a miracle that it has survived.

The architect was Charles Day, a Classical architect with a Catholic church already to his name in Bury St Edmunds. He designed the Shire Hall in Worcester where he was surveyor to the county of Worcestershire. His Jesuit clients put up most of the money for St Francis Xavier – £16,000, a huge sum for that time – and the Duke of Norfolk donated the land.

At the opening 'the leading county families were present' as well as a few Protestants who 'testified by their presence, a kindly sympathy with their Catholic brethren'. According to a local paper they were treated to 'A Grand Selection of Sacred Music'. Bishop Baines, the great champion of Classical architecture, led the procession round the church while a large choir sang the Hallelujah chorus. Pugin called it 'a pagan temple' and a 'Catholic concert hall'. Baines responded vigorously to this 'unauthorised and virulent attack' in the *Catholic Directory* of 1840.

By the late 20th century the fabric had deteriorated significantly. The roof was leaking badly and the fine organ, on which Sir Edward Elgar liked to play, was thought to be damaged beyond repair and was destroyed. The cost of restoring the church was going to be enormous. The Archdiocese of Cardiff had decided instead to sell the commercially valuable site, but the Friends of St Francis Xavier campaigned, funds were raised and the Archdiocese changed its mind. There was a debate about whether the church should be restored to its original Greek Revival look or to the heavy but impressive appearance that the later Victorian restoration had given it. English Heritage provided funding and expertise and a new priest, Father Michael Evans, saw

J J Scoles's shining tribute to St Peter's, Rome: at St Francis Xavier the tabernacle is flanked by Classical columns and Victorian wall paintings.

through a return to Classicism. Something may have been lost (though the Victorian wall paintings are still there under the new layers of paint, and two are visible to either side of the High Altar) but what we see today is one of the great achievements of modern church restoration.

A few steps from Broad Street lead up to a narthex – screened now from the main church by a wall of glass incised with papal coats of arms. Beyond the glass doors is an interior that is broad and rectangular with a dramatically coved ceiling. The space within is perfectly proportioned and subdued. Most of the natural light illuminating the interior comes from a glazed dome toward the east end, 60 feet above, painted with gold stars on a blue background. Light shines down on the marble High Altar and the tabernacle. The superb, towering gold tabernacle was designed by J J Scoles in about 1850 as an act of homage to the one designed by Bernini in St Peter's Rome. On either side of the altar are two large Ionic columns flanked by the two Victorian wall paintings of St Francis Xavier and the Virgin Mary.

To the right of the altar is a shrine to Father Kemble, an 80-year-old Herefordshire priest martyred in 1679 for no other offence than simply being a priest. During his gruesome death Father Kemble's hand was severed, and it is now preserved in a glinting silver reliquary on the side altar. There is a wall plaque with a gilt frame illustrating his martyrdom. He was canonised in 1970.

There is a new, electronic organ with discreetly mounted speakers; an arrangement that allows light to come in through the west window. During the two years of restoration the congregation was invited to hold Roman Catholic Mass in Hereford Cathedral – the first such celebrations there since the Reformation.

3 Pugin and his Followers:
The Enchantments of the Gothic Style

Tiles at St Augustine's Abbey, Ramsgate.

The return of colour, decoration and
enrichment: the crypt of St Chad's
Cathedral, Birmingham, '...the first fully
Catholic place of sepulture to be revived',
claimed Pugin.

Augustus Welby Northmore Pugin (1812–52), son of a French emigré,
converted to Rome in 1835. At an early age he was working on designs
for the new Palace of Westminster and he became not just a great and
famous architect but an influence on the thinking of his century. As
Britain's industrial revolution accelerated Pugin pointed backwards to the
Middle Ages. This, he claimed, was a time when craftsman and labourer
worked contentedly to erect the finest buildings the world has ever seen.
First of all Pugin pointed to the churches and cathedrals built in England
in the 15th century – the Perpendicular period – and then he switched
his passionate devotion to the 13th and 14th centuries. The architecture
of that time was Gothic and it was not just beautiful, it was moral.
The construction articulated the function and purpose of the building.
The design expressed how that had been achieved. These buildings were
flooded with glorious light from radiant stained-glass windows. In them
were treasures – crosses, roods, fonts, pulpits, carvings and statues of saints.
Post-Reformation zealots had torn these things out of the churches.
Sacred objects that had for centuries symbolised and enshrined the
devotional life of individuals and communities had been destroyed.
Pugin had better knowledge of these things than many of his
contemporaries. He had travelled in Europe, seeing at first hand the
medieval wonders about which he enthused. Pugin wanted not only
to build churches in the medieval Gothic way but also to adorn them.
The altars that had been stripped would be replenished, mystery and
beauty would return to worship; the working man and his family would
be given something wonderful. Pugin looked back to the medieval
parish church where the sanctuary sheltered mysteries and spiritual
energies so powerful and dangerous that – like a nuclear reactor – they
were separated from the rest of the church. The worshipper could only
glimpse the sanctuary through the arches of a screen.

Pugin was obstinate and bigoted as well as brilliant. He insisted on the
necessity of screens, long, distant sanctuaries and side aisles. Innumerable
churches were built following his principles. What did it matter if the
aisles of medieval churches and cathedrals were built for circulation, not

St Giles, Cheadle: Pugin's dream of a return to the Middle Ages.

for seating? What did it matter if people could not see what was going on during the Mass? 'So sacred, so awful, so mysterious is the sacrifice of the Mass', he wrote, 'that if men were seriously to reflect on what it really consists, so far from advocating mere room for its celebration, they would hasten to restore the reverential forms of Catholic antiquity, and instead of striving for front seats and front places, they would hardly feel worthy to occupy the remotest corner of the temple.'

If, as he said, Gothic was socially and aesthetically as well as morally the only possible Christian style, then Classical architecture was 'pagan'. It was the architecture of the Reformation ('a dreadful scourge') and Henry VIII. Classical was hierarchical, the architecture of power. Classicism derived from Rome ('built by slaves') for emperors and tyrants. Bring back Gothic and you bring back craftsmen and artists working in a community whose spiritual and aesthetic yearnings would be given expression and form. In an age that became tormented by the question of architectural style Pugin's ideas were very persuasive – more, as it happened, to Anglicans than Catholics. The foremost Anglican architect Sir George Gilbert Scott gratefully acknowledged that Pugin had got it right and embraced the Gothic. Pugin would be among the immortals on the Albert Memorial which he designed. (Scott insisted that Pugin, and not he, should have a full length figure on the memorial. Scott is shown only in a modest relief, behind Pugin). But there was some opposition. John Henry Newman had severe doubts which he expressed with some vigour. So had the influential Bishop Baines. Had not Classicism been the style of the Counter-Reformation, of Rome? Was not Rome the seat of authority to which all Catholics looked for moral and spiritual guidance? But Pugin – for a time – won the day. The principal style of 19th-century church building (and much else) would be Gothic.

Edward Pugin, like his father, was an architect given to destructive controversy and, in his case, ruinous litigation. They both died young, Edward of a heart condition that cannot have been helped by his taking a Turkish bath on the afternoon of his death. He too believed that Gothic architecture was the only Christian architecture, but later in life Edward would change and adapt it. Charles Francis Hansom, a devoted follower of the great man, was committed to 'correct' Gothic and long after the death of Pugin would have nothing to do with the freer, more adventurous interpretations of it that became fashionable. Matthew Hadfield was a less assured practitioner preferring to imitate Pugin and copy the medieval in a fairly literal way; something Pugin never did. John Weightman and Matthew Hadfield of Sheffield (both pious Catholics; Hadfield was a Liberal town councillor) built numerous and accomplished 'medieval' churches all over northern England. W W Wardell put his experience of working with Pugin in Gothic at Greenwich to good effect when he moved to Australia. His vast Gothic cathedral in Sydney had additions to it designed in 1851 by A W N Pugin.

For all that, a different sort of architecture that derived nothing from the Middle Ages was beginning its rise to eventual domination. At the Great Exhibition of 1851 the medieval court that Pugin and his friends and associates designed was much enjoyed by the visitors, but they tended to go in larger numbers to look at the hammers and whirring wheels of the industrial machines in the neighbouring courts.

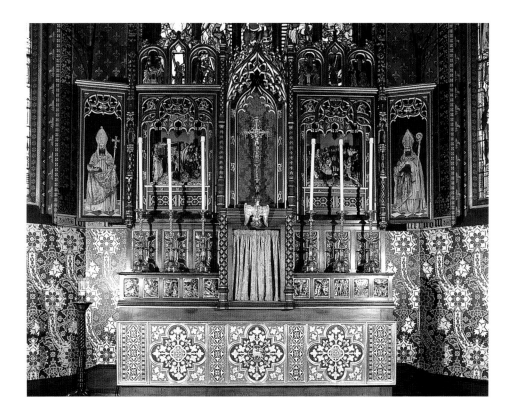

Pugin's first large-scale work:
the altar and sanctuary at Oscott
– the elements were designed or
donated by him.

Oscott College Chapel, Chester Road, Sutton Coldfield, Warwickshire (1837–8)

Oscott College is the seminary for the Archdiocese of Birmingham but trains students for the priesthood from all over England and Wales. It was built on a ridge of high ground overlooking what was then empty countryside. In the far distance, to the south, smoke from the chimneys of fast-industrialising Birmingham was just visible. Money came from the 16th Earl of Shrewsbury and the architect was Joseph Potter of Lichfield. It was vastly ambitious and expensive; Oscott was designed to be a beacon of the Catholic revival in the midlands. It is no wonder A W N Pugin was drawn to it. He arrived in 1837 with his patron the 16th Earl and a fast-growing reputation. Most of the building had been completed by Potter but Pugin designed Gothic lodges and the statue of Our Lady based on the 15th-century one he had given to St Chad's in Birmingham. But chiefly he took over the decoration of the chapel. Potter withdrew in 1840 leaving an unremarkable square box of a building; the opulence of the chapel's breathtaking decoration and furnishing owes everything to Pugin. Pugin lavished antiques, both medieval and baroque, upon it and he designed Gothic vestments for the spectacular service of consecration that took place in 1838. Present were bishops and a hundred clergy. There was a vast procession. Pugin made himself a *de facto* master of ceremonies and played a lordly role that many there thought should have been left to priests. With tears in his eyes he said 'it was the grandest day for the Church in England since the Reformation'. He would often stay at Oscott, styling himself as 'Professor of Ecclesiastical Antiquities', and there he gave his lectures that were published in London as *True Principles of Pointed or Christian Architecture* (1841).

The whole of the sanctuary is astonishingly colourful. The reredos has an exuberantly carved wooden frame designed by Pugin which encloses powerful, coloured medieval carvings of the Annunciation and Birth of Christ, the Adoration of the Magi and the Vision of St Hubert. Below are blue and white Limoges enamel panels illustrating the Life, the Passion and the Ascension of Christ. Pugin's design for the ceiling of the chapel is a riot of religious symbol and imagery intertwined with embellished 'M's (for Mary). The tall, highly wrought pulpit is by Pugin, the altar rails are 17th-century Baroque. (Pugin was yet to reach the full fanatical zeal of his commitment to the Gothic and allowed some Baroque.) The rails were bought in London as were the original Flemish 17th-century choir stalls.

Pugin wanted to reintroduce and reinvigorate crafts that had gone into decline or extinction since the Reformation. He designed the windows above the altar, his earliest stained-glass work. They were executed by manufacturer William Warrington of London who worked with Pugin to reinvent the medieval techniques of the craft and they show the Virgin Mary as Queen of Heaven, flanked by a multiplicity of saints in a great burst of colour and light.

Pugin also sought to revive the art of medieval paving tiles. He made contact with Herbert Minton and began a collaboration that lasted for Pugin's lifetime and reintroduced the craft to Britain. Pugin's further ambition was to reintroduce medieval ways of engraving and working with brass and metal. It was at Oscott in 1837 that he first met John Hardman and they became life-long friends. The Hardmans were Birmingham Catholics and very successful businessmen (the family firm made buttons and metal goods). John Hardman could provide Pugin (who initially had to work with venerable German metalworkers who still used medieval methods) with what he wanted. Hardman had the new machines and understood the techniques, not just for brass engraving but also for working with glass. The later stained glass in the chapel and the college is by Hardman & Co.

Pugin's son Edward designed the Weedall Chantry which was added to honour the co-founder of Oscott. It was completed in 1862. There are two side chapels but the space is dominated by a life-size alabaster statue of Our Lady *Sedes Sapientiae* or Seat of Wisdom. The statue was exhibited at the 1862 International Exhibition in London and was designed by Pugin's son-in-law, John Hardman Powell, a member of the Hardman firm. Behind the statue a Tree of Life was painted on the wall bearing on its branches brass memorials to distinguished Oscott alumni. The tree was eventually painted out but the brasses, rather oddly, remain *in situ*.

Two years after the Restoration of the Hierarchy in 1850, the synod met in the chapel. John Henry Newman preached on what was later published as 'The Second Spring' of Catholicism in England as it emerged from persecution. The synod wept at his words.

'...the most magnificent thing that Catholics have yet done in modern times': Pugin still in his Perpendicular phase at Derby.

St Mary, Bridge Gate, Derby (1838)

This was A W N Pugin's first large parish church. The 100-foot crocketed spire that he wanted was never built but its tall, slightly attenuated tower still dominates the city. Its height challenges the medieval tower of the church that became the Anglican cathedral – something which may have provoked Anglican clergymen to remark on the sinfulness of Protestants attending the opening ceremony of St Mary's. Relations were not improved when the Church of England's St Allemand's was built in 1846 – with a very tall spire – right in front of the new Catholic church. The Anglican church was demolished when the ring road, which now separates St Mary's from the city centre, was cut through in 1967. It is now best approached from the town by a modern footbridge.

The priest was Father Sing, an Old Oscottian and a great Pugin supporter. He was reputed to move easily in the best circles and such was his pulling power that 'some of the best families in the county would attend Mass conducted by him – wherever it might be held' reported an impressed contemporary. But as well as having an existing congregation the coming of the railways had led to a great influx of Catholic Irish into Derby. A big new church was called for. Bishop Walsh, who had done much to get Oscott going, wanted to see many more new churches built, and paid for this site himself.

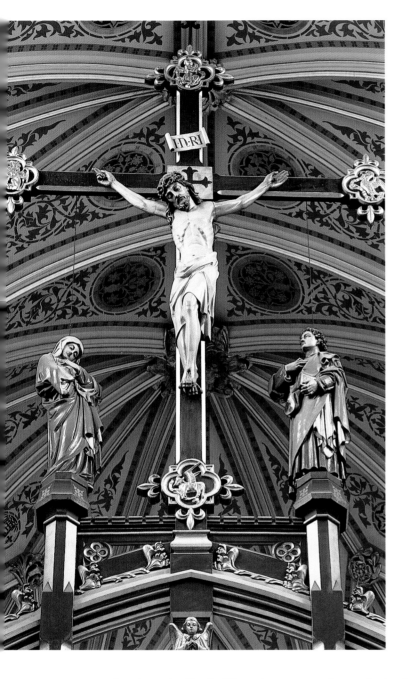

A carved wooden arch supports the rood with statues of Mary and St John.

During the elaborate opening ceremony Bishop Wiseman preached the sermon and seventy priests 'wearing splendid robes' and Bishop Walsh 'attired in gorgeous robes' took part. They might have been even more splendidly dressed but for a big falling out earlier in the day. Pugin had discovered that there was going to be an orchestral Mass rather than plainsong. He and Lord Shrewsbury walked out before the service had begun. They took with them the Gothic vestments that Pugin had designed and for which Shrewsbury had paid. For all that, the church, according to Dr Wiseman, 'was the most magnificent thing that Catholics have yet done in modern times in this country' and it '…would not have done dishonour to Rome'. There was a grand dinner. The days of the modest Catholic chapel were definitely over.

St Mary's is Perpendicular which was then Pugin's preferred style of neo-Gothic. The builder was George Myers of Hull who would work with Pugin at St Chad's Birmingham (see page 67) and elsewhere and become a life-long friend and associate. The interior is a wonderful, virtuoso display of light, shape and colour. The fluted columns seem almost dangerously thin as they reach up, uninterrupted by capitals, to the clerestory and nave roof. Between the nave and the sanctuary there is a slender wooden arch that supports the rood and the figures of Mary and St John. There is no screen below the rood, which Pugin would have favoured. The three vividly coloured apse windows based on the theme of the biblical Tree of Jesse rise up above a superbly carved altar and are by William Warrington. The elaborately carved stone reredos behind the High Altar replaced one by Pugin. There is a square tabernacle that breaks into the outline of the great east window with carved angels grouped around it and a piercingly crocketted pinnacle, also with angels with outstretched wings, above it. There are canopied sedilia.

The church was extended by E W Pugin in 1855 by the addition of a Lady Chapel. This is larger than many churches and its monumental altar of Caen stone and marble was designed by another of the architect's sons, Peter Paul Pugin. Above the altar is a more than life-size statue of Our Lady of Lourdes. The stained glass above is, like all the glass, excellent with other windows (1919–31) by Hardman & Co elsewhere in the church.

St Alban, Chester Road, Macclesfield, Cheshire (1839–41)

In September 1838 the 16th Earl of Shrewsbury wrote to Father Hall at the old St Michael's chapel in Macclesfield. The priest was planning a new and much larger church and was already talking to an architect, a Mr Hadfield. The earl wrote 'I am happy to say that Mr Pugin is just returned. He will call on you…should the committee agree to avail themselves of Mr Pugin's talents, I will add Fifty Pounds a year to my subscription.' Hadfield took the hint and Pugin designed a fine, large church in his currently favoured Perpendicular style. Nicholas Wiseman – later to be Cardinal Archbishop of Westminster – officially opened the church. The proceedings do not seem to have matched those at St Mary's, Derby. There was no grand dinner but a 'cold collation for the clergy at the Macclesfield Arms Hotel', reported the local paper.

At Derby, Pugin never got his spire and here he was frustrated in his plans to have a tall tower. The money ran out and St Alban still looks slightly sawn off at the top. The interior, however, is delightful both in its use of architectural space and in its furnishings. Once again Pugin created an inspiring display of light on delicate and slender painted stone columns that support a clerestory and the lofty roof beams.

Beyond a dramatically suspended rood, the climax and the focus of the church is the sanctuary. The raised altar is seen through one of Pugin's finest designs – a rood screen with eight panels and two large gates. The carved wooden figures on it are 15th-century Flemish and came from Louvain. It separates the nave from the High Altar in which are sealed relics of St Thomas of Canterbury. The reredos behind it – said to have been inspired by the reredos at St Alban's Abbey – has canopied niches for carved figures of Mary, Jesus and the twelve Apostles. There are inventively canopied sedilia marked *Sacerdos, Diaconus* and *Sub-Diaconus*. A gallery behind the rood screen leads up to an oriel overlooking the Lady Chapel. Rising above all this splendour is the east window by William Warrington. It has seven lights and was the gift of the Earl of Shrewsbury, whose arms accompany the towering figure of St Alban, proto-martyr of England.

The window in the Lady Chapel (1854) features the crowned figure of Mary with St Edward the Confessor and St John the Evangelist. They share the space with, bottom left, some parishioners and, right, Father Hall in his clerical robes. Children from the Catholic school collected money for the reredos, which was eventually installed and in 1930 enriched with gold. The walls have ten 'half angels' painted on canvas attached to them (by Hardman & Co of Birmingham). Architect Richard O'Mahony, was commissioned to re-order the church in 1982. He found Pugin's interior 'truly inspiring' and in the course of a sensitive re-ordering left the sanctuary unaltered.

Rood screen, sedilia and sanctuary: 'A screen', wrote Pugin 'teaches the faithful to revere the holy mysteries'.

St Chad's Cathedral, Queensway, Birmingham (1839–41)

This was one of A W N Pugin's earliest Catholic commissions and it was characteristically ambitious. He designed a big church that would reflect the confidence of a city proud of its growing wealth and industrial strength and would one day house the recently rediscovered bones of St Chad. St Chad's always seemed likely to become a cathedral. Pugin drew up the plans from his power base at Oscott. They were not received with unanimous approval. Local congregations in Birmingham were used to having their own ideas about what sort of churches they wanted and they prevaricated over Bishop Walsh's plans for a great ecclesiastical building. But with Pugin on the scene and Lord Shrewsbury's financial support in the offing, Walsh pushed the scheme through. Pugin had not the least interest in what the locals wanted. What they got was an enormous red brick (very Birmingham) church with two steepled spires on the west front that would have looked at home in a German port on the Baltic Sea. It was built of English bond brick. Pugin chose the material and the unusual Hanseatic look quite deliberately to make St Chad's stand out from the other churches of Birmingham. The soaring new St Chad's was erected in a very short period of time. The east side with its sanctuary, chapels, crypt and transepts all climbed picturesquely down a slope to a huddle of workshops round the canal basin, through which building materials for the church were brought by barge. St Chad's was opened with splendid liturgical ceremonies (thirteen bishops in the sanctuary) that lasted five days. Proceedings were concluded by a dinner at the Town Hall. After dinner the architect spoke at some length.

The interior space comes as a surprise. The exterior may be dark, weathered red brick but inside everything feels high and light. Attenuated stone piers soar upwards to a highly decorated, steeply pitched roof. Excellent stained-glass windows glow from all sides. William Warrington made the three apse windows in 1840 to Pugin's designs. On the north aisle is Pugin's monument to the cathedral's founder, Bishop Walsh. It was shown at the Great Exhibition of 1851. Above it is the magnificent Immaculate Conception window (1868) erected as a memorial to John Hardman, who can be seen, bottom left, wearing a cope. Further down the north aisle is the Glass Workers' window. It was a gift of employees of John Hardman & Co and shows exemplary medieval workmen virtuously busy, cutting and painting glass.

St Edward's Chapel was added in 1933 to designs by S Pugin Powell. Above the altar is a reliquary containing the tibia of the 7th-century

Not like other Birmingham churches: Pugin's Baltic design for the towers of St Chad's was deliberately chosen to make the building distinct from other churches in the city.

'All ornament should consist of enrichment of the essential construction of the building': Pugin's nave and sanctuary at St Chad's.

St Chad, the first bishop of the Midland see. The glass windows around the chapel graphically tell the story of how the saint's bones were removed from Lichfield Cathedral after the Reformation and hidden above a four-poster bed. The narrative concludes with the relics being carried in triumphant procession through the streets of Birmingham in 1919 with bespectacled clergy officiating.

The pulpit in the nave is 15th-century Flemish, probably from St Gertrude, Louvain. It is made of carved oak and was the gift of Lord Shrewsbury. The choir stalls were from Cologne. Pugin himself gave the 15th-century statue of Our Lady in the Lady Chapel. The roof of the crossing is exceptionally splendid and there is a ceiling panel on the south aisle roof commemorating the moment when, and the place where, a bomb pierced the roof in 1940. The explosion burst a radiator pipe and the consequent deluge put out the fire. The words 'Deo Gratias' are painted on the panel.

Pugin's High Altar in the sanctuary is stone, fantastically carved and painted. Above the reredos, flanked by kneeling angels is a gilt box containing more relics of St Chad. The tabernacle doors by J Hardman Powell are enamelled with the Agony in the Garden. Architectural historian Roderick O'Donnell considers that 'The whole ensemble is one of the most important mid-nineteenth century recreations of medieval furnishings, comparable to the throne ensemble in the House of Lords.'

The spacious crypt was 'the first fully Catholic place of sepulture to be revived' according to Pugin. It contains a series of chantry chapels. The Hardman chantry, with brass memorials to the family, is decorated in the high, Puginian mode. Louisa, Pugin's second wife, is buried here. The Romanesque arches were built to suggest an earlier age of construction than the cathedral above and so give a sense of slow, organic growth.

In the 1960s Birmingham was transformed by a system of ring roads and underpasses that now encroach on the cathedral. Until 1960 the Bishop's House that Pugin had designed stood next to St Chad's. In 1967 St Chad's was subjected to a vigorous re-ordering. Much of Pugin's legacy was removed. The rood screen, of which he was very proud, was taken away. It found a home in the Anglican Holy Trinity church in Reading. Pugin's tiled floor was replaced though some of the original tiles were put into the former baptistery. In a recent further re-ordering a Gothic-style forward altar has been installed. Recently, there has been action by the cathedral authorities to restore as much as possible of the colour, and the former glory of St Chad's.

Our Lady and St Wilfrid, Warwick Bridge, Carlisle, Cumberland (1841)

In 1840 A W N Pugin turned aside from building lofty churches and cathedrals for expanding cities to design this small and exquisite village church. He had a high opinion of the village church. The parish church transcended even the Reformation, he thought, and its grip on the national imagination had not faltered. 'Are not village spires, the church bells, the old porches, the venerable yew trees, the old grey towers, subjects on which poets and writers love to dwell?' he wrote in 1843. Little has happened to this church since it was built and it is a perfect example of how he could put his True Principles into practise.

It stands on slightly raised ground near the centre of the village. Not, it has been pointed out, too raised – not aloof from the village. There is no tower; just a bell-cote built in the local sandstone. There is a graveyard; churches that did not have graveyards, Pugin thought, omitted 'the very remembrance of death…lest visitors to these places be shocked at the sight of tombs'. There are modest buttresses and an inviting porch.

The interior of the church is more or less exactly as Pugin left it. His original decoration has escaped interference and change. The nave looks towards a rood and its screen. The screen is solidly carved and surmounted by six tall candlesticks put there to illuminate the rood above where Mary and St Wilfrid stand on either side of the crucified Christ. The ensemble, framed against the splendidly painted

The carved and gilded reliquary of St Chad above the High Altar at Birmingham.

Pugin's admiration for the English village church was brilliantly expressed at Warwick Bridge.

The Easter Sepulchre in the sanctuary at Warwick Bridge contains the remains of the church's founder, Henry Howard.

sanctuary roof and three lancet windows, is also painted and picked out in blue, gold and red. The screen is hinged. Drawn back, the lower sections become communion rails.

The benches are plain and simple but the Stations – gold and detailed – are spiky and ornate. There are large painted roundels on the walls commemorating various parishioners as well as the family that provided funding for the church, the Howards. Also remembered are the Benedictines who, before emancipation, 'served this mission in Warwick Bridge' and who still serve the parish to this day.

There is an Easter Sepulchre in the sanctuary within which are the mortal remains of 'Henricus Howard benefactor obiit ad 1842'. The sanctuary is ornately painted and stencilled walls frame an altar, a reredos, a piscina and sedilia – all to Pugin's design and all beautifully crafted. The altar is raised above the colourfully tiled sanctuary floor and to the right is the entrance to a small sacristy. From there a flight of stairs gave access to the pulpit. To accommodate the re-ordering a simple, but Puginesque-looking table stands in front of the original altar and houses a reliquary. The west end too has three lancet windows, a small organ and a chrysmatory where the holy oils are kept.

The church has relics, brought originally from the catacombs of Rome, of St Etronia a child martyr. It also keeps some very finely embroidered vestments, one of which was made by Mary Queen of Scots, during her captivity. The craftsmen who worked at Warwick Bridge were to go on to work at St Giles, Cheadle (see page 74).

St Barnabas Cathedral, Derby Road, Nottingham (1841–4)

St Barnabas 'when complete will be the most perfect revival of a large parochial church that has yet been accomplished…and to the minutest details this church will be a strict revival of Catholic antiquity' wrote A W N Pugin. It was one of his most daring designs in the Early English style. The Earl of Shrewsbury, Ambrose Phillipps de Lisle and Bishop Walsh put up most of the money. It became a cathedral in 1850. When it opened it was the biggest Catholic church in England.

St Barnabas stands on a busy main road. The tower and broach spire rise high above the crossing. The walls are of local sandstone and there are tiles and green slate for the roofs. The windows are lancet. It is very imposing and was all rather more than Shrewsbury had bargained for. He grumbled to the Bishop but Dr Walsh demurred. He had ambitions to make Nottingham, rather than Birmingham, England's central see and he wanted something big.

For his part, Pugin thought the narrow lancet windows made the place dark. Lancet was all right for country churches, but for a big city church you needed, he thought, something bigger. The cathedral can no longer be thought of as dark: the walls of the interior were painted white in 1993. Pugin's original rood screen and High Altar were destroyed in the late 19th century and there has been much rearranging and alteration since then. More recently, however, there has been an attempt to restore some of the former colour and drama to the cathedral.

The High Altar now stands underneath the crossing and the roof levels interact above it with different

The mosaic splendours of Ravenna in Nottingham: J Alphege Pippet's astonishing Blessed Sacrament Chapel at St Barnabas.

colours, angles and designs. Suspended from the roof is a decorated and solid-looking tester. The bishop's throne faces the congregation from the place where the High Altar once stood. The rood is suspended eloquently from the sanctuary arch. There is an ambulatory round the sanctuary with a crypt below it and the east end chapels still have their Pugin altars. The whiteness of the nave walls is relieved by gold outlining and roundels above the columns. Most of the glass was made by William Wailes of Newcastle to Pugin's designs but there is good modern glass by Joseph Nuttgens in the north and south transept, left and right of the sanctuary. Nuttgens said that designing glass for insertion in the high lancet windows was 'a very difficult business'.

The central tower and spire, canopied saints and lancet windows of Pugin's church in Nottingham, which was the largest Catholic church in England when it opened in 1844.

Nuttgens's friend and neighbour, sculptor Eric Gill carved the statue of St Hugh in the south-east chapel.

The true glory of St Barnabas is the Blessed Sacrament Chapel. Here Pugin's spectacular vision of the Middle Ages was brought lovingly back to life in the 1930s by J Alphege Pippet, directed by Bishop McNulty. Here is majestic iconography and shimmering decoration in gold and red to rival Byzantium as well as a magnificent arch above a radiant altar and tabernacle.

St Mary's Cathedral, Clayton Street West, Newcastle upon Tyne (1842–4)

Local Catholics voted in 1838 for a new church that would be 'an honour to their religion and an ornament to the Town' and could seat about 1,200 people. At St Mary's, A W N Pugin showed how confidently he could handle the Decorated style. The Gothic cathedral is centrally placed, a short walk from John Dobson's great Classical Central Railway Station with which it is almost contemporary. However, the enormous tower and spire are not by Pugin; he wanted one, but as usual the money ran out. In 1872 the necessary £2,000 was found and the tower was built by A M Dunn and E J Hansom. It soars above the three gable ends of what, in 1850, became the cathedral of the new diocese of Hexham (later Hexham and Newcastle). The baptistery chapel was added in 1902.

The townspeople had raised most of the money themselves by subscription but Pugin doubted if it was enough – there was no Earl of Shrewsbury waiting in the wings. Nonetheless work commenced, with George Myers as builder. The interior is uncomplicated. It has, so to speak, three roofs – one over the nave and one each over the north and south aisles. Above the columns carved angels on the corbels support the beautifully painted scissor-braced roof. There is no clerestory. The rood that was moved to the side as an 'experiment' during re-ordering was later voted back to its central position by the parishioners. The nave leads straight under it to the sanctuary which has no arch but where there is a High Altar designed by Pugin to take the breath away. It was originally in the Lady Chapel and shows, in exquisitely carved white Caen stone, a calm and beautiful Mary with the Infant Jesus standing on her knee. Beside her, in attitudes of breathless adoration, stand angels with torches and harps. Above this major work of art is a marvellously carved reredos, similarly in white stone, showing the Resurrection, the Crucifixion and Pentecost where St Paul has been allowed to be present among the Disciples.

Opposite: Puginesque tiles and a perspective towards the High Altar and reredos at St Mary's, Newcastle. The Tree of Jesse east window was designed by Pugin and made by William Wailes, a Newcastle man.

The seven-light east window completes an extraordinary ensemble. It is another masterpiece and it was made to Pugin's designs in 1844 by William Wailes, a Newcastle stained-glass artist. A complex and brilliantly coloured Tree of Jesse shows the ancestry of Jesus in formal and detailed glory: the patriarchs wear hats; the kings wear crowns; the vine reaches up to Mary who, again, has the Infant Jesus on her knee, and above her the Holy Spirit shines in the form of a dove.

Outside the east end is the newly opened Cardinal Hume Memorial Garden. At its centre is a statue of the cardinal by Nigel Boonham looking thoughtfully toward Central Station.

St Giles, Cheadle. '...my consolation in all afflictions': the pulpit amid Pugin's glimmering decoration.

St Giles, Bank Street, Cheadle, Stoke-on-Trent, Staffordshire (1840–6)

When the church was finally finished in 1846 the local people who came crowding in to take a look thought it was so rich in colour and decoration that it was like going into fairyland. Pugin might not have approved of their line of thought, but among the mills and factory chimneys of this northern town they had indeed seen something amazing: Pugin's most successful and famous church.

The 16th Earl of Shrewsbury had bought a prime site in the town and he commissioned Pugin giving him carte blanche to design whatever he liked without financial constraint or patronal interference; Pugin joyfully accepted. There had been disappointments at Derby and Birmingham but, he wrote, 'Cheadle, perfect Cheadle. Cheadle is my consolation in all afflictions.' He hoped that 'learned people would flock to the church as a model', and they did. John Henry Newman, who was to become a critic of Pugin, was reminded by the Blessed Sacrament Chapel of *porta coeli* – the gates of heaven. Anglican architect Sir George Gilbert Scott came. Other architects, artists and designers came, not just from Britain, but from all over Europe.

At Cheadle, Pugin designed a 200-foot tower and spire to dominate the town. It is made from the local red sandstone and is a marvel of detail with pinnacles, niches and an abundance of crockets climbing up the sides of the slender spire. Shrewsbury provided the materials and the men to do most of the work, but it was still a colossal and very expensive (£20,000) project. The west door was made by John Hardman & Co and is a glowing tribute to the church's aristocratic patron. The Talbot arms of lions rampant form the gold hinges to a startlingly grand, red-painted oak door.

But it is the interior that takes most visitors' breath away. Pugin has decorated, stencilled, painted every inch of the ceiling, walls, arches and columns. The floor is tiled in a rich complex of patterns (by H Minton). The windows (by W Wailes) burn with colour. The screen is still in place – beautifully and delicately carved – and so are the loft and rood. Everywhere there is heraldry, sculpture and religious iconography. The inside of St Giles is not bathed in light as were the churches of Pugin's Perpendicular days but benefits from a muted, respectful diffusion of light through clerestory windows.

The sedilia, surmounted by gables and pinnacles, richly foliated, for priest, deacon and sub-deacon to sit in during the chanting of the Gloria and Credo.

Above the sanctuary arch is a Last Judgement painted on canvas by Eduard Hauser. Among the saved is Gwendolyn, daughter of the 16th Earl. Beyond the screen there are more riches – sedilia, an Easter sepulchre, altar and reredos – all wonderfully painted and embellished. There are side chapels and a bulky, carved font and pulpit. In the south chapel the decoration reaches a climax with gorgeously designed symbols of the Lamb of God and the Eucharist.

St Giles made visible at last Pugin's dream of a church returned to the glory of the Middle Ages. He wrote: 'Oh! Then, what delight! What joy unspeakable!…the stoups are filled to the brim; the rood is raised on high; the screen glows with sacred imagery and rich devices…the lamps of the sanctuary burn bright; the saintly portraitures in the glass windows shine all gloriously; and the albs hang in the oaken amburies…and pix, and pax, and chrismatory are there, and thurible, and cross.'

St Peter, St Peter Street, Marlow, Buckinghamshire (1845–6 and 1970).

Opposite: St Peter's viewed through Pugin's arch and the cemetery: '…nothing can be calculated to awake solemn and devout feelings more than passing through the resting-places of the faithful departed'.

Pugin's admiration for the traditional English parish church found further expression at St Peter's. Approached from the street, through wrought-iron gates (designed by Pugin), is a venerable-looking cemetery. Beyond is a church with walls in traditional knapped flint and a stone broach spire. It might have been there for centuries. It was one of the architect's last churches, but St Peter's has another claim to fame. It possesses the relic of the left hand of St James the Apostle. Famously, the rest of the saint is venerated in the cathedral of Santiago de Compostela in Spain. The hand is kept locked away and out of sight. An extension, which is bigger than the original church, was built in 1970 to the designs of Francis Pollen (1926–87), designer of the chapel at Worth Abbey (see page 208), to accommodate an expanding congregation no longer able to squeeze into Pugin's church.

The fan-shaped, modern extension to Pugin's church, built in 1970 to the designs of Francis Pollen.

It was not always so. A year before the opening of the church a Mass held in the old premises attracted a congregation of three. One was the priest's sister, another an 'old Irish lady from Cookham' and the third was Charles Scott Murray, Bart, BA (Oxon), Conservative MP for Buckinghamshire. While acquiring the BA at Oxford he had come under the influence of John Henry Newman. Scott Murray was 'county' and it

caused a local sensation when he was received into the Catholic faith during a visit to Rome. It was strongly suggested that he should resign his parliamentary seat. He chose not to do so; he merely took the newly prescribed declaration for Roman Catholic MPs. Furthermore, even though Bishop Wareing advised him that there were no Catholics in Marlow, he appointed a priest, started a Catholic mission and set about erecting a church.

There is a memorial to Scott Murray and his family in the south aisle. It is an ornate marble affair, much crocketed, with angels blowing golden trumpets and an abundance of coats of arms. Next to the monument is the screen that Pugin designed and George Myers built from Caen stone. Above is a rood of carved and painted wood with Mary and St Peter beside it. The altar beyond and the reredos were designed by Pugin. The altar shows carved profiles in relief of impassive biblical figures seated at lecterns on a blue background with delicately traceried, golden arches above them.

The simplicity of the nave walls is contrasted by some vividly painted Stations (1926) carved in Oberammergau, and at the back there is a Pugin-designed chrismatory for holding the consecrated oils used in baptisms. The windows are by Hardman and the best is the east window above the altar. However, daylight through it is now completely blocked by the new extension. (It can be seen if the fluorescent light installed behind it is switched on.)

Francis Pollen's thoughtful extension is approached through what used to be the Lady Chapel. Here a doorway was cut through and a passage leads to what is, in effect, a new church. It is wedge shaped and the congregation, much grown with the expansion of post-war Marlow as a major commuter town, has an uninterrupted view of the altar from raked benches. Behind the altar is a largely unadorned, curved brick wall which has been given drama by the gift of a large mosaic of the Risen Christ. The whole is lit by a series of clerestories and the altar by a cunningly cowled window above it.

St Augustine's Abbey, St Augustine's Road, Ramsgate, Kent (1845–50)

This is A W N Pugin's most personal church. He not only designed it but also paid for it, spent years building it, lived next door to it and was eventually buried, with members of his family, beneath it. 'I have never had the chance of producing a single, fine ecclesiastical building', he wrote, 'except my own church, where I was both paymaster and architect.'

St Augustine's: Pugin's font glimpsed beyond the columns. It was shown at the Great Exhibition and admired by Queen Victoria.

Pugin liked the sea and he liked to visit his aunt in Ramsgate to get away from the frequent conflicts he was having with patrons and priests. 'There is nothing worth living for but Christian architecture and a boat', he stated.

The church is dramatically sited, high on the chalk cliffs south of the town. There was to have been a noble spire on the tower that would signal to all on land or sea the presence of this Catholic church, but it was never built. It is faced with knapped flint. Pugin personally selected and chose the position of every stone. For this labour of love Pugin gathered around him the people and friends who had worked with him over the years of his greatest achievements: George Myers was builder and contractor; John Hardman made all the glass; Herbert Minton the tiles.

The interior is, as Pevsner says, 'a marvel, movingly strong of structure and profuse in the decoration everywhere.' The nave walls are faced with stone and sandstone (very good for the acoustics of chanting, Pugin reported) and is embellished with carvings and mouldings. The sanctuary is as long as the nave and there are large side chapels. There is a bulky pillar to the right of the nave, so designed to bear the weight of the spire that never was. Left of the nave is a statue of St Augustine, designed by Pugin himself, holding a model of the church. This was Pugin's ideal church and he designed an appropriately intricate oak screen, carved by

Myers. Screens were vitally important to Pugin: 'When such a boundary is erected round the place of sacrifice in church it teaches the faithful to reverence the seat of the holy mysteries and to worship in humility', he wrote. Despite that, the screen was moved to a position in front of the Lady Chapel as part of the re-ordering in 1970. The altar, throne and tabernacle were similarly removed. Throne and tabernacle may be seen now at Southwark Anglican Cathedral, London.

The glorious east window was designed by Pugin and executed by John Hardman. It shows Christ in Majesty surrounded by angels with the four Evangelists at the base. A writhing grapevine holds the whole composition together.

St Augustine's from the cliffside. Pugin selected and positioned every stone.

The Lady Chapel has a fine stone altar and, somewhat obscured by the repositioned rood screen, there is another screen, probably the finest in the church, in metal, designed by John Hardman Powell. It was commissioned, in Pugin's memory, by fellow architects.

At the west end of the south aisle is a huge font designed by Pugin that was exhibited at the Great Exhibition and was given to the church by George Myers. It is a virtuoso exercise of medieval-style carving with scenes from the Bible and adorned by many angels. A very tall, spiky, gravity-defying canopy can be raised up to ceiling height for baptisms.

The Pugin chantry in the south transept is lit by a vast window that shows St Augustine and other saints. In a lower panel is Pugin himself, dressed as a Benedictine oblate, as well as his three wives. Below the window is a life-size, recumbent stone effigy of Pugin, designed by his son Edward. Pugin is wearing a medieval-looking cloak and his hands are clasped in prayer. His feet rest on two martlets, the Pugin emblem, and below him, carved into the sides of the monument, are figures of his children weeping and kneeling in prayer. The floor is covered with colourful Minton tiles bearing more emblems of martlets and his initials. The tiles carry the inscription 'Pray for the soul of Augustus Welby Pugin, founder of this church'. 'Pugin', said John Hardman Powell, 'delighted in the monuments of great men'. Pugin died in 1852, exhausted and after bouts of insanity. Below the chantry is a sealed vault where the architect is buried, together with members of his family. His son Edward died in 1875 and he too lies here. He also had a tempestuous life and had expressed a wish that 'On my tomb I should like written, Here lies a man of many miseries.'

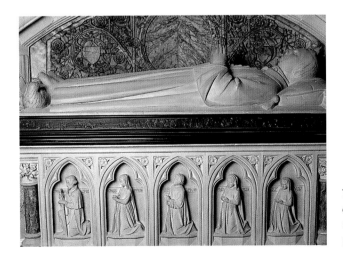

The life-size effigy of Pugin designed by his son Edward. Below him are carved figures of his weeping family.

Our Lady and St Alphonsus, Blackmore Park, Hanley Swan, Worcestershire (1844–6)

This church owes its existence to an old Worcestershire recusant family called Hornyold. Thomas Charles Hornyold was a determined Catholic campaigner in the early 19th century and he, and his nephew John Vincent Gandolfi, built this church. The Gandolfis were a grand Genoese family, some of whom had come to England for the silk trade. John Vincent was so well in with the Catholic hierarchy in Rome that at the age of 21 he was made a papal knight. The Hornyold family fortunes were low. To make ends meet, Thomas Hornyold developed Malvern Wells which was on the edge of his estate. He donated the site and John Vincent paid for the church and the adjoining monastery.

The final result could not be more pastoral and English. There is a lychgate with a broad tiled roof and a path winds through venerable-looking gravestones. The church itself has low stone walls and a very high pitched roof. A cloistered passage leads off to what was once the house of Redemptorist priests.

The monastery, joined to the church by a cloister, once housed a community of Redemptorist monks.

The architect was Charles Hansom (1817–88) who had been a pupil of his elder brother, the great Joseph Hansom. Charles was much favoured by Bishop Ullathorne and the English Benedictines. Ullathorne suggested that the design should be based on the famous Early English church at Skelton, near York.

A W N Pugin was brought in to design the furnishings; Pugin called in H Minton for the tiles, W Wailes for the windows and J Hardman for the furnishings. Consequently, an already significant interior with a stencilled and rib-vaulted nave is wonderfully enriched by its carved altars, reredoses and rood screen. There are altar crosses made from enamelled copper and brass, brass candlesticks, an incense boat and much more – all Pugin and Hardman. Minton's tiles for the floor were also Pugin designed. Above the screen to the Lady Chapel is a stuffed owl. It has no iconographic significance, but was put there to deter bats.

The English pastoral scene at Blackmore Park, paid for by profits from the Genoese silk trade.

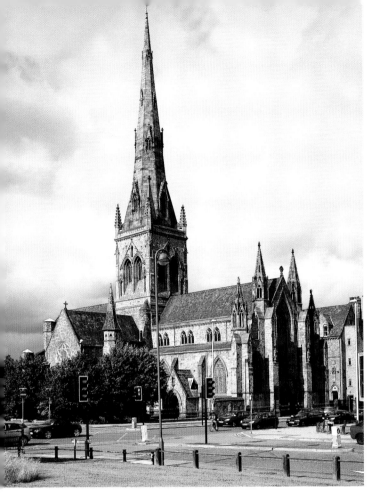

Cathedral of St John the Evangelist,
Chapel Street, Salford, Greater Manchester
(1844–8)

A symbol of Catholic renewal, St John the Evangelist towered above the factories, mills and wretched housing of 19th-century Salford.

The tide of urban regeneration has yet to ripple out from Salford Quays and the Lowry Museum to the cathedral's surroundings, which still look grim. It was built on land purchased after the sale – to the railway company – of the land on which the old Catholic chapel had stood. Funds were donated by a local industrialist and major employer, John Leeming. The architect was Matthew Hadfield of the Sheffield firm Weightman and Hadfield.

The architect studied different northern medieval buildings as a preliminary to designing the church that became Salford Cathedral in 1850. In the end the tower was based on Newark, the nave on Howden and the choir on Selby. Pugin might have disapproved of this somewhat slavish copying of medieval examples, but the elements come together effectively.

There is a strongly shaped, broad 200-foot nave. Above the columns are what were once vividly painted saints in crocketed Gothic niches below a clerestory. The walls are largely white plaster and the space has a slightly stripped look to it. Since the vigorous reorder-ings of 1972 and 1983 (both removing or damaging original furnishings) nothing obstructs the eye between the raised forward altar, the ambulatory screen and the colossal window which spreads across the east wall. It was made in 1856 by William Wailes of Newcastle and sets out to tell no less than the story of Catholicism in England from the conversion of King Ethelbert by St Augustine in 597 through to 1850. As well as angels and most of the company of heaven, just about everybody who played a major part in the story is there, including Henry VIII (bottom near the right) who is looking sourly at the papal legate. To his right, a faithful Catholic is about to be hanged. But all ends well with the Restoration of the Hierarchy and a competent-looking cardinal taking control of things again.

A window featuring architects Matthew Hadfield holding a plan of the church (left) and George Goldie holding a drawing of the reredos he designed for St John the Evangelist.

The floor of the chancel has a very beautiful pavement of mosaic featuring the papal arms and the Dove of Peace. The Lady Chapel, behind the screen where the original High Altar used to be, has an alabaster altar with elaborate carving and a statue of Our Lady of Fatima. Next to it, separated by a screen, is the Leeming Chantry. John Leeming continued to be generous to St John's all his life and he and his family are buried and commemorated here. There is a raised arch in white stone erected to his memory over his bronze memorial. In 1923 a marble tablet was erected to a descendant, Henry Leeming. The inscription records that he was the first Colonel Commandant of the Salford Catholic Boys' Brigade.

On the south aisle the Blessed Sacrament Chapel (by Peter Paul Pugin, 1884), the only part of the church to retain something like its original character before re-ordering, provides some uncharacteristic and welcome colour amid all the white plaster. There are gorgeous paintings on gold of the Apostles and an ornate marble altar (designed later by J A Pippet). Below is an effigy of St Aurelius. Cardinal Vaughan brought back relics of the saint from Rome which are entombed here. The saint's recumbent effigy was so realistic that it bordered on the macabre and frightened the children. A curtain now hangs in front of it.

Nearby is a large window featuring the architects Matthew Hadfield and George Goldie. Hadfield is holding the plan and Goldie a drawing of the reredos which he designed a few years after the cathedral was built. (That reredos and the screen which stood alongside the sanctuary were destroyed during another re-ordering in 1990). Between them in the window, St John himself holds the model of the church.

Our Lady Star of the Sea, Crooms Hill, Greenwich, London SE10 (1846–51)

The Catholic chapel that preceded this church was a wretched affair set in the midst of Greenwich's most loathsome slums. Father North was determined to build something much better. He had a hard time raising the money and when he had gone some way to his goal his bank foreclosed. With all his funds lost, Father North started again. There was no show of generosity from the local Catholic gentry. In contrast, the poor of the parish subscribed regular portions of their meagre incomes. Father North resorted to writing hectoring letters to the Catholic press, touching on the debt the country owed to Catholic Irish sailors, heroes of Trafalgar, now pensioners in the nearby Greenwich Hospital, who were obliged to worship in a dreadful place.

Against the odds Father North succeeded. To much muttering from local Protestants, the graceful spire of the church was erected; a landmark to mariners on the Thames and to landsmen in Greenwich itself. The raising of the cross to the top of the tower was watched by hundreds of spectators, including pensioners 'with spectacles on nose and many an aged eye was dimmed with joyful tears', according to *The Tablet* in 1849. In 1851 the church was opened (tickets from one guinea to half a crown which must have excluded the pensioners) and Cardinal Wiseman preached the sermon. Some Protestants marked the occasion by burning effigies of the pope and the cardinal outside. The architect was William Wilkinson Wardell (1823–99), and A W N Pugin designed most of the decoration of the church and some of the fittings.

Much has happened to the church since its foundation but Pugin's exuberant rood screen, of carved Caen stone with marble columns, has survived. The rood is still there too, of painted oak, with Mary and Mary Magdalene on either side. Wardell designed the High Altar, possibly with Pugin and George Myers lending a hand. It was made by Boulton and Swailes and was exhibited at the 1851 Great Exhibition. To the left of the sanctuary arch, in a canopied niche, is a superb white stone statue of Our Lady Star of the Sea, designed by Pugin and made by Myers. Pugin designed the altar and tabernacle in the Blessed Sacrament Chapel and the

Wardell designed the church at Greenwich and A W N Pugin contributed to the interior. The stone rood screen was designed by Pugin as was the statue of Our Lady Star of the Sea (to the left). Beyond the screen is Edward Pugin's monument to the church's founder, Canon North.

beautifully stencilled roof owes its inspiration to Pugin's carved wooden cornice which is emblazoned with Latin phrases. There are stone sedilia and a piscina in the sanctuary which are probably by Pugin, as are the pulpit and east window.

The church was built in fulfilment of a vow Father North had made to his mother, as she and her infant sons were saved from drowning. When North died, Edward Pugin is thought to have designed his tomb (1861). He lies under an arch which divides the sanctuary from the Lady Chapel, next to his brother who succeeded him at the church as priest. A fine brass memorial by the altar records their achievements. There is an unusual votive lamp in the shape of a boat which hangs to the side. It was given by Mrs Knill, the church's benefactor, designed by Pugin and made by Hardman.

In recent years great changes have been inflicted on parts of the church. Cork tiles now cover the encaustic tiled floor of the nave and the ceiling of the main church. Wardell left for Australia in 1858. There he designed Catholic cathedrals for Sydney and Adelaide.

Wardell's great tower and spire at Greenwich; a beacon to mariners and landsmen alike.

Weightman and Hadfield's nave at Sheffield. On the columns are carvings of the heads of saints.

St Marie's Cathedral, Norfolk Row, Sheffield (1846–50)

When Father Pratt and his fast growing congregation needed a new church to replace the chapel they had outgrown, they wanted Gothic style and commissioned the reliable Sheffield partnership of J G Weightman and M E Hadfield. The firm had built dozens of Gothic churches in the north. Hadfield, who played the major role, and Father Pratt went on a trip through the north and east of England to seek inspiration. What they liked best was the 14th-century church of St Andrew Heckington in Lincolnshire. The plan and 'Decorated' style of that church would be echoed in the church that became Sheffield's Roman Catholic cathedral in 1980.

In 1850 there was a grand opening day 'in the presence of … many Catholic gentry from around the country'. The church's records tell us 'Bishop Gillis preached for an hour'. It was a day with added cause for celebration because this was the year of the Restoration of the Catholic Hierarchy and the beginning of a new and confident era for the faithful. Father Pratt, however, had died a few months before.

The tower and spire of St Marie's soar above the business quarter of the city. Inside there

An important church with powerful sponsors, St Marie's still dominates Sheffield's business quarter.

are clerestoried aisles, low transepts, a splendidly decorated roof and a long sanctuary. It is tall and light. A W N Pugin's rood screen was removed but the dramatic rood remains, outlined against a beautiful sanctuary ceiling of elaborate ogee wind braces, painted with stars and angels. Pugin's serene and moving reredos remains – somewhat altered. The panels show, among other scenes from the New Testament, graceful reliefs painted in gold and blue of the Annunciation – with a very human-looking Mary thoughtfully reading the book of Isaiah, the childhood of Jesus, and Jesus carrying the Cross. In front of the reredos is the bishop's throne, carved from the old choir stalls, and above is the extraordinary east window designed by George Goldie and made by William Wailes. It is enormous and has 1,000 panes. It shows the life of Mary as well as images of many saints, popes, kings, angels, archangels and virgins. During the last war it was dismantled and stored, in a coal mine, by a dedicated parishioner.

Removed from its original position beside the sanctuary and placed in the Mortuary Chapel is an effigy of Father Pratt. He is wearing priestly robes and lies with an angel at his head, his dog at his feet and a model of the unfinished church in his hand. Above is an altar. The central carving shows the Deposition which is flanked by the words, in late Victorian script, 'de profundis clamavi…'. On the walls are panels with pictures and text painted in a faded, attractive, late Victorian style, asking for prayers for the church's dead clergy. The chapel has a spirited carving of a heavenly choir of angels.

The glass in St Marie's was made and designed by some of the biggest names in the business – W Wailes, J Hardman, J F Bentley, A W N Pugin and, from the 20th century, Patrick Reyntiens. The windows show many aspects of the life of Mary, an abundance of northern saints and English and Welsh martyrs.

The Munster (Lady) Chapel is remarkable. J F Bentley designed the window (1884) which commemorates Carolina Bernasconi, who died aged 16, and shows the Annunciation. The altar is made from polished slabs of Sicilian stone. The white marble statue of Mary was carved in Rome. There is an icon of Our Lady of Czestochowa by Stanislaw Frenkel and, beneath the icon, a memorial to the Polish troops who died in the Second World War. St Marie's became the parish church for the many Polish families who settled in Sheffield after that war.

The Priory of Our Lady and St Michael, Pen-y-Pound, Abergavenny, Gwent (1858–60)

Catholic worship never ceased in Abergavenny during the penal years. Franciscans, Benedictines and Jesuits all played a role in sustaining Catholicism there. At one stage Mass was openly celebrated in the town centre in a long attic. The attic was rediscovered in 1907 and a picture found in it is now on show in the local museum. Abergavenny provided two martyrs, St David Lewis and St Philip Evans. Following the 'Popish Plot' allegations of Titus Oates, both Lewis and Evans were accused by informers and executed in 1679. They are commemorated in this church.

The priory was designed for the Benedictines by architect Benjamin Bucknall (1833–95) of Stroud. He had been a pupil of Charles Hansom and was far from being a cut-off provincial. He designed many churches and had translated some of the writings of the influential Viollet-le-Duc into English. He gave the Benedictines a large church in the Decorated Gothic style and, though slightly apart from the centre of the town, it makes its considerable presence felt: tall and dominant outside and spacious inside.

Its principal success is the east end. The reredos was designed, some 25 years after the church was opened, by Edmund Kirby of Liverpool, a maestro of the reredos, and was carved by A B Wall of Cheltenham.

It stretches from wall to wall and climbs through crocketed pinnacles up to and over the base of the east window. There is nothing else like it in Wales. Ecstatic choirs of angels adore the Blessed Sacrament in the tabernacle in a wonderfully carved stone tableau of veneration. One panel on the far right shows a section of the heavenly choir with angelic musicians raptly performing on pipes and stringed instruments. The crowning pinnacles are surmounted by statues of the seven archangels. The actual east window (by Hardman) can more than stand the competition. It fills the wall and has gloriously coloured full-length portraits of Mary holding the Christ Child in the company of various saints under a rose window.

To the right of the sanctuary hang two large oil paintings, recently restored, that were found abandoned in a cellar. One shows a lively heaven with the symbols of the Passion being displayed by enthusiastic angels. God the Father and God the Son sit more thoughtfully in the background. The other, dated 1861, shows St Michael. It is a copy after Raphael by Kenelm Digby. The forward altar cunningly incorporates the old altar rails from the re-ordering.

A local solicitor, John Baker-Gabb, discovered that one of his ancestors had been a famous Benedictine mystic, Dom Augustine Gabb. Baker-Gabb converted to Catholicism and gave the money for the reredos. He also paid for the chantry chapel of the Sacred Heart in the south aisle (added in 1894 in memory of the Catholic martyrs) in honour of his father. There is a roundel of Baker-Gabb looking distinguished in the uniform of a papal chamberlain. Opposite him is an oil painting of St David Lewis. Under it is a small wooden statue of the saint in travelling clothes. St David Lewis was born locally, became a convert to Rome and joined the Jesuit order. He was commissioned to look after the many Catholics on the Welsh borders and was known as the 'Father of the Poor'. He was betrayed and was executed (by the blacksmith – no one else would do the job) at Usk after giving a stirring and unapologetic speech to the crowd. St David Lewis is also shown in the stained glass of the chapel in company with St Benedict and St Ignatius of Loyola.

In 1978 St Michael's came under the jurisdiction of the Benedictine abbey of Belmont. The medieval vestments kept at Our Lady and St Michael are some of the greatest treasures of Wales. They are not on display, but are worn on important feast days and are exhibited from time to time.

Angelic instrumentalists amid the crockets of Abergavenny's stupendous reredos, designed by Edmund Kirby.

4 The Great Catholic Revival: Consolidation and Expansion

So much did Pugin's advocacy of the Gothic triumph that it became for decades almost the only style used by Catholic and Anglican architects. Apart from the work of the big name architects, thousands of lesser Victorian churches would be built in the Gothic style. Their first task – rather than to express exquisite refinement of taste – was to accommodate the ever-growing congregations of the cities and towns. Anglican architects like Sir George Gilbert Scott could build churches with artistic ambitions (Scott built more than 140) in the suburbs and better parts of town for middle-class Anglican congregations. Catholic churches were built where their mostly working-class congregations, very often Irish, had crowded into the slums of cities that were being transformed by the new railways, coal mines, gas works and factories. The worshippers in these congregations had no means of transport and so the new churches and their schools – like their workplaces – had to be within walking distance of home. Second churches were sometimes built to accommodate the immigrant newcomers who did not always receive a generous welcome from the existing Catholic community. Most of these churches were gaunt and cheap. But however impoverished their budgets, nearly all of them were Gothic and they reflected the pride that wealthy patrons and hard-up congregations alike felt in their religion.

Not all commissions for church architects were limited to satisfying the needs of the poor and the working class. The building boom was also propelled by a church that had re-established its hierarchy, was absorbing large numbers of converts, had indubitably become a major part of the ecclesiastical and political landscape and had the self-assurance to express itself in buildings that reflected just how much things had changed for Catholics in a hundred years.

Inspired by Ruskin, some church architects became fascinated by the materials of which their buildings were made – what Mark Girouard has called 'the stoniness of stone, the brickiness of brick and the flintiness of flint'. The industrial revolution had produced new building materials and the railways enabled them to be transported all over the country.

Jesuit affirmation: the elaborately carved altar of the Annunciation and the reredos depicting Our Lady and Child surrounded by 17 Jesuit saints at St Francis Xavier, Liverpool.

The forcefully carved tympanum at St Wilfrid, York, controversially sited opposite the Minster.

There was a price to be paid for all this, however. The enthusiasm of designers to exploit the materials was not always matched by their talent to do so. Architectural detail and polychromatic brickwork were blackened and obscured by coatings of smoke and industrial filth. The same industries that rendered churches black (as well as proud new town halls, banks and railway stations) also released money into the towns and cities which they polluted. Some of that money was put to use in building churches of considerable scale and confidence.

Giles Gilbert Scott's iconostasis-like reredos at Lancaster Cathedral.

Landmark churches were deliberately big and were placed prominently to give evidence, if that was still needed, that Catholicism was back. J A Hansom's St Walburge, built to serve a suburb of Preston, is a church of Wagnerian scale and ambition. It was paid for by the congregation, and that congregation's needs, as well as the Jesuit patrons' traditions, were taken into account in its design. Whatever other qualities St Walburge may have, it has excellent, unobstructed sight lines to the extraordinary pulpit and the altar. The emphasis of the church plan had begun to shift to the liturgical requirements of the people.

The new technologies of the age not only made an obsession with the minutiae of medieval church design begin to seem irrelevant, but also enabled architects like Edward W Pugin (1834–75) to develop beyond his father's edicts and build churches – for what Edward called a 'perfect auditory town church' – with broad naves and continuous aisles that ran counter to the limited sight lines of A W N Pugin's aisled buildings.

Another extraordinary Catholic talent was Joseph Aloysius Hansom (1803–82). For a time he partnered E W Pugin and he too was part of a dynasty. He worked with his younger brother Charles and his son Henry John. He was a radical socialist. He designed the Classical town hall for Birmingham, founded *The Builder* magazine and invented the Hansom cab. He made no money out of that, but his churches – St Walburge, in particular – show his continuing and brilliant inventiveness. His brother Charles designed churches all over the midlands, Wales and the south, and his son John went into partnership with Archibald Matthew Dunn (who had trained under Charles) and they worked together at Downside and Cambridge.

Joseph John Scoles would concentrate on the Gothic and his work would be continued by his sons – both became priests as well as architects. Notable Catholic churches were built by S J Nicholl, a pupil of Scoles, Henry Clutton, George Goldie of York and his son Edward, and Benjamin Bucknall of Stroud. All were Catholic and all were Goths. So much did they succeed in stamping that style on their age that even today some Catholics feel uncomfortable about worshipping in a church that is not Gothic. Gothic somehow feels right.

Immaculate Conception, Farm Street: Charles Goldie's painting of the death of St Francis Xavier on an island off the coast of China.

Immaculate Conception, Farm Street, Mayfair, London W1 (1844–9)

Even before the full force of the Catholic revival was under way the Jesuits had planned this large 900-seat church for the fashionable part of Mayfair where they had their English headquarters. They gave the job to J J Scoles, a favourite of theirs – an eclectic Catholic architect who could turn his hand to both Classical and Gothic. In this case he went for sumptuous Gothic. Other architects added to, or altered, the church over the years that followed but Scoles deftly set the scene for a series of spaces, added over the years, which together make up a magisterial whole. All around the central nave there are glimpses through the arches in mysterious, dimly lit side chapels of paintings, marble, mosaics and glinting religious objects.

The west front was based on the south transept of Beauvais Cathedral. It was badly damaged during the last war. The east window was based on the one at Carlisle Cathedral. This window was raised higher up after its construction to be clear of the altar and reredos below and it now, incandescently, fills the wall. There is no screen to interrupt the view of it or the High Altar, which was designed by A W N Pugin and is among the best things he ever did. When the east window was raised in 1864 the floor of the sanctuary was also raised by several feet. Hitherto the congregation had been on the same level as the altar and had had a correspondingly poor view of it. George Goldie panelled the walls with large sheets of green marble and alabaster. Between the reredos and the window, vivid Venetian mosaics telling the story of the Annunciation and the Coronation of Our Lady were put in place in 1875. Pugin might have questioned this but the frontal of the recently installed forward altar is a successful act of homage to him, a plaster cast of the original altar that he designed.

In 1858–60, following a fire, Henry Clutton rebuilt the Sacred Heart Chapel south of the sanctuary. It has a wonderfully carved altar by Thomas Earp of Lambeth incorporating bronze reliefs of Joseph and his brethren by Theodore Phyffers, a protégé of Pugin's from Antwerp. The mural behind it is by Peter Molitor, an artist from the Rhineland. On either side of the tabernacle are carvings of two small angels designed by the then hardly known John Francis Bentley, Clutton's one-time pupil.

Clutton also added a south aisle in 1876–8 which he divided into different chapels and which he, and other architects, decorated. In one of them the artist Charles Goldie painted an arresting picture of the Death of St Francis Xavier on the shore of the island of Sancian. In the background is the coast of China and with St Francis are his Chinese and Indian followers.

The north outer aisle was added in 1898–1903 by W H Romaine Walker. This incorporates a chapel to St Ignatius of Loyola, founder of the Jesuit order, as well as a large statue of the saint. He holds a book of the Spiritual Exercises with the Jesuit monogram showing.

Romaine Walker was obliged by lack of space outside the building to use internal buttresses for his widening. He cunningly turned this space restriction to advantage by incorporating comfortable-looking confessionals into the buttresses between the chapels.

The west rose window was destroyed by blast during the Second World War and in 1953 glass by the Irish-born artist Evie Hone (who lived and worked in London) was installed. Below it is a Bishops' organ. The Immaculate Conception is as famous for its music as for its architecture.

The noble and sumptuously detailed interior of Farm Street. Stencilled vaulting, granite columns and magnificent clerestory windows frame the Tree of Jesse east window and solid Caen stone altar.

J J Scoles's church for the Jesuits, with the later tower, rises above the Everton neighbourhood.

St Francis Xavier, 2 Salisbury Street, Liverpool (1848 and 1885–7)

Before the Second World War St Francis Xavier's was the largest Catholic parish in the country. Its origins go back to a meeting in the nearby Rose and Crown pub between eight Catholic businessmen who raised money for a new church for the neighbourhood. The new church was offered to the President of Stonyhurst College, the Jesuit Provincial, and has been staffed by the Jesuits ever since. The architect selected was J J Scoles (1798–1863), a favourite architect of the Jesuits. The spire was added in 1883.

The church, which was designed to seat a thousand worshippers in what was then a fashionable part of Liverpool, was soon found to be too small and the Sodality Chapel, itself the size of a good-sized church, was added in 1885–7. Next to the church was the first Catholic secondary grammar school in the country (1876–7) and a Poor School was soon added. During the 1920s and 1930s the Everton neighbourhood changed and became much more working class. St Francis Xavier's thrived in the new conditions. Although damaged during the Blitz it survived the war in good heart. All this fell away in the 1960s when much of the local population was compulsorily shifted and resettled in other parts of the city. The area fell into general decline but this magnificent church survived, though only just; the diocese tried to demolish it in the 1970s. The Jesuit college buildings to the east of the church, designed by Henry Clutton, have also survived. They are still in use as part of Liverpool Hope University College which shares the church, and they provide a touching continuity between past and present.

The stone and slate Gothic church is now surrounded by car parks and some indeterminate open spaces. It makes a somewhat daunting first impression. Inside, tall and slender polished columns of Drogheda limestone (painted white) support a wagon roof. These columns have, in contrast to their slim width, heavily foliated capitals and massive bases. To the right is the Sodality Chapel. This was designed by Edmund Kirby (1838–1920) who designed the Catholic church at Parbold (see page 116) and who, coincidentally, was related to the publican of the Rose and Crown. The High Altar, in the polygonal apse, was designed by J J Scoles in 1856 and shows, in brilliant white stone carvings, scenes from the Bible. Above the altar, the stained-glass east window shows St Francis Xavier on his travels attended by people of many races. The surrounding chapels to the Sacred Heart and the Rosary have similarly narrative altars. The painted rood hanging above is the work (1866) of William Earley of Dublin.

The Sodality Chapel is a surprise, not just because it rivals the main church in size but because of its original and lofty design. Again, there are very slender shafts (this time of Purbeck marble) supporting a polygonal, plaster vault. Around it are the flamboyantly decorated altars of the sodalities – associations of lay Catholics. In the sanctuary is the altar of the Annunciation with carvings by J R Boulton of Cheltenham of Mary and Jesus with seventeen Jesuit saints. There is a gilt tabernacle door with reliefs by Conrad Dressler. To the left is an unusual chapel to St Joseph. The altar shows scenes from his life and death and is surrounded, appropriately, by walls of wood which culminate in a virtuoso display of oak carving around the altar itself.

Christ with the Afflicted: detail from the Sacred Heart Chapel. The carving is based on a painting by Dutch artist Ary Scheffer.

At the west end of the church a window designed by Linda Walton commemorates all those thousands of hidden saints who worshipped here. It was unveiled in 1999, the 150th anniversary of the church, and includes

The Rosary Chapel with its virtuosic 1850 altar and reredos; the pulpit is of Caen stone.

some of the men and women's organisations, altar servers, school teachers, priests, sacristans, choir-boys and bell-ringers who played a part in the church's story, featuring also emblematic roses and a crown – after the pub in which the founders met. Another window in the west organ gallery depicts Christ the King presiding over the Court of Heaven. The Jesuits are well represented.

St Walburge, Weston Street, Preston, Lancashire (1850–4)

It must have looked astounding when it was built in the 1850s; a huge, dark, sandstone church with the tallest parish church spire in Britain (only Salisbury and Norwich Cathedral spires are taller) in contrasting white limestone. The spire was completed in 1869 and pierced a sky made smoky by the encircling chimneys and cotton mills of the furiously expanding industrial town. It was said to have been built partly from Portland Stone railway sleepers and its foundations embedded in great bales of wool. Even when it was built its Jesuit founder priests were criticised for going a bit over the top, a case not so much of Catholic triumphalism as Catholic hubris. *The Ecclesiologist* attacked the plan as a Counter-Reformation church in Gothic form, 'the flaunting off-spring of the unhappy nuptials of Oratorianism and true Christian ecclesiology'. It is rather cut off now from the town by a railway cutting but, isolated and magnificent, it still astounds.

Incredibly, no rich patron paid for St Walburge, but a largely working-class congregation subscribed their pennies with 8,000 people promising to pay £1 a year. To help with the cost, Irish workers, who provided most of the congregation and were the victims of a $2\frac{1}{2}$-year lock-out at the local mill, did much of the work.

As Pevsner says, 'nothing prepares you for the shock of the interior'. It is immense, a

A landmark church: at over 300ft, the great limestone spire of St Walburge is taller than those of most cathedrals.

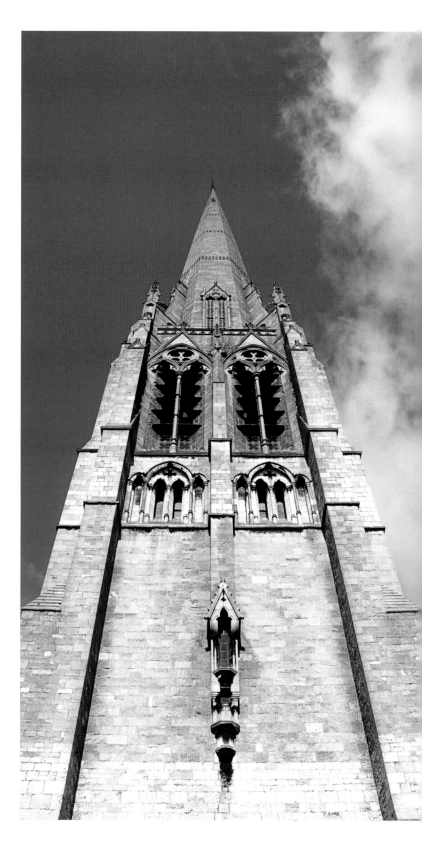

At St Walburge's, Joseph Hansom's magisterial hammer-beam roof is tipped by colourful carvings of the saints.

spectacular medieval great hall above which lowers a vast hammerbeam roof – more like Valhalla than a parish church. ('Walpurgisnacht' derives its name from St Walburge, an 8th-century English saint who distinguished herself by her piety as well as her administrative skills as abbess of Heidenheim in Germany). There are no aisles and no columns support the steeply pitched roof. The architect the Jesuits employed was J A Hansom (1803–82). Hansom experimented with ways of constructing such a roof on the building next door where he lived for two years and which became a school (now the Institute). It resembles most a secular building like Westminster Hall and was intended to create a single open space with perfect sight lines, in contrast to the divided aisled interior favoured by Pugin. As if to compensate for the rather worldly effect, the hammerbeams are tipped with brightly coloured carvings of saints in religious-looking, crocketed niches. To the left of this great chamber is a raised pulpit that is approached – very unusually – up a flight of arcaded steps inside the wall. Savonarola would feel nervous preaching in such a spectacular setting.

The apse was added in 1872 by S J Nicholl and the position of the east windows thrust back into a semi-circle. Much of the glass is by Hardman & Co and not all of it has stood the test of time, but the altar and reredos hold their own in the vastness. On the south side, above four statues of saints and one of Mary, is a gallery once used by the nuns who served the church. It surmounts an ugly (and problematic) heating system. The west end has a big circular window under which is an exuberantly carved gallery (Pevsner calls the columns supporting the gallery 'rogue' columns but then he called the roof 'a bad dream'). The gallery holds an appropriately sized organ.

There is a very human touch amidst all the grandeur. Under a triptych of the Crucifixion, painted on a gold background, are the names of the men of the Royal Lancashire Regiments – the Pals – who lost their lives in France during the two world wars. There are a lot of them and almost all were privates. 'He loved them unto the end', reads the inscription.

The back-to-backs where the largely Irish local population lived have mostly gone now and a congregation that once exceeded 1,400 has shrunk to fewer than 300. The west half of the great space is used for secular purposes. Next to the church is a presbytery designed to accommodate eight priests. There is now only one.

A difficult site: Shrewsbury's cathedral poised on the cliff-like edge of town.

Cathedral of Our Lady Help of Christians and St Peter of Alcantara,
Town Walls, Shrewsbury, Shropshire (1853–6)

The 16th Earl of Shrewsbury wanted to build a cathedral in the famously historic town from which he derived the name of his title. But there was more than just aristocratic noblesse oblige driving the project. The Catholic population was growing. Irish immigrants were laying the railway lines that were connecting parts of England and Wales through Shrewsbury. The earl wanted his favourite architect, the elder Pugin, to design the building. But A W N Pugin died in 1852 and then the earl died also. His successor Bertram, the 17th Earl, took over the financial responsibilities from him. Edward Pugin (1834–75) took over the architectural commission. Bertram was twenty and Edward was eighteen. Given their inexperience and the difficulties of the site they wisely engaged A W N's old friend George Myers to assist with the building.

The cathedral stands on the high, cliff-like edge of Shrewsbury. There is no tower but a large bell-cote rests on a very high gabled nave and aisle.

It was opened in 1856 by Bishop Wiseman – after some anti-Catholic grumbling in the town – to considerable ceremony. Bertram had died two months before the cathedral was opened but he had chosen the dedication to St Peter of Alcantara (1499–1562), a Spanish mystic and friend of St Teresa of Avila.

There is a large, rose-red porch (later, 1906) beyond which is a nave with aisles to either side of tall and slender columns. The ceiling is painted and panelled. A large and dramatic rood with an unusually elaborate cross hangs from the entrance to the sanctuary. It is much later than E W Pugin. Beyond, in the shallow sanctuary, is the original High Victorian reredos. Much was taken away or resited during the 1980s re-ordering, not least Pugin's High Altar, the altar rails and the font. The new stone High Altar (1985) was quarried in Shropshire. Behind it – splendidly filling the wall – is the great east window by Hardman & Co of Birmingham.

On either side of the chancel are two fine side chapels. The one to St Winefride contains a tabernacle which originally stood on the High Altar. It is an astonishing work of craftsmanship in carved wood, burnished with gold. The chapel of the Sacred Heart (1885) was decorated by J A Pippet of Hardman & Co and glows with mysterious, enigmatic paintings of the Apostles and saints.

No less grave and formal are the Stations of the Cross, commissioned in 1954 from Philip Lindsey Clarke. The octagonal and highly carved font by Pugin was moved to its present position in the re-ordering. It was given to the church by the Countess of Shrewsbury as a memorial to her son Bertram.

A great feature of the cathedral is the glass designed by Margaret Rope, a local doctor's daughter who became a nun, studied art and turned her hand to making stained glass. She designed the west window, much of the glass in the aisles and in the chancel a window commemorating the Eucharistic Congress in London in 1921. It features a red London omnibus of the times.

St Vincent de Paul, St James Street, Liverpool (1856–7)

St Vincent de Paul's looks across a main road towards abandoned or half-heartedly converted warehouses and waste land. Behind it is new housing in the area around St George's Square that was bombed in the war. The church itself has a strikingly tall, attenuated bell-cote on the west gable of a very steep pitched roof, but has a closed look about it. So the shock of a superb interior is the more surprising. At both the east and west ends there are large windows and the massive clerestory windows on either side of the nave allow an extraordinary amount of light to

Margaret Rope, a nun, designed much of the glass in the cathedral in Shrewsbury. This detail is in the sacristy.

High Victorian Gothic: Edward Pugin's nave and east window, relishing the 'Decorated' style at St Vincent de Paul.

The impassive alabaster figures set in a row of marble niches of E Pugin's reredos at St Vincent de Paul. The altar was added later in 1927.

irradiate the church. This is E W Pugin (1834–75) on form, relishing the 'Decorated' style that he adopted in the middle of his short career.

The church replaced a wooden shed that was used for services and was paid for by its largely Irish dock-land congregation. E W Pugin had an office in Liverpool and his ability to build large buildings on a modest budget was never put to better use than here. There are substantial columns with foliated capitals and there are reliefs of angels (recently painted gold) above the arches. The west end has a choir loft under its huge window. The nine-light east window fills the wall. The stained glass dates from 1925. Below is a very formal, serious alabaster reredos. From wall to wall, expressionless statues of saints and biblical figures stand in an impersonal row of niches. Designed by E W Pugin in 1867, they were carved in alabaster by William Farmer.

On either side of the sanctuary there are side altars which, though created later, continue Pugin's sober mood. Most striking is the Lady Altar of 1899, to the left of the sanctuary. Mary stands under an extravagantly pointed canopy with a round carving in stone of the Annunciation behind her. The sacristy is beautifully fitted out in varnished wood.

St Peter's Cathedral, East Road, Lancaster (1857–9)

Most 19th-century Catholic churches were designed by Catholic architects. Anglican architects tended to work on churches of their own denomination. But it was an Anglican, Edward Graham Paley (1823–95), with a flourishing church practice in north-west England, who designed St Peter's. Perhaps because his practice was so manifestly successful he was an inevitable choice. His church, which became a cathedral in 1924, stands on a hill to the east of the city and looks towards Morecambe Bay and the Cumbrian mountains. The graceful 240-foot tower and crocketed spire tactfully adorn, rather than dominate, the Lancaster skyline.

Inside the cathedral the feeling of well-mannered elegance continues; St Peter's has one of the most beautiful church interiors in the north. There is a light, clerestoried nave with an unusually shaped arch-braced roof looking towards three bright east windows. There is a rich, screened sanctuary below them. The sanctuary has been through some testing changes in recent years. The Blessed Sacrament was moved from the altar during re-ordering and much else was removed or resited. In 1995 Bishop Brewer, assisted by English Heritage and architect Frank Roberts of Preston, endeavoured to restore what had been lost. Cunningly, a new Blessed Sacrament Chapel was created behind a new and extremely well-designed metalwork screen, an arrangement which enables both the High Altar and the Blessed Sacrament to be seen by the congregation. Also triumphantly returned to centre stage is Giles Gilbert Scott's mighty reredos – a 32-panel triptych that enfolds the altar in a miracle of carving and painting. It resembles a Greek iconostasis and shows – with tremendous and solemn formality – the Passion, the Apostles, saints and the souls in purgatory. On the wall behind and beside the triptych are more sacred scenes – this time painted on the unusual medium of linoleum (Lancaster was a lino-producing town). The restored High Altar, with a relief in marble of the Last Supper and a wrought metal tabernacle, was created for the golden jubilee of the church in 1909 by Giles (later Sir Giles) Gilbert Scott.

The fine medieval-looking choir stalls and their misericords in the sanctuary were carved in 1899. A shining *corona lucis* is suspended above the forward altar which is of recent design – along with the cathedra and ambo.

The baptistery is octagonal and approached through wrought-iron gates. It was designed like a chapter house in 1901. The glorious stained-glass windows (by Shrigley and Hunt) are very much of their period and give dim and subtle illumination to the ample marble font and its remarkable oak roof, shaped like an octagonal church spire. One arresting window just outside the baptistery unusually shows King Herod. He has sword in hand and a child at his feet.

Sandstone, ashlar and slate: the tower and spire of St Peter's adorn the Lancaster skyline.

A robed and tormented-looking King Herod with his foot resting on a dead child: window by the entrance to the baptistery of St Peter's. The colours are muted and there are symbols of cunning (the fox), betrayal (apples) and the devil (snake). The window is a masterpiece by Lancaster firm Shrigley and Hunt.

Herodes iratus occidit multos pueros

The windows in the apse are by Hardman & Co as is also the Te Deum window. The Catholic martyrs are commemorated in many of the cathedral's windows, in particular St Thomas More who was Chancellor of the Duchy of Lancaster. A relic of his hair shirt is kept in the chapel dedicated to his memory. In the north aisle is a large seated figure of St Peter, a copy in wood of the famous statue in St Peter's, Rome.

Our Lady of Reconciliation de la Salette, Eldon Place, Liverpool (1859–60)

This church was E W Pugin's solution to providing a very big space, on a very slim budget. Nearly 2,000 people crammed into Mass here after it opened. It was built near the docks for a rapidly growing population – largely of immigrants from Ireland but later, also from Lithuania. A talented Canon Hughes spoke several languages and preached to the Lithuanians in their own tongue. The church could comfortably seat 800 and because Pugin designed narrow aisles with tall arcades that have widely spaced columns, all the sight lines were good. The Lithuanians had a good view, not only of Canon Hughes, but of the altar in the Lady Chapel that they had presented to the church.

The stone exterior is unadorned but looks impressive, especially in the way the striped masonry of the east wall and the slate roof curve around the apse. Lightening what might have been an overwhelming density of mass is a small, conical bell-cote above the rose window on the west end. Edward Pugin was moving on from the limiting Gothic imperatives laid down by his father, and the church was described in *The Tablet* as being 'a complete revolution in church-building'. It went through a drastic re-ordering during the 1970s in which, among other things, a new ceiling was suspended from the roof, at about a third the height of the church. Under it, the congregation faced sideways to an altar placed on the south aisle. To general rejoicing this has all been removed and, although the original reredos was destroyed in a fire, the church has regained much of its original appearance. The interior space is tall and bright again with large clerestory windows shedding most of the light. The height of these windows was important and reflected the fact that the houses and streets hemming in the church were originally very dark and narrow.

The roof runs continuously from nave to sanctuary. Pugin's drawing of that roof shows his own pleasure at the panache with which he has organised the intricate and elegant scissor bracing of the vaults.

The reredos is an unadorned wooden screen, but in front are altar rails made of complicated and sinuously carved Belgian oak that commemorate the dead of the First World War. Some of the first priests of the church were Belgian and the connection is also marked by the Stations of the Cross, which are Belgian. To the

Top: E Pugin's elegant bell-cote on the steep west gable at Eldon Place.

Above: Belgian craftsmanship on the carved altar rails.

right is the altar of St Joseph with scenes carved in marble of the Nativity and the saint's death.

Our Lady of Reconciliation de la Salette was not the original dedication and there was, until recently, no statue of her in the church. Now there is a very expressive and highly coloured statue of the weeping figure that appeared to two children in the Haute-Savoie.

St Francis of Assisi, Pottery Lane, London W11 (1859–60)

When Henry Manning (later Cardinal Archbishop of Westminster) acquired this site for the Oblates of St Charles Borromeo, Notting Hill was famous for its desperate poverty and deprivation. Father Henry Rawes, one of the oblates, was sent to do missionary and educational work among the poor around Pottery Lane, many of whom were Irish immigrants. He paid for the church himself. The architect was Henry Clutton (1819–93) who was assisted by John Francis Bentley (1839–1902). Clutton designed a small brick building in the French Gothic style and Bentley supervised the construction work of the church. It soon proved to be too small.

Bentley would go on to great things both as architect and as a designer of church furnishings, but this was one of his first independent commissions. Yet it was Bentley that Father Rawes asked to design additions and fittings and the commission enabled him to leave Clutton and to set up his own practice. He added a Lady Chapel, a baptistery, a porch, a presbytery and a school. He also took command of designing and commissioning much of the decoration of the church. The result is one of the best loved and most splendid small churches in London.

Bentley converted to Catholicism in 1862. When the baptistery he designed was completed Bentley was the first person to be baptised in it. The font is granite and the oak canopy was given by Bentley as a thank-

Rich design and decoration at St Francis of Assisi for the slum dwellers of Notting Hill.

offering for his conversion. *The Building News* of 1863 was enthusiastic. The baptistery promised to be 'one of the most complete little chapels in England'. The stone vault is born up by marble columns with superbly carved capitals. Some of the details were finished later in 1910 by Hardman & Co working with Bentley's son, Osmond.

The Lady Chapel was added to the too small church by the ingenious device of pushing the aisle through to the back of the apse. It contains the altar of St John, designed by Bentley. Thomas Earp of Lambeth made the alabaster frame of the reredos which contains a painting by Nathaniel H J Westlake. Below are paintings on encaustic or slate of Daniel and St John by Westlake. The altar has intricate inlays of marble and gold. The piscina and the altar of the Lady Chapel were also designed by Bentley and the paintings of Our Lady of Dolours and various female saints on the altar front are by Westlake, who also painted the seven Dolours of Our Lady around the walls.

The High Altar and reredos are opulent, dramatic and hold together the heart of the church with its oddly dispersed elements. There is alabaster cunningly inlaid with mosaic and marble, and columns with ornate capitals and ornament and pattern interleaved with a suggestion of Art Nouveau. The brass tabernacle door is encrusted with enamels and precious stones. All are enfolded by the luminous paintings by Westlake.

The church has been redecorated and re-ordered (1984) but has kept much of its character and beauty as a result of the retention of the original furnishings.

A riotous profusion of pinnacled crockets and niches; E Pugin's superb reredos at Ripon.

St Wilfrid, Coltsgate Hill, Ripon, Yorkshire (1860–2)

After St Walburge, Preston, this was a relatively modest design by the architect J A Hansom (1803–82), but he rarely let the opportunity to astonish pass by. Here he designed a sanctuary much higher than an already tall nave. Through the windows of an octagonal tower, brilliant light pours on to the other spectacular feature of St Wilfrid's, the exuberantly carved reredos designed by Edward Pugin.

The Catholic community in Ripon had been growing steadily since the Catholic Emancipation Act of 1829, but local hostility still made it prudent to bid for the land on Coltsgate Hill through a Protestant friend of the parish priest – Father Garstang. He was succeeded by Canon Vavasour who, with his family and friends, paid for the church, the presbytery and school. The cost was said to have been about £5,000. The brick exterior shows the strong design of the church, with its odd and intriguingly shaped tower and sturdy-looking presbytery.

Hansom's chosen style was early French Gothic and the church is said to have been inspired by a 12th-century church at Les Saintes de Mer in Provence. There are four wide arches on either side of the tall nave. The capitals on the columns have prolix carvings of foliage and above them, in the spandrels of the arches, are medallions (made in Venice) showing mosaic portraits of saints – including St Wilfrid.

St Wilfrid is also the subject of E W Pugin's inspired reredos. He is shown, in a much crocketed niche, carved in relief, preaching before two kings and attended by sorrowing monks on his deathbed at Oundle. In addition, there are superb carvings of bishops, abbots and monks. The High Altar is of Caen stone with much coloured marble and carvings of various biblical scenes. The alabaster tabernacle has brass doors and above it are two angels who direct the eye up to the reredos and the blazing, immensely lofty east windows.

Canon Vavasour is commemorated in a window above the High Altar which shows him being presented to Christ by St Philip. Another notable benefactor to the church was the Marquis of Ripon, a former Viceroy of India, who converted to Rome in 1874 and was the first Catholic mayor of Ripon since the Reformation. Several remarkable windows in the nave designed by John Hungerford Pollen were dedicated to his memory.

Charles Hansom designed the Gothic tower and spire that rises above Classical Bath.

St John the Evangelist, South Parade, Bath (1861–3)

Just over a hundred years after the Gordon Riots had destroyed or wrecked Catholic chapels and homes all over the city, this High Victorian assertion of the faith was opened. Four years later, a 222-foot high Gothic spire was added. It soars up over the south side of predominantly Classical Bath. It was built by the Benedictines of Downside Abbey, who handed over the church to the Clifton Diocese in 1932. The walls are of Bath stone and have a rough look to them as if just brought from the quarry. The roof is complex, with gables and narthex jutting out and a five-sided apse. Sanctuary and nave are the same height and of the same width as each other.

The architect was Charles Francis Hansom (1817–88), brother and one-time pupil of J A Hansom. He was a prolific church architect who, nearly 20 years earlier, had designed the village church at Hanley Swan (see page 80). This was a much bigger building and he regarded it as the best thing he ever did.

The stately interior is a good reflection of mid-Victorian taste. The nave is separated from the aisles by columns of colourful polished marble with unrestrained capitals of carved flowers and foliage. Above, in the spandrels between the arches, angels in roundels play on a variety of musical instruments. The sanctuary is more muted and has an exquisite screen painted in blue and gold and delicate communion rails. The eagle is commonly the symbol of St John but the wrought iron screen here has on its top, under the rood, a pelican – feeding its young with its own

Marble columns, foliated capitals and a deeply carved pulpit – High Victorian style at St John the Evangelist.

blood – a symbol of Christ. The High Altar is made from white marble with coloured columns. The panels on the reredos show scenes from the life of St John as well as his vision of the Apocalypse. The saint also appears above on the stained-glass east window at the foot of the cross with Mary. There is a blazing and triumphant white tabernacle and the ceiling above it, and the east windows that curve round the apse, are wonderfully and intricately painted. The Blessed Sacrament Chapel also features the pelican above the tabernacle. The altar shows the Last Supper and the sacrifice of Abraham.

All the chapels have something to admire. There are altars carved by Thomas Earp, glass by Hardman & Co and, rather hidden round the back in the baptistery, an ornate shrine designed by Edward Hansom in 1871 to contain the relics of St Justina of Padua.

St John the Evangelist was bombed in 1942. Four people died and the south aisle was completely destroyed. It was rebuilt in the traditional Gothic style of the church, to the disappointment of some enthusiasts for the modern. The note of tradition was further maintained by the inscription on the wall commemorating the air raid being carved in Latin, when the church was 'HOSTILI INCURSIONE DIRUTA...'.

St Wilfrid, Duncombe Place, York (1862–4)

St Wilfrid's has not always had a good press. It was built
directly opposite the Minster and its idiosyncratic
tower has been thought to compete aggressively, and
unsuccessfully, with the genuinely medieval towers of
one of Britain's greatest buildings. It was designed to be
the pro-cathedral of the diocese of Beverley and it
remained so until 1878.

There was a thriving Catholic congregation in
the mid 1850s in a city which had a history of repression and recovery during penal times. St Margaret
Clitherow was martyred by being crushed to death and
her shrine is not far away from St Wilfrid's in the
Shambles. In 1686 the Institute of the Blessed Virgin
Mary started the Bar Convent in a private house and
Catholic worship has been practised there ever since.
A large number of York Catholics were openly
worshipping even before the law officially permitted
them to do so. After emancipation their numbers were
swollen, as was often
the case in northern
cities, by Irish immi-
grants fleeing from
famine. They were
not made especially
welcome by the
indigenous Catholics
and further space was
sought to accommo-
date them all. By the time St Wilfrid's was being built there was already a
large and well-designed Catholic church by J A Hansom just down the road.
The architect for St Wilfrid's was George Goldie (1828–87), who had impec-
cable credentials for the job. He was a York Catholic. His father was a staunch
member of the Catholic community and he was the grandson of Joseph
Bonomi, an architect famous enough at the time to be mentioned in Jane
Austen's *Sense and Sensibility*. Goldie specialised in the High Victorian style of
which St Wilfrid's is his most remarkable example; his touch was not light.

Goldie had to work in an awkwardly shaped site. The unusual and
controversial tower has a steep hipped roof and there are gargoyles, lancet
windows, finials, crockets and a tall cross on the top. The west front too has

Right: the font at St Wilfrid's, like
the church itself, is bulky and
expressive of the confidence of
York Catholics of the time.

Below: complimenting or
competing with York Minster?
Goldie's idiosyncratic tower
confronts its neighbour.

much detail and is enlivened by a forceful tympanum (carved by Thomas Earp of Lambeth), which shows in Cumberland sandstone, on either side of the seated Christ, scenes of the Fall and Redemption with the expulsion from Eden and the Annunciation.

Goldie's interior is no less robust. The most striking features are the great sandstone columns. They are huge, with shaft rings bulging out halfway up their height, which emphasise their bulk. Their bases are substantial as are their capitals, which are heavily carved with angels amidst dense foliage. The sanctuary sustains the mood. Around and behind the reredos is an arcade with stone figures of the evangelists jutting out and, unusually, seated at desks. Above them are large paintings on a gold background (by Goldie and Knowles). Central is the Crucifixion which is flanked by four scenes of biblical events. The opulent High Altar gleams whitely against the grey reredos. It bears a monumental tabernacle. The arches to the sanctuary have large carved figures standing in front of them and the walls above the arches are thickly painted. There is glass by William Wailes, but the windows that once completed the ensemble in the sanctuary were blown out during the Second World War.

The font is appropriately strongly built and weighty, embedded with large, jewel-like roundels. The carvings on the confessionals are unexpectedly delicate; they are what remains of the old pulpit. The Lady Chapel has densely carved panelling and an altar showing Mary and Jesus with two angels. The Sacred Heart Chapel has a charming statue of St Joseph the Worker.

All Saints Friary, Barton-upon-Irwell, Greater Manchester (1862–5)

West of Manchester, where retail and business parks finally give way to the Manchester Ship Canal's swing bridge, aqueduct and conservation area, stands an isolated masterpiece. It is one of Edward Pugin's most successful designs and best funded commissions. It was built to serve as a parish church and as a mausoleum for the local grandee, Sir Humphrey de Trafford. He had married the Earl of Shrewsbury's daughter and the earl, an unstinting fan of the Pugins, had recommended Edward as architect for the chantry chapel Sir Humphrey was planning to build.

The de Trafford family was firmly inter-twined with local Catholic history. One de Trafford, an abbot, had participated in the 1536 uprising, the Pilgrimage of Grace, and had been executed. Another became an apostate and vigorously persecuted Catholics. But in the 18th and 19th centuries the family were great supporters of the faith and of their Catholic

E Pugin's isolated and now endangered masterpiece, west of Manchester.

tenants. Sir Humphrey gave the land for the church and indicated to Pugin that £25,000 would not be too much for a family chantry chapel, which would then develop and expand into All Saints church. It was finished in 1868. At the opening, the congregation listened to Beethoven and a sermon preached by Archbishop (later Cardinal) Manning, whose train was carried by Sir Humphrey's six-year-old son. Thereafter the great west door of the church was kept open for parishioners and visitors and on Sundays the private door to the side was opened for the de Traffords when they arrived in their carriages and occupied the chantry chapel.

This is a strikingly unusual and individual church. Above the rose window on the west side there are brooding sculptures of religious figures and above them, on an exaggeratedly steep roof, a bell-cote tapers into a slender, white stone spirelet and cross. The inside is polychromatic; the tall arches and the columns are formed from bands of Mansfield red and Painswick white stone. The capitals are carved into joyously abundant foliage. The roof is superbly coloured and gilded. Through the arches, the murals on the aisle walls are visible. These have faded with time but this, for the moment, rather enhances their antique appearance.

Pugin's sanctuary has one of the most dramatic reredoses in the county. It is a fantastic tableau of angels, seemingly airborne above the tabernacle, bearing aloft a jewelled and golden crown. The artist who carved it and the no less exuberant altar, as well as the altar in the chantry, may have been either J R Boulton of

Angels exhilaratingly aloft above the tabernacle of the now threatened sanctuary.

Cheltenham or E E Geflowski of Liverpool. The chantry chapel is screened off from the sanctuary by double columns. The altar shows the carved figures of the Virgin and Child surrounded by angels and saints and below it is an effigy in white marble of the dead Christ in the sepulchre. The floor was magnificently and colourfully tiled by Minton's: each tile has the de Trafford monogram and arms on it. The fine glass of the window in the chantry, as in the sanctuary, is by Hardman & Co.

On the wall of the sanctuary a large mural shows bishops, clergy, nuns and patrons kneeling before the Lamb of God. Prominent among the company, near to his patron, dressed as a cleric and holding plans of the church, is Edward Pugin. At the east end of the south aisle is a portrait of Father Kolbe, a Franciscan who died in Auschwitz. There is also a statue of him wearing clerical dress, but with a striped concentration camp uniform draped over one shoulder.

The de Traffords left Lancashire, and the church was left empty until it was taken over by the Franciscans in 1962. It had meantime fallen into near dereliction. A huge national effort was made (by English Heritage, a surviving de Trafford and the borough of Trafford amongst others) to raise the colossal sum of money needed for restoration. The work started in 1981 and took six years: the bell-cote which had developed an ominous lean was taken down, reassembled and then put back again; the roof was removed and the dry rot which threatened the roofs and walls was drastically treated; the murals were restored; and modern glass was put into the rose window.

Tragically, the dry rot and damp have returned and once again threaten the roof, the magnificently tiled floor of the chantry and the murals. Consequently, at the time of writing, the sanctuary and chantry chapel are screened off from worshippers and visitors.

Our Lady Help of Christians and St Denis, Priory Road, St Marychurch, Torquay, Devon (1865–81)

'…worthy of Our Lord': Joseph Hansom's church for Marychurch.

In 1864 Bishop Vaughan of Plymouth invited Mother Margaret Hallahan to bring her nuns to south Devon, to a site near Torquay. Mother Margaret arrived with the intention of building a new church of sufficient grandeur to be worthy of Our Lady. A wealthy newcomer to the district, William Chatto-Potts, offered to pay for whatever was required and Joseph A Hansom was the commissioned architect. Work began immediately, but then slowed; Hansom's son, also called Joseph, went off to Rome in a burst of pious enthusiasm to help defend Pope Pius IX from Garibaldi, and his anxious father followed him.

A convent for the nuns, a cloister and an orphanage were built simultaneously with the church and it was not until 1881 that the whole complex could be opened.

The church is solid stone, in self-assured Gothic, and exudes confidence. It stands on a hill above the St Marychurch community and has a big, complicated tower and spire with gables and attendant spirelets. The west front is particularly impressive. The entrance has a carved stone arch, a tympanum, many crockets and, from various angles and niches around the walls, statues of the saints scrutinise the visitor.

The interior is long and lofty with a clerestory to one side, a triforium and a gallery on the west (which was for the use of the orphans). The columns have unusually deeply carved capitals. At the tower end there is a veritable forest of bulging supporting columns and a thicket of carved vegetation in the capitals. They are said to have been inspired by the garden of Mr Chatto-Potts. Young Joseph Hansom designed (1881) a font in local marble made by a Mr Blackler which stands near the entrance of the crypt.

The sanctuary at the east end is, for a Hansom church, relatively unflamboyant. The altar itself is simple, with a carving of the Last Supper on its front.

Hansom's sanctuary, altar and reredos, with a stone tower climbing up towards the high east windows.

Holy Name of Jesus, Oxford Road, Chorlton-on-Medlock, Manchester (1869–71)

That J A Hansom could do a big thing in a big way is nowhere better demonstrated than by this astonishing church, just south of the city centre in what was once a fashionable Georgian part of town. It was not built on the pennies of the poor. The Jesuits wanted something large and emphatic and had at their disposal a generous sum of money they had received from two Catholic spinsters in Worcester. The land was given by

Adrian Gilbert Scott's octagonal tower of 1928 surmounts the 19th-century French Gothic of the Holy Name.

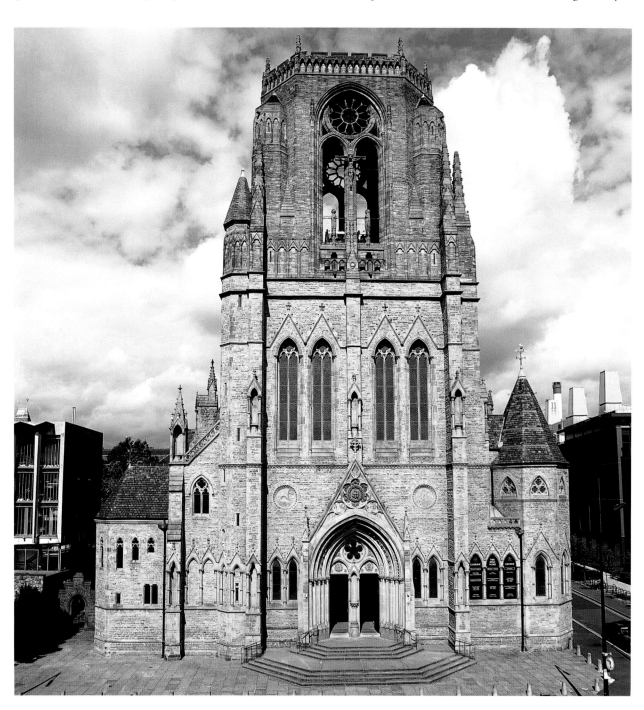

Opposite: Pushing Gothic to its limits: Joseph Hansom's vast interior space at the Holy Name.

Formidable Gothic arches frame the Holy Name's substantial and comfortable confessionals.

Lady Stapleton-Bretherton, another great benefactor to Catholic causes. The scale, the style and the architectural ambition of the church made a great impact at the time and would influence the design of Manchester Town Hall and the university buildings near the church. Hansom designed a great tower to be topped by a steeple. It was never built; the land was unsuitable. The smaller octagonal tower was added by Adrian Gilbert Scott in 1928.

Hansom was pushing Gothic way beyond a respectful copying of medieval precedents. The Holy Name has a spaciousness and clarity of structure that has prompted speculation that he must have been influenced by Viollet-le-Duc, the Frenchman who was not only the great theorist of Gothic but also a prophet of architectural Modernism. Hansom was collaborating with his son and future partner Joseph Stanislaus Hansom; the Holy Name was being built at the same time as Arundel Cathedral (see page 113).

Hansom was a master of creating overwhelming interior space. Here he designed a very broad nave, with a much narrower sanctuary, transepts and a rib-vaulted ceiling of daring width. To achieve this Hansom used local terracotta for the vaults which considerably lessened the weight bearing down on the spans.

The individual elements within the huge church, which is remarkable for the completeness of its 19th-century furnishings, are not diminished by the colossal scale. The High Altar is the focal point (the sight lines are excellent) and it was never moved to accommodate any re-ordering. It was designed by J S Hansom in 1890, after he had taken over the firm. It is of alabaster inlaid with green Russian malachite and its frontal is based on Leonardo da Vinci's *Last Supper*. Behind it the Caen stone reredos rears up in a great white, stalagmite-like cliff of crocketed spikes. Within its niches are statues in alabaster of ten Jesuit saints by R J Boulton. The glass in the window above is by Hardman's (1899) and shows a resplendent Coronation of Our Lady. An ambulatory curls round behind the altar and reredos, where there is an unusual stairway leading up to the throne.

Many of the side chapels in the Holy Name are individual masterpieces. The three chapels on the south aisle were unfinished by Hansom when the church opened and John Francis Bentley was asked to complete them. He knocked the chapels into one but this weakened the whole structure and the space was re-divided into three parts in 1997. However, the delicately coloured and superbly designed chapel and altar, dedicated to the Madonna della Strada, Our Lady of the Wayside, were restored and put back into position. Below the altar in St Joseph's Chapel is a reliquary designed by J A Hansom.

The pulpit (1886) is made of alabaster inset with mosaic portraits of the 16th-century English martyrs and has a carved wooden canopy. The baptistery was completed in the 1890s with money from the de Trafford family. It is a splendid stone octagonal space, with a lofty ceiling and statues of the saints and pictures of Jesuit missionaries preaching and praying in exotic parts of the world. The font is alabaster and the immense canopy of carved oak can be raised and lowered through a formidable system of counterweights.

On the north aisle Hansom designed eight confessionals. Each has a fireplace and – for the priest at least – they provide an unusually comfortable and urbane space. The organ by Hill & Son (1871) is very fine.

Cathedral of Our Lady and St Philip Howard, Arundel, West Sussex (1870–3)

The great ridge of the cathedral roof shares the hilltop skyline of the town with another of Henry 15th Duke of Norfolk's *grands projets*, Arundel Castle. Cathedral and castle rise above the flat lands where the river Arun runs towards the English Channel and together they make up one of the great townscapes of England. The Duke was head of the most prominent of the English noble families that had remained loyal to the Catholic faith at the Reformation. It might be thought that the Fitzalan Chapel at the castle would have been big enough for his religious needs, but Henry wanted something special to mark his 21st birthday. He commissioned architect J A Hansom to design a colossal, fabulously expensive church in French 13th-century Gothic style in honour of the Duke's patron saint, St Philip Neri. A lofty tower was planned but never built. For all that, the stone walls of the cathedral rise with effortless superiority above the rooftops of the town, with an epic tympanum on the west front and a massive roof that is girdled round by delicate pinnacles.

The pinnacles and gables of Arundel Cathedral, which has one of the most extraordinary church roofs in Britain.

The nave is tall, narrow and light; none of the nave windows have stained glass. The clustered columns, like those at Bourges Cathedral, have enormous capitals. There are roundels with reliefs showing the features of the English saints. Chapels, with splendid glass, radiate off. Much of the stained glass was designed by Nathaniel Westlake and some of the other glass was made by Hardman and Powell. The vista culminates in a sombre, dignified apse and sanctuary, lit from behind by five deeply coloured windows high in the ambulatory. St Philip Neri, founder of the Oratorians, is remembered in the south transept by a tall statue on the altar under an exaggeratedly elongated canopy that stretches up towards the shadowy ceiling of the chapel. Similarly tall, thin lancet windows relate in pictures scenes of the saint's life and death.

The Duke was an Old Oratorian and he wanted the cathedral to honour the founder of the order – even if the honour was to be conferred in the Gothic rather than the Roman Classical style usually preferred by the Oratorians. The dedication was eventually changed. Two new windows (1986) designed by John Lawson in the south aisle show the current dedicatee of the cathedral, St Philip Howard as well as his wife Anne Dacre.

St Philip's father was the 4th Duke of Norfolk who was beheaded by Elizabeth I for plotting to marry Mary Queen of Scots. His son Philip, nonetheless, became a brilliant, worldly courtier. He sat in on the formal debates that took place between Catholic prisoners and Anglican divines. He was very moved and became reconciled to his family's faith. Philip was incarcerated in the Tower of London until he died, perhaps poisoned, eleven years later. He was canonised in 1970. The church became a cathedral in 1965 and the dedication was changed in 1973 to Our Lady and St Philip Howard.

In 1971 the relics of St Philip Howard were brought from the Fitzalan Chapel to a new altar tomb in the north transept. A wrought-iron screen, incorporating a motif of chains, surrounds the shrine. In front of a vivid red curtain a striking wooden statue of the saint stands on the stone sarcophagus.

The Lady Chapel has what is believed to be the first tabernacle to be produced in England after the Reformation. It was made for the Duke of Norfolk in 1730.

Arundel Cathedral seen across the Sussex meadows.

The grand interior Charles Buckler designed for the Dominicans. The stone gallery he wanted was never built and he disowned the iron one that was erected instead.

St Dominic, Southampton Row, Haverstock Hill, London NW5 (1874–83)

In 1862 the Dominicans, back in England for the first time since the Reformation, bought three acres on the outskirts of Kentish Town in north London. They built a priory and laid the foundation stone of a chapel. Work was slow as money was short. Their architect, G R Blount, died having only laid the foundations for the east end. The Blount designs were abandoned when work really began under the direction of architect Charles Alban Buckler (1824–1905). Buckler and his three brothers had converted to Catholicism and, as they had all joined the Dominican order, Charles was well positioned to get the commission. Cardinal Wiseman laid the foundation stone of what was one of the largest Catholic churches in London in 1863, 20 years before it opened.

The Dominicans wanted a church large enough to cater for a rapidly growing congregation and one that would signal that the order was back in London and very much back in business. It has no tower, as the Dominicans were rather against towers, but there is no need for one. St Dominic's is 100 feet high and 200 feet long. It has an unbroken roofline, is built mostly of brick ('the Dominicans do not despise brick and slate' observed Buckler), is simply designed (the Dominicans favoured simplicity) and effortlessly makes an impact on the surrounding urban landscape.

The narthex is austere and lofty enough but the interior of the church is vast. Great columns soar up to the vaulted roof high above. Light beams through distant clerestory windows and from lights above the many chapel altars. In keeping with a long Dominican tradition stretching back to the Middle Ages, the sanctuary is very much a continuation of the long nave. There is no screen. There is an abundance of chapels, twenty-three, all round the church. The individual chapels were paid for by private patrons. Fifteen of them are dedicated to the Mysteries of the Rosary to which the Dominicans have a particular devotion.

The High Altar was designed by Buckler and is not of Dominican simplicity. It has eight mosaic panels showing Dominican saints. A series of spiky gabled arches rise up, giving maximum drama to the monstrance throne held at their centre and above which is a spirelet that reaches up in front of the east window. John Hardman designed the five tall windows of the apse that show the Crowning of Our Lady, the fifth Glorious Mystery.

The other chapels in the series gleam with stained glass that illuminates statues of saints, altars, devotional pictures, rich iron work and commemorative brass. Before concelebratory Mass became standard these altars would have been busy each day with priests saying their Mass; the sense of an ancient faith being vigorously renewed must have been potent. Buckler himself gave the Annunciation Chapel as a thank-offering for his own reception into the Catholic faith. The three panels of its reredos show Gabriel, the lily flower and Mary. The window above also shows the Annunciation. Mr and Mrs Buckler are shown as being present and below there is a cenotaph bearing the Buckler coat of arms.

A chapel dedicated to St Dominic has a reredos with the saint's death painted by Philip Westlake. N H J Westlake painted the large, serious Stations of the Cross. Buckler wanted to put in a gallery below the clerestory with a stone parapet but an incongruous iron walkway was built instead.

St Michael, St Michael's Road, Ditton, Widnes, Lancashire (1876–9)

The huge tower of the church broods over the modern developments that surround it on the flat lands north of the Mersey. It is built of dark red sandstone punctuated by lancet windows. Grimacing gargoyles jut out under an unusual saddleback roof. It looks German, and indeed it was built for a community of German Jesuits who had been expelled from the Rhineland in 1872. Lady Stapleton-Bretherton, who had been so generous to Manchester's Holy Name of Jesus (see page 110), paid for St Michael's. The architect was well-connected Catholic convert Henry Clutton (1819–93), a relation of Cardinal Manning and friend of Cardinal Newman. Four of his children became nuns or priests.

Clutton's church may look spectacular, even menacing, from the outside, but the interior is by contrast light and welcoming. It is cruciform with a very high roof of oak and pine supported by daringly elongated columns. The roofs of the nave and the sanctuary are the same height and are rounded off by a flat and shallow east end with yellowish sandstone walls.

The carved wooden tester that took the place of the original altar after re-ordering more than holds its own in the east end of Henry Clutton's church in Ditton.

One of the formidable grimacing gargoyles on the tower of St Michael's.

The altar was moved from the east wall during the re-ordering and has since vanished. But the extraordinary tester that was salvaged from the pulpit when that was destroyed at the same time now holds and surrounds the tabernacle in the centre of the wall. It is multi-levelled, an exhilarating display of wood carving virtuosity and has become the focal point of the church. When it was reassembled in its present position a pencilled note was found in it saying that 'Peter Eckers, lay brother of the Society of Jesus, carved this.' The structure is topped off by a silvery statue of St Michael wielding a triumphant sword. The sanctuary lamps were also the work of a brother and look German; so too were the carved wooden altars of the two inviting side chapels either side of the sanctuary. Paintings in gold and blue glimmer above them.

The Jesuits left Widnes in 1900 and St Michael's is now a parish church.

Our Lady and All Saints, Lancaster Lane, Parbold, Lancashire (1878–84)

In the late 19th century Parbold was still an isolated village in the Lancashire hills. The church of Our Lady that overlooks the village is a large and sophisticated exercise in Victorian Gothic which would more than hold its own in Manchester or Preston. It was designed by Edmund Kirby (1838–1920), a prolific north-country architect from Liverpool who had been a pupil of Edward Pugin. He designed a big church, next to Lancaster House, the home of his patron, Hugh Ainscough.

The Ainscoughs were an old, aristocratic Catholic family who had been through hard times after the Reformation. In the 18th century they revived their fortunes through business, particularly flour milling, and by the mid-19th century they were rich again. They

The rose window featuring only female saints and the reredos with life-size angels at Parbold.

wanted a church that reflected the pride they felt in the reassertion of the faith in their county and one that would be a grateful symbol of their association with the Benedictines of Ampleforth College. The Benedictines too had a long association with the district during the years of persecution and there was a choir of 20 Benedictine Fathers at the consecration of the church in 1884.

The sandstone church has a tall, pinnacled tower which supports an octagonal and slender slate spire. (Ainscough instructed Kirby that the spire should be taller than the one on the Anglican church situated a little higher up the hill). It is certainly impressive, as is the interior. The nave, sanctuary and side chapels work in unity. The arcades have tall pointed arches supported by quite short columns. A rood hangs from the sanctuary arch beyond which is a large rose window. It celebrates only female saints; one depicted is St Sativola, patron saint of millers.

The High Altar reaches up in front of the reredos to the east window. To counteract any possible gloom thus caused, Kirby put gabled dormer windows into the sanctuary roof – an unusual feature. The substantial reredos he designed in a spirit of Neo-Gothic exuberance (and he designed a great many); it fills the whole of the lower east wall. Within large, spiky niches stand eight life-size angels. Each one carries an object associated with the Passion. The altar is tiled with designs based on the rose and the fleur de lys – symbols associated with the Manchester Regiment. There is in a side chapel a monument to Cyril Ainscough of the 5th Battalion of the Manchester Regiment who was killed in the Dardanelles during the First World War.

Richard Ainscough, Hugh's brother, was also killed in action. There is a touching window to their memories in which both stand before an armed but not very ferocious St Michael, who holds the devil in chains. Also remembered in glass is St John Rigby, a Lancashire martyr from the parish.

Edmund Kirby's grand tower and spire for the Benedictine parish symbolised pride in the survival and reassertion of the Catholic faith in Lancashire.

5 Alternatives to Gothic

A W N Pugin may have stamped his architectural convictions on the look of the age but he had formidable critics. John Henry Newman saw his obsession with an idealised medieval past as absurd. He remarked that Pugin was excluding half of Christendom from his vision. That half included St Peter's Rome and the Vatican. He wondered how Pugin could exclude from his thinking the Classical churches 'from which so many saints had received their inspiration'.

Bishop Baines – Vicar General of the Western District – had lived in Rome and liked it. He took a strong line on churches that were in 'what is called Gothic architecture and are unfortunately unlike anything else in creation'. When Pugin attacked the Classical church of St Francis Xavier in Hereford, Baines vigorously defended it, chastising him for an 'unauthorised and virulent attack'.

Pugin did not even care for Perpendicular Gothic. It smacked of the late, declining Middle Ages, of the Renaissance and the end of the Age of Faith. So to build in that style or in the earlier Romanesque Gothic style also went against the party line. But architects did build in those styles. And later on, the architects and the Fathers who built the Birmingham and Brompton oratories would seek to reflect the glamour and authority of Rome and its pope rather than a medieval dream world. A Classical dome could make a tremendous silhouette above a town or city and be just as capable of expressing the authority of Rome as any spire.

There were other objections to Gothic. Long, aisled naves, narrow, dim and distant chancels, muttering priests hidden from view and celebrating inscrutable mysteries behind choir screens might capture some aesthetic imaginations, but there was a growing demand for more functional spaces, clearer sight lines, more involvement with, and understanding of, the service by the congregation. What was the point of aisles if those in them could see nothing of the proceedings? New techniques meant that aisles could be abandoned as one of the means of keeping up the roof. Newman found that a Pugin altar was too small for Pontifical High Mass. East windows in the 13th-century style dazzled the congregation during the Benediction. Classical buildings were good at accommodating the demands of a changing ritual in changing times.

*'Laudate Dominum'…*Classical arches and decoration at the Brompton Oratory. Pugin's critics believed that Classical forms of architecture were preferable to the Neo-Gothic model when it came to the expression of Catholic worship.

Above: a tortoise supports this ambitiously carved column at Clifford.

Below: the tower at Clifford is a landmark for miles around in this historically Catholic county.

St Edward the Confessor, High Street, Clifford, West Yorkshire (1845–8)

This is a big church for a village. It dominates Clifford and its tall, individual spire is a landmark for all the surrounding countryside. This part of Yorkshire was a stronghold of the Catholic faith and Clifford was well represented in the 1536 uprising, the Pilgrimage of Grace, and during the Civil War. But by the early 19th century only a few Catholic families lived there. This changed when Ralph Grimston started a flax mill in the village in 1838. He was a Catholic and he made a point of employing Catholic workmen, who were often otherwise discriminated against by employers. The Catholic population increased accordingly. Grimstone also had the ambition, as well as the means, to found a church.

In this he was assisted by Joseph Maxwell, a local magnate and friend of Father Clifford, who ran the local mission. They were visiting an aristocratic Catholic family in Traquair, Scotland, where they met a high-achieving shepherd's son called Ramsay who had studied architecture in France. Ramsay was dying of consumption and Maxwell was touched. The young man had produced some drawings for an imaginary church, and Maxwell bought them for fifty pounds. When the church was commissioned these drawings were handed, as the basis of what might be built, to the now celebrated architect Joseph A Hansom. It was said that Hansom was not over zealous in attendance at Clifford ('proper working plans were never made out' and Hansom 'could hardly ever be got to look after the work' say *The Chronicles of a Wharfedale Parish*, a 1909

account of the church's history). But Hansom made the drawings practical and a local builder, George Roberts, saw the project through. This village church was thought grand enough for Cardinal Wiseman to open and it had supporters in some unlikely places. Among those who contributed to the building, apart from Mr Grimston, were the King and Queen of Sardinia, the Grand Duke of Austria and the Queen of the French.

The extraordinary tower came later (1859), designed by George Goldie, architect of St Wilfrid's in nearby York (see page 106). Grimston paid £1,000 for the tower which, 'though an object of beauty itself, is out of proportion to the rest of the building, being far too high', said the *Chronicles*.

The church is built of light coloured limestone and, considering its origins, the French-Norman look is not so surprising. Romanesque was briefly fashionable at that time and the glorious interior of St Edward the Confessor makes one wish the style had had a longer run. This space has heavy components (viewed best from a substantial gallery), but the effect is not in the least dour or heavy. Clerestory windows brighten the stone walls and the remarkable columns. These are very thick, in some cases carved, and were inspired by no less than the massive columns in Durham Cathedral. One pillar rests on a carved stone tortoise and is decorated with colourful emblems of the Evangelists. The capital is extravagantly foliated.

The sanctuary is unusually and strikingly arranged with columns and rounded arches screening the Blessed Sacrament Chapel. During the re-ordering some columns were removed and repositioned on the side walls of the Lady Chapel. This chapel contains one of the church's biggest attractions, a marble statue of a thoughtful-looking Mary with crossed hands: 'the most beautiful statue of the Mother of God to be found in Christendom' say *The Chronicles*. It was carved by Karl Hoffman, a Jewish sculptor working in Rome in 1844. He was persuaded by Maxwell and Father Clifford (who met Hoffman on a visit to Rome) to turn a block of marble which he had left over into a statue of the Virgin. This led Hoffman to study his subject and, legend says, he consequently became a Roman Catholic. The statue 'was for some years unpaid for'. Eventually Mr Grimston paid for it.

From the gallery: Hansom and Ramsay's French Romanesque interior. The columns are modelled on those at Durham Cathedral.

The Oratory of St Philip Neri, Hagley Road, Edgbaston, Birmingham (1860 and 1903–9)

John Henry Newman was ordained priest in Rome in 1847. He had come to admire the Oratorians there and decided to set up the institute devoted to St Philip Neri in what had become his adopted city, Birmingham. The first houses – one was in a former gin distillery – were primitive affairs in poor districts. Pope Pius IX then let it be known that he wanted Newman to extend his mission to where his special genius lay, among the educated classes. The Oratorians moved to Edgbaston, a much better part of town. A splendid church was planned in the Classical style, but funds allowed only an unambitious church with a roof taken from a derelict local factory. This was added to over time with a chapel (1858) by John Hungerford Pollen and a heavy, Romanesque red brick cloister by Henry Clutton.

Our Lady's Altar, with altar rails from Rome, columns of Siberian onyx and altar lamp from Munich. The statue of Our Lady is a replica of one in Paris.

Opposite: The authority and glamour of Rome in Birmingham: Doran Webb's immense and sombre interior.

Newman died in 1890 and it was felt that a new, more appropriate church should be built to his honour in the place where he had lived for so long. The architect appointed was E Doran Webb (1864–1915) and the style chosen was again Classical. Doran Webb is not widely known, but here at Birmingham he built something exceptional. It is almost invisible from the Hagley Road being screened off by the red brick façade of the school. Even the dome is barely visible from the street. Past the cloisters and the Classical west front broods Doran Webb's sombre basilica. Fitful light from dormer windows casts a muted radiance on the tunnel roof, the marble columns and the shallow apse to reveal a serious, awe-inspiring interior. It is fifty years on from Birmingham's Gothic St Chad's Cathedral (see page 67); it is another world.

The twelve tall, coloured columns have very big Corinthian capitals and were each shaped from single blocks of marble. They are nearly 18 feet high. They were quarried in northern Italy, roughly shaped on site, taken to the port and there given final shape. A small boat then brought them, two at a time, to England where they were shipped by canal to Birmingham. Their arrival in the Hagley Road stopped the traffic.

The quality of the materials is sustained throughout the church. The pulpit is a formidable construction of white marble, porphyry and mosaics and the stairs up to it are made of alabaster. The Stations of the Cross are painted on ornately copper-framed Limoges enamel (by Hardman & Co). The walls of the sanctuary are made from red African onyx with bands of Siena marble. The altar front has panels of Connemara marble and plaques of lapis lazuli. The baldacchino came from Rome. The dome, though not especially high (120 feet), is still a powerful element in the overall scene, with mosaics on the pendentives of the prophets Ezekiel, Jeremiah, Isaiah and Daniel. The roof of the nave was stencilled and decorated, in a similar spirit to the rest of the church, in 1986.

There are many chapels along the sides of the aisles. Not one lacks abundant decoration. St Philip's Chapel is all that remains of the old church of 1858 where Newman said Mass. The commission for the alabaster altar was given by Newman to architect George Gilbert Scott junior, soon after his conversion to Catholicism. The altarpiece is a copy of the painting by Guido Reni of St Philip Neri.

The Oratory has an important organ and organ gallery. There is a remarkable baptistery (by Dunstan Powell) with walls of white plaster, baroque cherubs and a font of alabaster with a bronze canopy. St Athanasius' Altar in copper, mosaic and marble contains the body of St Valentine. It was presented to Newman by Pope Pius IX. The Shrine of St Philip Neri, made of white marble with a waxen effigy of the saint, contains relics of St Philip – also given to Newman in Rome.

Processional figures of saints have been, and still are, carried through the streets of Clerkenwell in honour of Our Lady of Mount Carmel.

St Peter's Italian Church, Back Hill, Clerkenwell Road, London EC1 (1862–3)

The Pallottine Fathers who founded the church, as well as Cardinal Wiseman and Pope Pius IX who was taking an interest, wanted it to be for 'the faithful of all nations', not just the large, impoverished Italian community who lived around Hatton Garden and Clerkenwell in the 19th century. But St Peter's principal mission was to Italians and very Italian it has always been. It has an Italian-style loggia (added by F W Tasker in 1891) facing the Clerkenwell Road. Above the entrance is a bronze memorial (1960) to more than 400 Italian detainees who were torpedoed by a German submarine as they were being shipped to internment in Australia in 1940.

Father Raphael Melia travelled extensively throughout Europe raising funds to build a church for the Italian Catholics of Clerkenwell. The proposal was to build a very large church indeed, which would be dedicated to St Peter. The scale of the scheme, and the potent dedication, were not well received in some quarters; in the House of Lords it was sourly remarked that London already had a cathedral, St Paul's. Nevertheless, in 1852 land was bought and work began the following year to the designs of Francesco Gualandi of Bologna, based on the classic Italian basilicas of St Chrysogono and Santa Maria in Trastevere in Rome.

Ten years later, in 1863, the crypt was opened on Christmas day and then, a month or so later, the church, to a more modest design by John Miller Bryson, was opened too. The original plan had envisaged accommodation for 3,400. Bryson's solution was for a mere 2,000. For all that, when it was opened St Peter's was much admired for its size – it claimed to be the largest Catholic church in Britain at the time – and for being the only church in the country built like a Roman basilica.

The columns of the spectacular nave are made from York stone painted to look like marble. Above their Ionic capitals is a large, arched triforium. There are galleries behind the arches which were originally designed to provide additional seating but these were blocked off in 1886. The galleries have paintings of St Peter and St Paul.

F W Tasker added the Italian-style loggia to St Peter's in 1891.

The vast interior was eventually highly painted and decorated but in the 1950s white paint was liberally applied and now its impact is very much brighter, if less textured and detailed, than it used to be. But it is dramatic enough. It has a broad nave and two wide aisles, chapels, transepts, and two arches that tower over the sanctuary with Latin inscriptions and a painting of Pius IX. On the flat ceiling above the nave there is a large painting of the Conversion of St Peter.

There is nothing about St Peter's that is austere or minimal. The High Altar, the tabernacle and the steps are made from variously coloured Italian marbles. Above, the baldacchino is supported by four marble columns decorated in black and gold. Above that there are four gilded statues of angels. At the centre of the apse behind the High Altar is a painting of the Annunciation by Viennese artist B Einler. The communion rails are ornate. Two side chapels are dedicated to St Joseph and St Vincenzi Pallotti. They are flanked by four terracotta statues of the Evangelists. Few of the artists and craftsmen employed at St Peter's are household names in this country.

Many of the paintings and frescoes in the church, vividly Italian in style, were by Gauthier of Saluzzo and Arnaudo of Caraglio from Piedmont. It took them ten months (1885–6). In 1953 Don Giuseppe de Fillipi added some more. Strong in charm amid all the marble grandeur, is the carved wooden Neapolitan crib in the north aisle.

Our Lady Queen of Martyrs and St Ignatius, Chideock, Dorset (1872)

This is one of the most delightful and unexpected Catholic churches in Britain. It is screened off by trees to the point of invisibility from a quiet Dorset lane north of the village. Beyond the trees there is what looks like a medieval Italian church. No famous architect had a hand in its design and because of that, perhaps, it is little known.

This part of west Dorset is drenched in its heroic Catholic history. No less than five local Catholics were martyred in the persecutions. The powerful Catholic Arundell family lived in Chideock Castle (now destroyed) and led a stubborn local resistance to the Protestant settlement. The castle, its chapel and priest's hole were a staging post for large numbers of missionary priests entering England through the nearby harbour of Lyme Regis.

In 1802 Thomas Weld of Lulworth Castle, a relation of the Arundells and of an ancient Catholic family himself, bought the Chideock estate. He gave

The Tuscan-looking west front at Chideock records Charles Weld's achievement in Latin script.

it to his sixth son, Humphrey, who built the manor house and turned the old barn into a chapel. His son, Charles Weld, was the driving genius behind the present church. He incorporated the barn into the transept of the new church and not only designed the church in the Italian Romanesque style but also did much of the work himself as a labour of love.

The church's west front would look at home in Tuscany. There is a very large, heavily carved roundel in painted terracotta above the entrance. Below, a long Latin inscription records Charles Weld's labours.

The interior is one of the most idiosyncratic and personal statements of Catholic faith in the country. The barrel-vault roof has panels of saints and religious imagery stencilled to the designs of Charles Weld. The shafts have capitals with, among many other sacred images, the Crown of Thorns and the instruments of the Passion that Weld carved into the stone foliage. Above the arches and below the clerestory windows are paintings on both sides of the church of the English Martyrs. The Chideock Martyrs are nearest the sanctuary on the right. All the paintings were done by members of the Weld family while Charles was painting the altar, the sanctuary wall, roof and dome. Various patron saints of the family are represented on the reredos. Dramatic light cascades on to the altar from the dome above it. It illuminates a statue of the Virgin who stands on a tortuously carved column in a position of adoring ascension.

Among the riches of this amazing church are the paintings which cover the sacristy wall and which, again, Weld painted. They have faded into a happily unrestored simulacrum of their medieval fresco inspiration. From the gallery the family could look down on the sanctuary at Mass. It is still furnished with homely family photographs and tired-looking but comfortable chairs. The church has fragments of the True Cross and the hair shirt of St Thomas More as relics. There is also a small museum. Not every exhibit is devoted to Chideock's anguished Catholic past. There are fading photographs of long-forgotten football teams, village fetes and scout camps.

Charles Weld's faded wall-paintings in the sacristy.

London Oratory of St Philip Neri, Brompton Road, London SW7 (1878)

Newman did not think much of the area or the site. He wrote 'essentially in a suburb…a neighbourhood of second-rate gentry and second-rate shops'. He favoured somewhere in the West End where the Oratorian mission among the educated might better flourish. And not only Newman disapproved. The Anglican vicar of Holy Trinity next door objected to the close proximity of so many Catholics. But Father Faber had led his Oratorians from the midlands to London in 1849 and they wanted to build a 'good, large and stately church' in the Italian manner and a better address was proving too expensive. The Fathers began by building Oratory House as their residence, the Little Oratory as their chapel (by architect J J Scoles) and making do with a temporary church.

The Counter-Reformation in Kensington: the Oratory's heroic stone façade rises above the Brompton Road.

By about 1875 the Oratorian Fathers were seeking funds and preparing plans for a proper church. In fact, it was said, they 'developed a fever for architecture' and there were soon 'almost as many plans as Fathers'. In 1878 a competition for a church designed 'in the style of the Italian Renaissance' was announced. There were thirty competitors and the non-Catholic architect Alfred Waterhouse was employed to keep an eye on the proceedings. But he was not to select the winner: that was reserved for the Fathers. They chose an unknown, Herbert Gribble (1847–94), a 29-year-old Devonian. He had been a pupil of Joseph Hansom and had worked with him at the Holy Name, Manchester, and at Arundel Cathedral. Through Hansom, Gribble had come into contact with the Duke of Norfolk who was an old Oratorian and whom the Fathers were hoping would contribute to the church. Even before the competition, Gribble had published an impression of what he thought the church might look like. He wanted, he said, 'those who had no opportunity of going to Italy to see an Italian church…to come here to see the model of one'.

The church was opened in 1884. It is Roman Baroque, its ashlar façade rising cliff-like in Portland stone above the Brompton Road. The steel-framed dome over the crossing was added later in 1896 by George Sherrin and the lantern by Edwin Rickards, but Gribble constructed the inner dome. This he did by laying a continuous ring of concrete in a spiral. Suffering sleepless nights over his own daring, he used concrete for the vaulting, the saucer domes and the haunches of the nave bays. In this he was inspired, he said, by the temple of Minerva Medica in Rome.

The Fathers wanted a church as grand and spacious as St Philip Neri, their founder, had demanded for the Chiesa Nuova in Rome, and with Gribble's help they achieved it. Here in Kensington, it might seem, are the very stones and marbles and spirit of Counter-Reformation Rome. The extraordinarily opulent interior is all that Gribble and the Fathers can have wished for. The epic nave is very broad (51 feet – the third widest in England after only Westminster Cathedral and York Minster) with coupled pilasters, coupled columns and much Devonshire marble. The theatrically baroque statues of the Apostles (*c.* 1680–5) leaning forward from niches in the walls between the chapels were carved in Carrara marble by Giuseppe Mazzuoli (1664–1725). They had been thrown out of the Duomo in Siena, during a period when the Baroque was out of fashion in Italy, and were happily acquired by the Fathers.

The Fathers had wanted good, deep chapels around the church, not mere altars. Gribble designed some of them but others played a part. The altar of the Lady Chapel came from Santo Domenico in Brescia and was constructed by Francesco Domenico and Antonio Corbarelli in 1693.

Much of the impression the church gives now is the result of decoration carried out by Commendatore C T G Formilli in 1927–32. He was an Italian living in Kensington and was, if anything, even more Roman in his Catholicism than Gribble and the Fathers. He wanted to make the interior 'still more in keeping with the traditions of the Catholic Church'. Pope Pius XI kept an eye on all this and approved of his plans. Formilli designed the stucco Stations of the Cross, the stencils in the dome, the figures in the spandrels representing the Virtues, the explosive groups of cherubs over each arch and the colossal mahogany pulpit. In the vaults above are his panels with angels who hold the instruments of the Passion.

The sanctuary is deep, with a High Altar in marble and gilt. The seven-branched candleholders were designed by William Burges and were given by the Marquess of Bute in 1878.

The whole foreign-looking sumptuousness of the Oratory had its critics, but the Fathers made no apologies. One wrote at the time of Formilli, 'we could have had British labour and a thoroughly British scheme of decoration. But we did none of these things, and I for one do not regret it.' So it remains, un-reordered, with no forward altar, a monument to the ultramontane tendency in Victorian Catholic England – especially perhaps to the converts' enthusiasm for Rome.

On the sanctuary wall of the Oratory is this large, 1925 painting of St Philip Neri blessing students of the English College in Rome, who were to leave for eventual martyrdom.

St Wilfrid, Chapel Street, Preston, Lancashire (1878–80)

St Wilfrid's was transformed from being a stark, Nonconformist-looking barn built in 1793, to a marvel of self-assured opulence in 1878. The architects of the change were Father Ignatius Scoles (1834–96) and S J Nicholl (1826–95). The church they designed for their Jesuit clients has one of the great Classical church interiors of Britain.

Catholic Preston had a heroic history of recusancy and martyrdom. Years after the Reformation it was reported that 'Popish priests meet on Market-Days' and the 'best Estates in this County are in the hands of Papists. Their priests swarm in', wrote the Anglican vicar in 1713. Long before the relaxation of the Penal Laws there was already a large local Catholic congregation. The church of 1793 was the largest Catholic church of its time in Britain. It was opened confidently on June 4th, George III's birthday, to the strains of Handel's *Messiah*. By the 1870s it was no longer large enough and, furthermore, its appearance was thought to be insufficiently distinguished for its central role in the life of the town. In 1877 Father Jackson told a public meeting that they were going to have a substantial new church, that it would be beautiful in the Italian style, and emphatically Jesuit.

The town was going through a bad period and there was so much unemployment that street collections were tactfully discontinued. The money was found, however, and the church was opened in 1880. The architect, Father Scoles, was the deacon at High Mass, which ended with forty days' indulgence for all present.

At first the *Preston Herald* did not like the exterior ('not much to look at'), but S J Nicholl recast it in terracotta and brick. It is now in what was described as the North Italian Renaissance style but still has, at a glance, something of the look of a counting-house about it. However, there are Christian symbols in abundance all over it: the west front has a spirited tympanum over the entrance with a strongly carved relief of Christ in Majesty surrounded by saints, St Wilfrid prominent among them. High above the doors there is an elaborate round window with engraved symbols around it of the four Evangelists.

Above: Christ in Glory amidst the saints in the tympanum of St Wilfrid's.

Work on the inside had been proceeding too. The result was a basilica to rival the Oratory in Birmingham. The interior evokes Classical Italy. It shines with different coloured, polished marbles, mosaics and alabaster, in a space defined by massive Corinthian columns of Shap granite and a tunnel vault. Father Scoles designed the High Altar: more rich marble and mosaic, lit from above. In the apsidal sanctuary there are lustrous chapels. The four white pilasters there are of Vein Carrara. A frieze round the apse had inscribed on it the appropriate text: 'AT THE NAME OF JESUS LET EVERY KNEE BOW'. This was not retained in the redecoration of the 1960s. The firm of Pugin and Pugin designed the Lady Altar, which was carved by R L Boulton of Cheltenham. St Wilfrid's never moved the position of the High Altar during the liturgical changes in the 1960s.

The centre of Catholic life in this very Catholic town: the terracotta and brick exterior.

Right: St John Fisher's portrait in gold mosaic: a detail of the opulent interior.

6 'Twilight Saints and Dim Emblazonings': The Late Goths

'The Relief and Solace of the Holy Souls in Purgatory' at Our Lady and the English Martyrs, Cambridge.

Opposite: A sombre masterpiece of late Victorian architecture: the colossal nave of Norwich Cathedral.

The Gothic Revival had a long sunset. As it changed and developed in the late 19th century, it was taken to new levels of splendour in the hands of Anglican architects like Pearson, Bodley, Street and Butterfield. They were more adept as the inheritors of the tradition than their Catholic counterparts and, on the whole, they had bigger budgets. But some generous Catholic patrons like the 15th Duke of Norfolk and Mrs Lyne-Stephens were very wealthy indeed. They wanted Gothic and found Catholic architects who would give it to them. What they commissioned at Norwich and Cambridge were massive achievements, but by the time they were finished they had begun to look like extraordinary but isolated anachronisms.

Things were stirring and the old architectural certainties expressed in stone would be challenged, gently at first, with the new century and then swept away. The old conflicts about style would seem increasingly irrelevant. Strangely perhaps, the last great Gothic structure to be completed in England would be the mighty Anglican cathedral in Liverpool, with a Catholic architect – Sir Giles Gilbert Scott. He had built in Romanesque Gothic as late as the 1920s and completed the Gothic of Downside Abbey church as late as 1938. But it took an architect of his stature to bring off such triumphs. For most, the Gothic game was up. John Francis Bentley's Holy Rood at Watford is an undisputed masterpiece of Gothic but in his hands it feels different and new. Bentley was prepared to move into the Byzantine style when he accepted the most important Catholic commission of the century – the cathedral at Westminster of the Most Precious Blood.

The red-brick church and presbytery stand four-square to Shefford's high street.

Mrs Yolande Lyne-Stephens, former star of the ballet in Paris, depicted in a window holding the church she gave to Shefford.

St Francis of Assisi, High Street, Shefford, Bedfordshire (1884)

Shefford was a centre of Catholic worship throughout the centuries of oppression. In 1791, after the second Catholic Relief Act permitted public worship and the building of licensed Catholic chapels, a small chapel was built behind the house of a local Catholic family. Barely a century later the foundation-stone of the present church was laid on the place where the house had stood.

The red brick, late Gothic style of the front of St Francis of Assisi stands four-square to the high street, flanked by the presbytery and the building that was its Home for Poor Catholic Boys. The church was designed by the London architect S J Nicholl (1826–95) and it was largely paid for by Mrs Lyne-Stephens, the former dancer, who also paid for the great Catholic church in Cambridge.

The interior is intimate rather than grand. The walls are panelled with cedar wood, which is punctuated by carved and painted Stations of the Cross. The pews are the original ones of 1884. Under a canopy there is a statue of St Francis. The roof of the nave is muted in colour but the sanctuary roof blazes with gilded angels and bosses set against a vivid blue background.

There is no screen and the view of the extraordinary reredos is unimpeded. It is very tall. There is no east window so the reredos rises up to the ceiling in a masterful display of Gothic stone, alabaster and marble – almost filling the space between the sanctuary walls. The wall against which it stands is painted deep red, in vivid contrast to the white stone of the carved saints and their niches.

There is good stained glass. Mrs Lyne-Stephens gave money for some of it and one of the windows on the west side shows her holding a model of the church. On the north window, the Agony in the Garden of Gethsemane is a memorial to 24 old-boys of the Home who died in the First World War. It is attributed to Hardman & Co.

Beyond a narrow cloister beside the Lady Chapel is all that remains of the old chapel. What was once St George's is now a dark, wood panelled sacristy with an equally dark, illuminated memorial to the donors of the original church. This room became the schoolroom of the Home which was closed in 1975.

St David's Cathedral, Charles Street, Cardiff (1884–7 and 1959)

Cardiff had as grim a Catholic history as anywhere in Britain. Fifty recusants died in the dungeons of the castle or the city gaols. St Philip Evans and St John Lloyd, the Cardiff Martyrs, were hanged, drawn and quartered in 1679. Even in the 19th century Catholics on their way to Mass might expect to be stoned by their neighbours. Nonetheless, the Catholic population grew. What had seemed quite a large church when it was built in the 1840s (designed by J J Scoles) was soon too small. Funds to build a new one were raised from the impoverished congregation as well as from local grandees. The architects were Peter Paul Pugin and Cuthbert Pugin, and St David's opened, with great ceremonial in 1887. In 1920 it became the cathedral of the new diocese of Cardiff.

St David's was designed in the Early English Gothic style of the late 13th century, in dark Penant sandstone with a four-stage tower and a large west window. More remarkable was the 148-foot-long and 70-foot-wide nave, which has no aisles and hence no supporting columns. Its unified space was the antithesis of the church with narrow sanctuary and medieval-style aisles that A W N Pugin had advocated. Photographs suggest the original High Altar (by Messrs Boulton of Cheltenham) was well worth looking at. It was elaborate in marble and gold, its reredos rising up in three crocketed peaks with mysterious dark niches and attendant angels. Around the sanctuary arch the walls were stencilled and there was an imposing pulpit and tester.

The cathedral was bombed and all but destroyed during a German air raid in March

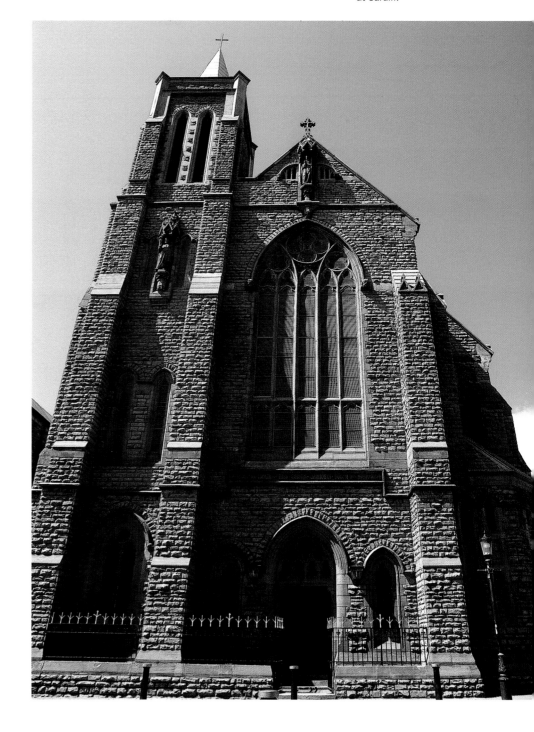

Dark stone frames a large west window and supports the tower at Cardiff.

1941. Post-war reconstruction in the shell of the old church was carried out by Messrs F R Bates and Son. Although rebuilding such a broad roof with no supporting columns was still a technical challenge, it was decided to stick to the original Pugin and Pugin plan of unrestricted views, which had now become even more liturgically fashionable. Furthermore, since the Pugins' day, St David's had become a cathedral and lacked a sanctuary spacious enough and dignified enough for pontifical ceremonies. The new sanctuary is no longer an area designed to evoke the Middle Ages, but is a functional space characterised by its clarity and light. It has a marble floor and a large, no-frills, pointed reredos with diagonal banding in vivid contrast to the pale simplicity of the walls. Elsewhere there are contemporary Stations of the Cross by Adam Kossowski, a massive balcony across the west wall under the great west window and some stained glass of *c.* 1900 that survived the Blitz.

Other reminders of the old church are side chapels with original altars and the baptistery which was retained. There are statues of Cardiff Martyrs St Philip Evans and St John Lloyd.

The Duke of Norfolk's thank-offering for his "most happy marriage": the epic nave at Norwich.

Cathedral of St John the Baptist, St Giles's Gate, Norwich (1884–1910)

In 1877 Canon Duckett wrote to Henry, 15th Duke of Norfolk, of 'our present great need of a new church. Oh, that God would inspire your grace to build one for us!' The Duke was an enthusiastic builder and the church he had built in Arundel to mark his 21st birthday would become a cathedral. Now he wanted to celebrate his recent marriage to Lady Flora Hastings: 'Shortly after my most happy marriage I wished to build a church as a thank-offering to God' he wrote. He agreed to pay for a great new church in the county from whence he derived his title. In 1976 this church too would become a cathedral.

Despite local opposition to the project, a site was found. The old gaol, which stood on a commanding height west of the city was purchased. From here Canon Duckett's new church could look symbolically down on Norwich's medieval cathedral. He wrote 'the impression made on the non-Catholic mind of Norwich & the neighbourhood would be much greater by a fine church built on a most magnificent & elevated site than by one built in a hollow'. George Gilbert Scott junior (1839–97), eldest son of the eminent Anglican architect Sir George Gilbert Scott, and thus a member of one of Victorian England's most influential architectural dynasties, was commissioned. George junior had been received into the Catholic church by Cardinal Newman the year before the commission in 1881, and he wrote to the Cardinal enthusing about the project, the site and the Duke's desire that the church should be built in the Early English style. However, neither he nor the Duke's young wife lived to see the church completed. Lady Flora died three years after work began and George Gilbert Scott junior succumbed to drink and insanity. He resigned from the job in 1894 and fled to France. He was confined in an asylum for a time before he died, aged

The crossing at Norwich. John Betjeman called the architect George Gilbert Scott junior "the greatest genius of the Gothic revival in England".

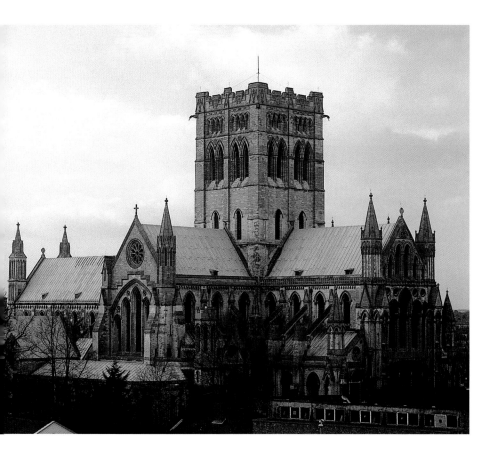

A dominant presence in the city: now a cathedral, St John the Baptist was the grandest parish church in England when it opened.

58, at the St Pancras Hotel in London which his father had designed. His successor at Norwich was his brother, John Oldrid Scott.

The nave was opened in 1894. Shortly afterwards the Duke wrote to say that he was having financial problems and doubted his capacity to go on at the same level of generosity. The city council and the neighbours began to express concern about the size of the project. But work went on, if more slowly, and what emerged from the collaborations (the Duke was no passive observer of the progress of his projects) was probably the grandest Catholic parish church in England. It was consecrated in 1910.

St John the Baptist has always seemed cathedral-like, 275 feet long and over 80 feet high, and though now somewhat cut off from the town centre by a ring road, it is still a huge and dominating presence: pinnacled, even forbidding. The interior is an immense and sombre space, described as 'unflinchingly Early English' by Bryan Little and 'Melancholy' by Gavin Stamp. The nave (by G G Scott) stretches away for 153 feet, its ten-bay arcade supported by immense cylindrical columns with capitals (locally carved) surmounted by the triforium and clerestory. The dominant colour is deep grey, with carvings between the arches of such worthies as Cardinals Newman and Manning. It is enlivened toward the east by the large and painted rood that hangs from the sanctuary arch. The original High Altar designed by Adrian Gilbert Scott was moved from the sanctuary (by G G and J O Scott) in the re-ordering. The Stations of the Cross were carved by Ferdinand Stuflesser's studio in the Alto Adige. He also carved the statue of John the Baptist.

The cathedral windows are magnificent: '…diamonded with panes of quaint device, And twilight saints and dim emblazonings…' as Keats put it . The windows in the Walsingham chapel are by Clayton and Bell. Most of the rest are by Hardman & Co, designed by John Hardman Powell in the nave and Dunstan Powell in the east end. The great north window was destroyed in the Second World War and restored by Hardman & Co. There is a memorial window that commemorates the first Duchess in the south chapel. The chapel to Our Lady of Walsingham, on the east side of the north transept, was given by Gwendolen, the Duke's second Duchess in 1909 and designed by John Oldrid Scott.

This extraordinary expression of Catholic pride and tribute to the Middle Ages was completed at the same time that Giles Gilbert Scott, the son of George junior, was finishing his church not very far away on the Norfolk coast at Sheringham. This was Gothic, but designed in a freer style and in a very different spirit. Pevsner observed that the church in Norwich, for all its impressiveness, was 'an end, not a beginning'. But what an end.

Our Lady and the English Martyrs, Hills Road, Cambridge (1885–90)

This is a very big church, a landmark for miles in a flat county. But it came late to a city that, at the beginning of the 19th century, had few Catholics. Catholics were unable to enter the university and Cambridge was famously Protestant. Although St John Fisher, beheaded by Henry VIII for his opposition to the Royal Supremacy, had been chancellor of the university, the character of the city was better defined by the group of graduates who used to meet at the White Horse Inn in the 1520s to discuss theology. They included William Tyndale, translator of the New Testament into English and Thomas Cranmer, as well as Hugh Latimer and Nicholas Ridley. All became architects of the Protestant Reformation. Some were themselves to become martyrs, with a different loyalty to those this church commemorates.

The heavy, vaulted, complex interior of the opulently decorated and furnished Cambridge church.

By the end of the first half of the 19th century, Cambridge Catholics were sufficiently numerous to make a church necessary. A small one, an early design by A W N Pugin, was built. Even Pugin disliked it. Towards the end of the 19th century the bishops were relaxing their hostility towards young Catholic gentlemen becoming undergraduates and something bigger and better was planned. Providentially, the money was forthcoming for one of the most ambitious churches to be built during the great Catholic revival in England.

Mrs Lyne-Stephens was the widow of a banker and landowner who had become immensely wealthy when he patented glass dolls' eyes that could move. She told Canon Scott, who led the Cambridge mission, that she would pay for a new church. The Newcastle firm of A M Dunn (1833–1917) and E J Hansom (1842–1900), who had been successfully working together at Downside (see page 156) and Stonyhurst, won the design competition in the Decorated style of Gothic. A local firm, Rattee and Kett, were appointed builders. There were bitter manifestations of anti-Catholic feeling that were not appeased when it was realised just how big and dominant the church would be.

Seen across the Downing College lawns or from the main road it looks stunning; huge, with a lantern tower and a spire the height of Ely Cathedral across the fens. There is much stone carving with saints and martyrs jutting from the walls, as well as portraits of Canon Scott and the bearded architects Dunn and Hansom on the south side. There are more saints on the north side and an inscription round the transept seeking our prayers for Mrs Lyne-Stephens. The benefactress is again remembered with her carved head on the right side of the porch. The carved head of the ever generous 15th Duke of Norfolk (who donated the site) is to the left. In the ante-chapel there is a wooden statue of Mary with the Christ Child which is said to date from the 16th century. It was discovered in the grounds of Emmanuel College in the 1860s and given to the church as a gesture of ecumenism.

The huge vaulted interior is tall, complex, dark and long – 155 feet. It is opulently decorated and substantially furnished. Emphasis is given to the English Martyrs, who are commemorated in the great west window by John Hardman Powell and elsewhere in the church. The narrative of their lives, and sometimes their deaths, is poignantly told in the north and south aisle windows. Cranmer, Henry VIII and St John Fisher

Our Lady and the English Martyrs: seen across the lawns of Downing College with Dunn and Hansom's spire and crossing tower.

The sanctuary at Wimbledon: the re-ordered High Altar of one of the most impressive churches in south London.

are shown together in a fateful tableau in the third north window. There is a large, arresting painting by N H J Westlake of Christ in Glory on the wall above the sanctuary arch. The rood shows Christ as High Priest and crowned as King. The stone High Altar contains relics of martyrs, and there is a gloriously carved oak baldacchino (by Boulton of Cheltenham and painted by Westlake) above it. In the niches of the piers of the baldacchino are intense carvings of the martyrs. The sanctuary was re-ordered in 1973 by Gerard Goalen, the architect of the church of Our Lady of Fatima at Harlow (see page 199). By him, too, is the new altar, placed at the centre of the crossing.

In the north transept, there is a wooden figure of the crucified St Andrew, the gift of A W N Pugin. It came from the old church, and was placed here in memory of Canon Scott.

Sacred Heart, Edge Hill, Wimbledon, London SW19 (1886–1901)

This part of Wimbledon was still quite rural when Mrs Edith Arendrup, a wealthy member of the Courtauld family, tried to persuade the Jesuits of Roehampton to take on a substantial church that she would pay for. They were not keen. One priest said that he would 'die of ennui in such a God-forsaken hole'. Mrs Arendrup dangled the potential need for a middle-class boys' school in the area. The Jesuits succumbed and Mrs Arendrup commissioned Frederick Walters (1849–1931), a pious Catholic who lived with his family not far away in Croydon, as architect.

The choice of site on the slopes of Edge Hill by Mrs Arendrup was brilliant. A great tower was planned but, as so often, never built and hardly necessary. Even without it, from such a commanding position it was a lofty symbol of the faith's triumphant return. This did not endear it to all. 'Wimbledon was looked on as a stronghold of Protestantism', wrote one of the Jesuits. Some of the neighbours suggested that working-class south Wimbledon had greater need of their mission.

So the Society of Jesus paid nothing for one of the most extraordinary churches in Greater London. It is very impressive, very long and 60 feet tall, with an unbroken roofline. The west front looks as though it might front an abbey with its twin turrets, a huge traceried window and a great door.

There is a long sweep down the nave, past stone columns surmounted by statues of Jesuit saints, to the sanctuary with the rood (1887) suspended from the arch above. Beyond is the polygonal apse with three stained-glass windows that show the Annunciation, the Crucifixion and the Resurrection and were designed by Hardman & Co of Birmingham. To the left is a precisely carved pulpit (1901) with emblems of St Peter and the four Evangelists designed by Walters himself. A brass plaque to its left commemorates Father Morris, who died while preaching from the pulpit in 1893.

The sanctuary was completely re-ordered in 1990 by architect Austin Winkley (designer of St Margaret's Twickenham, see page 212). It was a controversial re-ordering. The church had known controversy before. An altar for the north aisle was commissioned from a Mr Drysdale rather than Frederick Walters in 1915. When Walters saw it, 'he burst into tears' and the bishop refused to consecrate it. In 1990 the altar rails, by John Francis Bentley, which separated the nave from the sanctuary, were moved to the side. The High Altar was moved to the Blessed Sacrament Chapel and the baldacchino was removed altogether. The new High Altar contains relics of the English Martyrs. The ambulatory behind the sanctuary has three chapels leading off into the apse. The middle chapel once contained the altar that Mrs Arendrup had at home in her private chapel. It was destroyed in 1968. The windows are a memorial to her and her son Axel, who died young and is shown here as an altar boy.

To the right of the nave is a chapel commemorating with statues, plaques and glass the martyrs of England and Wales. A window by N H J Westlake shows Saints Edmund Campion, Thomas More and John Fisher. As well as saints and martyrs, there are windows in memory of parishioners and old boys of Wimbledon School who died in the First World War. One window depicts a boys' rugby match.

The Stations of the Cross are picked out in gold and were designed by Bentley. The church was originally lit by gas – something which apparently impressed the first visitors just as much as the sacred statuary and furnishings.

The Jesuits wanted a tower, but the Sacred Heart's dramatic hillside position meant that it hardly needed one.

St James's: two of nine Old
Testament figures featured on
the reredos of Our Lady's
Chapel, designed by Bentley.

St James, Spanish Place, London W1 (1887–90)

The church occupies an odd site, standing at an angle to the street that runs behind the Wallace Collection. It is partly concealed behind its own presbytery, but for all that its size and ambition are clear. Its architect was Edward Goldie (1856–1921) the son of George Goldie of York and, by happy coincidence, great grandson of Joseph Bonomi who had designed the embassy chapel that this one replaced.

The Spanish embassy had maintained a Catholic chapel that any Catholic might attend throughout penal times. The one Bonomi designed became too small and a competition was held – Catholic architects only – to design its successor. The little-known Goldie practice won against some big names. In such a location, this was a very prestigious commission. Building land in this part of London was hard to get and, then as now, expensive. But the site, opposite the old chapel, was successfully acquired (for £30,000) after much prayer and fasting. King Alfonso XII of Spain gave some of the money. It attracted a distinguished congregation.

The church is built of stone in the early Gothic style. It is big, almost 200 feet long and 67 feet high and will seat 2,000. The arches of the long nave are supported by marble columns that are themselves supported by smaller, dark marble columns. The lofty, vaulted stone roof and the double windows in the apsidal sanctuary look French, and the whole massive ensemble is lightened by innumerable, decorated chapels. The furnishings are ravishing and J F Bentley designed many of them.

The sanctuary walls are lined with marble and gorgeous *opus sectile* designed by Bentley. The outstanding reredos of hammered iron (by Thomas Garner) is decorated with flowers and gilt scallop-shells and is flanked by bronze statues of St James the Apostle and St Anne. The floor is covered with gold mosaic. Two gilt crowns on the sanctuary wall indicate that the places below are reserved, should they wish to come, for the King and Queen of Spain. In the nave is a large marble statue of St James wearing the scallop-shell of a pilgrim and affirming again the association of the church with Spain and the pilgrimage to Santiago de Compostela.

The Lady Chapel contains some of Bentley's best designs. The reredos dominates the whole chapel and is carved and gilded with angels, musical instruments, vines and grapes framing a copy of a painting by Murillo of the Immaculate Conception. The panels in the triptych of the reredos in the Sacred Heart Chapel show scenes of the Life of Christ and are also by Bentley. The altar of Our Lady of Victories, again by Bentley,

The French-looking apse and altar at St James's.

is in carved marble and alabaster. The reredos shows the Virgin and Child amid angels. There is also a much-venerated and much-travelled statue of Our Lady of Fatima.

The War Memorial Chapel has a wrought-iron screen and touching stained-glass windows commemorating the fallen. The reredos (1925) is by J Arnold Crush and the Stations of the Cross are by Geoffrey Webb. They were carved from alabaster and gilded.

There is a vast, carved marble and alabaster pulpit that was a gift from Lady Sykes, wife to Sir Tatton Sykes, a Protestant who at one time considered paying for Westminster Cathedral, and in the baptistery there is a fine, elegant wooden font in its original position.

A statue of St James of Compostela with symbolic scallop-shell and pilgrim hat affirms the church's Spanish connections.

Below: 'A masterpiece', Bentley's carved rood against a gold and green vaulted sanctuary.

Opposite: Bentley's superb designs, fittings, and vibrant colours in the sanctuary; late Gothic style but pointing to a freer architectural future.

Holy Rood, Exchange Road, Watford, Hertfordshire (1889–1900)

Not far from Watford's centre is one of the most beautiful churches in England. Cardinal Vaughan liked it so much that he commissioned the architect, John Francis Bentley (1839–1902) who had just a few churches to his name, to design the most important Post-Reformation Catholic building in Britain, Westminster Cathedral. Cardinal Manning laid the foundation stone for the Holy Rood in 1889. Every element of Bentley's design and furnishing for the Holy Rood is, as architect Goodhart-Rendel put it, 'perfection'. To architectural historian Peter Howell, the church is a 'masterpiece', showing the continuing vitality of the late 19th-century Gothic Revival, reinvigorated by the Arts and Crafts movement.

Bentley was 50 when Stephen Taprell Holland, a member of a building firm to which Bentley had once been apprenticed, asked him to build a new church in Watford. Holland would pay for everything and so the Holy Rood was built with few budgetary constraints in the late Perpendicular style. Bentley preferred to work in earlier Gothic, but all the components here are handled with such freedom and relish in the use of materials and details that the church does not feel in the least bit like an exercise in the archaic. Instead it is entirely of its own time – grand yet intimate.

The site is a difficult one, but Bentley fitted the church and presbytery on to an unremarkable street corner. The walls are of Hertfordshire flint with cleverly handled stripes of stone in the Hertfordshire vernacular tradition.

Bentley's fittings and materials are sumptuous, but not overwhelmingly so, and they combine to enhance the meticulous, miraculous spaces that he created. The nave is wide, and two-tiered arcades separate it from the shallow transepts. There are beautiful roundels of angels with golden haloes and head-dresses surrounded by bewitching decoration on the spandrels. The broad sanctuary is seen beyond a wonderfully carved and coloured rood and rood beam. Both are painted red and gold. The reredos on the altar, a triumph of detailing in reds and golds, extends up to the radiant, freely interpreted Perpendicular east window above which the vault, in softer patterns of green and gold, completes the *mise-en-scène*.

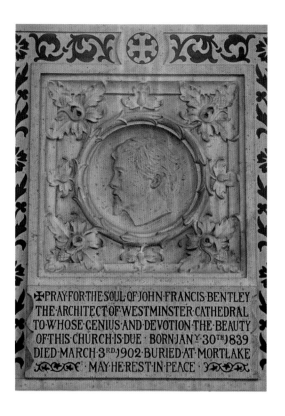

Above: Henry McCarthy's monument to the architect.

Right: the reredos above the High Altar at Holy Rood; a triumph of detailing.

There is a splendid vaulted baptistery under the tower with intriguing details and a shallow font. There are vistas through the arcades into the nave and transepts that show how great a master Bentley was at creating irresistible combinations of volume, light and space: what Sir John Soane called 'the poetry of architecture'. The west window is by Messrs Burlison and Grylls (1904) and the Stations of the Cross are by N H J Westlake. Other than that, Bentley's hand was on everything: he designed the rest of the glass, the pulpit, altar rails, side altars and shrines. He designed even the electric lights that hang from the ceiling; the light bulbs are exposed but the flat, ornate and complex pendants make electric lights seem the most natural thing in the world to find in a Gothic church.

One of the windows shows two elevations of the church which is framed by a wreath with two angels. The inscription invites our prayers for Mr Holland. There are memorials to Cardinals Vaughan and Manning (featuring their hats) and one to the architect himself. Bentley was very ill when the church was opened and he died of cancer not long after. Westminster Cathedral never got round to commemorating him, but over the south-west door at Watford he is remembered in a fine, carved monument by Henry McCarthy.

Holy Ghost, South View, Basingstoke, Hampshire (1902)

The church of the Holy Ghost stands on the corner of a quiet, suburban street, a little apart from, and looking down on, the ring roads and multi-storey car parks of modern Basingstoke. It was designed and paid for by the man who was, for the last years of his life, its priest: Father (later Canon) Alexander Joseph Cory Scoles SJ, third son of the more famous architect J J Scoles. Like his brother Ignatius, Father Scoles was a qualified architect. This church was his last and is, for many, the best of his churches.

Father Scoles went for the Early English Gothic style, built in flint with stone dressings. On the roof he put a small, octagonal bell tower with a slate roof. Though the materials may make the church look faintly rustic, this moderately sized church is urbane and sophisticated. No less an artist than N H J Westlake was responsible for the decoration and he produced an effect of great power, with paintings of saints and angels on gold backgrounds that fill the panels of the vaulted sanctuary roof. Below the nine east windows, more gorgeously painted panels of biblical scenes with gold backgrounds arch round the carved marble of the apse. The altar is polished stone and above it is an amazing tabernacle in white, in strong contrast to all the gold, which stretches up to the curving splendour of the roof.

To the left of the sanctuary is a Lady Chapel, with similar detailing and a fine altar and reredos. In the south aisle, one of the windows has a stained-glass panel dating from the 16th century. It came from the chapel of the Vyne, Basingstoke. Canon Scoles is buried outside the church.

The apse at Basingstoke: saints and angels on a gold background, biblical scenes and an astonishing white tabernacle.

7 Monks, Schools and Seminaries: The Return of the Monks

Detail from an altar at Downside Abbey.

Opposite: the profile of a monk carved for Mount St Bernard, Leicestershire.

After Henry VIII's dissolution of the monasteries, the majority of their buildings were abandoned and their communities dispersed. Many monks retired with a pension into secular life, while a small number suffered death for their resistance to the monarch. Some chose exile in France or Belgium and set up monastic communities with churches and schools where they trained priests who would later return to Britain to minister to the Catholic faithful. Apart from a period of respite during Queen Mary's reign (1533–58), hundreds of priests came to England, striving to avoid detection at the channel ports and the attentions of informers once they had arrived. They might pose as domestic servants or tutors in the great Catholic houses where they secretly celebrated Mass for the families who sheltered them.

As religious intolerance in England waned, in the late 18th century the French Revolution precipitated a furious wave of anti-clerical and anti-monastic violence in that country. Whole monastic orders moved back to the now relatively hospitable shores of England. Thomas Weld of Lulworth offered sanctuary in Dorset to the French Cistercian monks of La Trappe in 1778. Many of the monks were formerly exiled Englishmen and they lived very simply in a set of farm buildings on the estate. Mr Weld's generosity did not go unnoticed by his Protestant neighbours. He was roundly attacked. One critic thought the establishment was 'a gloomy abode of ignorance and nastiness'.

Over the following years secular priests and seminarians from the English College at Douai returned to England. In 1798 the college came to Old Hall Green in Hertfordshire where the faithful established St Edmund's College. 'The oldest Catholic school in England' is still open. Not long after St Edmund's was founded the northern bishops took their seminarians away to the north, eventually to settle in County Durham. English Benedictine monks from Douai went to Downside, Somerset and Ampleforth where, in the 1850s, the Hansom brothers would build a chapel for them. Irish monks were invited to Mount St Bernard in Leicestershire. German monks came to Devonshire. When there was a further wave of anticlericalism in France in the late 19th century, the ultra austere Carthusians bought 200 acres of Sussex and began to build. Similar pressures drove Benedictine monks from Solesmes to Quarr Abbey on the Isle of Wight in 1901. Monasticism once more had a substantial presence in the English countryside. Women too would play a role of growing importance as the 19th century progressed – female religious in scores of communities would teach and nurse in the expanding cities.

All these communities started off in cramped accommodation. Most went on to build large complexes of religious buildings of symbolic confidence and grandeur – as if to replace the glories that Henry VIII had destroyed. They are now a respected element in the religious life of the country to which they returned to rebuild the monastic life and to teach.

A Catholic education had been illegal for two centuries. Now, educating the Catholic young as Catholics was of prime importance to the priests and parishes of Britain. Schools were often built first, before the new churches. Education offered some sort of chance in life to the illiterate children of the teeming city slums, and it should be a Catholic education. Teaching was no less important to the returning monastic orders, with their special mission to provide a strong Catholic education for the young. In their case there was a tradition, nurtured in exile, of teaching the sons of the great Catholic families. The Jesuits, mindful of the importance that St Ignatius of Loyola had attached to teaching the young during their first seven years, had opened a school in St Omer, France, in 1593 and continued to teach as well as maintain their mission during the penal years. In the late 18th century they moved the school to Stonyhurst in the hills of Lancashire. The Benedictines took their school, after a difficult time with the French revolutionary militia, to Shropshire and then to Downside in Somerset 'on account of solitude and delightful walks'. In these schools, the sons of the Catholic gentry would receive an education modelled on the traditional English public school, with doctrinal correctness thrown in. The schools and seminaries had chapels – in some cases, magnificent chapels – designed by the very best architects and at great expense.

Giles Gilbert Scott's nave for the Benedictines at Downside.

St Peter, Stonyhurst College, Stonyhurst,
Blackburn, Lancashire (1832–5)

Few churches have a grander approach than St Peter's.
A long, straight drive passes through a broad park, past
innumerable playing fields, towards a heavy mass of school
buildings. To their right is the church. Its Perpendicular
exterior, with pinnacles and crockets outlined against trees
and sky, is reminiscent of King's College, Cambridge. It was
the first important work of the architect J J Scoles
(1798–1863) and the beginning of his long and successful
association with the Jesuit order.

When the Jesuits were openly re-establishing their
mission after the years of exile, education was high on their
list of priorities. Stonyhurst, formerly a private house,
became a Jesuit college in 1794. It succeeded their college at
St Omer and became perhaps the most prestigious of all the
Roman Catholic boarding schools – the school of first
choice for many wealthy Catholic families; a doctrinally
sound Eton in the Lancashire hills.

J J Scoles was a great Catholic architect. He could do
Classical (Holywell and, more grandly, Prior Park at Bath)
but mostly he worked in Gothic. St Peter's won the praise of
the still-Protestant A W N Pugin who was, it is thought,
referring to this church when he wrote: 'A very good chapel
is now building in the north and when complete I shall
probably recant'. He did convert to Rome shortly afterwards.

There are gardens behind the west front, and at the east
end a cloister connects the chapel to the school. Inside it is lofty in the Tudor style and grand for what is both
a parish church and a school chapel. The elongated columns and the arches are stencilled with patterns painted
in green and gold and lead up towards the clerestory. The east window fills most of the wall in the
Perpendicular style and there are effigies of saints on either side. The High Altar, much later than the church
(1893), was designed by Edmund Kirby. It is strongly crafted from different coloured marble, alabaster and
mosaics. The donors specified that only the very best materials should be used. The great brass candlesticks
were designed by Scoles. To the left and right of the sanctuary, in the chapels dedicated to St Ignatius of
Loyola and St Francis Xavier, there are very large paintings, vividly portraying dramatic moments in the
lives of the two Jesuit saints. They are said to have originally been frescoes by Fischer and Worms of Munich.
They were painted over in oils when the church was redecorated in 1954. The stained glass is excellent.

In the school itself there is an exquisite Boys' Chapel (by Dunn and Hansom) which is open to the
public only on request. A cabinet of important liturgical silver from Stonyhurst can be seen at Liverpool's
Walker Art Gallery.

The opulence of the school
chapel at Stonyhurst College.

Mount St Bernard Abbey, Coalville, Leicestershire (1843–4 and 1935–9)

'We shall be able to astonish': Pugin's choir and Eric Gill's choir-stalls for the monks at Mount St Bernard.

'Here then we are. I with my little company…on this land in the Charnwood Forest, which I have named Mount St Bernard', wrote Father Odilo Woolfrey in 1835. He was the leader of a small group of Cistercian monks who had been invited by a local squire to found a monastery. The squire was Ambrose Lisle (later de Lisle) March Phillipps, a zealous convert who wanted to restore the contemplative monastic life to England and atone for the part his ancestors had played during the Reformation in its destruction. (The family home, Garendon, had been on the site of a Cistercian house.) He provided the monks with 225 acres of wild countryside. Today there are farm buildings, fields with grazing animals, gardens where guests can wander contemplatively and, high up on a rock overlooking it all, there is a dramatic stone Calvary: Mount St Bernard looks the very image of the monastic ideal.

The first monastery the monks built soon proved too small but John, 16th Earl of Shrewsbury, was so impressed by the progress the monks had made that he promised to help them with a new one on a site nearby. Not surprisingly, with Shrewsbury and Phillipps paying the bills, the choice of architect was not in question. Furthermore, A W N Pugin offered his services for free: 'It is one of the cheapest buildings ever built' he wrote, 'We shall be able to astonish everyone with what we can build'.

When it opened in 1844 it was the first working monastery in England for centuries and the curious and the pious poured in to take a look. They still do. The monastery was visited by Cardinal Wiseman, Cardinal Newman and Bishop Ullathorne as well as such celebrities as William Wordsworth, Florence Nightingale and Mr William Gladstone on an early ecumenical mission in 1873. The monks coped with the visitors but also offered help to thousands of the needy poor.

'The whole of the buildings,' Pugin wrote, 'are erected in the greatest severity of the lancet style… Solemnity and simplicity are the characteristics of the monastery and every portion of the architecture and the fittings corresponds to the austerity of the Order.'

Pugin's church successfully achieved that simplicity, although only the seven-bay nave and aisle designed by him were built before money ran out. The same spirit was evident when the church was radically and successfully extended in 1935 by architect F J Bradford. Pugin's church became the monks' choir and a new nave for the laity was created opposite it, copying Pugin's design. The much enlarged interior is a clear, light, unfussy space which conveys all the solemnity that Pugin and the monks wanted. Bradford extended Pugin's austere thinking throughout the new

The post-war tower and Pugin's church of Mount St Bernard standing in the Leicestershire countryside.

additions. Straight, smooth, white columns rise, uninterrupted by capitals, to the pointed roof. The walls are bare of ornament. The whole church is lit by lancet windows that are mostly clear glass. The perspective from the west end takes the eye past the altar on a raised sanctuary (placed centrally beneath the crossing in the 1930s – early for such a liturgical arrangement) to the three lancet windows of what was Pugin's church. It is there, in choir-stalls of 1938 designed by Eric Gill, that the monks sing the divine office – moving to the altar to concelebrate the Mass with the laity who sit in the nave. Dramatically suspended above the altar is the tabernacle, delicately wrought in stainless steel, with the sanctuary lamp above it.

Almost all the glass in the windows is clear except for a splash of bright colour from a very high rose window in the transept designed by Joseph Nuttgens. The stone side altars are very simple but have some fine relief carving. Above them there are thought-provoking reliefs, also carved in stone, by Father O'Malley. They are very powerful; particularly those of the Crucifixion and the Risen Christ.

A strong, square, barely adorned tower was added after the Second World War (architect Albert Herbert from Leicester). It holds its own in the wild landscape of Charnwood Forest.

Chapel of St Cuthbert's College, Ushaw, County Durham (1844–8 and 1882–4)

The origins of the college date back to 1568. William Allen, an Oxford exile from Queen Elizabeth's Settlement of Religion, opened a foundation in Flanders which quickly became an important missionary college. It was

The spectacularly decorated collegiate chapel of Ushaw. Pugin's and Hardman's windows from the old chapel were reinstalled in the later one.

part of the new Catholic university of Douai. As time went by a school was opened and English Catholic aristocrats and gentry began to send their sons there. The French Revolution drove the institution back to England. After many tribulations the present site was bought and work began in 1804 on an ambitious complex of college buildings in the Gothic style for what was to be the seminary for the whole of the north of England. The chapel of 1844–8 was designed by A W N Pugin. By 1882 it was too small and architects A Dunn and E Hansom of nearby Newcastle were called in to design a new one twice the size.

The college went on growing until the 1960s, when a national decline in the number of young men seeking ordination obliged St Cuthbert's to adapt to new circumstances and become a new sort of institution – still a seminary but also a conference centre, a hall of residence for Durham University and an institute providing education not just for seminarians but also for clergy and religious and lay people.

Structurally, much remains as it was, an impressive range of buildings romantically isolated on the outskirts of Durham. Pugin's chapel was dismantled rather than destroyed and elements were incorporated into the 1884 rebuilding which was undertaken by its designers in a Puginesque frame of mind.

The chapel, like one in a very superior Oxbridge college, has a very large and solemn antechapel. The doors are from Pugin's original chapel as is the choir screen, though it has been enlarged. It was decorated by J F Bentley in 1894, who was extending the decoration he had done for St Bede's Chapel (to the north) where he had designed the altar. Nearby is the statue of Mary carved from a single piece of marble by Karl Hoffman in Rome. The windows of the antechapel (A W N Pugin and his old collaborator John Hardman) are from the original building and celebrate the Saints in Glory. Pugin's original Lady Chapel was reconstructed and the furnishings are mostly by him – decorated by Bentley. Impossible to miss is the very tall paschal candlestick (by Pugin and Hardman) inscribed with lions, angels and featuring the women going to the sepulchre. It was shown, to great acclaim, at the 1851 Great Exhibition.

At Ushaw, however, the chapel itself is its crowning glory. The interior is a real *coup de théâtre,* a space that makes one marvel at the magnificence that was thought appropriate for a theological college at the time. Under a vast and lofty vault, the choir-stalls face each other in formal, collegiate fashion. They have misericords and birds, beasts and foliage carved on them in abundance (mostly designed by Pugin). The Magnificat is inscribed in gold lettering on the wooden walls above the choir. The lectern, also shown at the 1851 Exhibition, is from a Pugin design.

Pugin and Hardman's splendid windows in the sanctuary were taken from the old chapel and reinstalled in an effective double row. St Cuthbert's life is celebrated in the central east window. The tabernacle is gilt and studded with crystals. The High Altar is ornate marble and the reredos (by Peter Paul Pugin, 1891) rises up with spiky energy to cut into the bottom view of the east window and wraps itself around the wall of the apse, framing gilded and painted wooden panels.

Built through the zeal of a Catholic convert, turned down by the Jesuits and adopted by the Benedictines: Belmont Abbey across the meadows.

Belmont Abbey of St Michael the Archangel, Belmont, Hereford (1854–6, 1860 and 1882)

Until 1916, the abbey was the monastic pro-cathedral run by the Benedictines for the diocese of Newport and Menevia. It still has the feel of a small cathedral standing in pleasant countryside south of the county town. The land was owned by Francis Richard Wegg-Prosser MP, a rich, well-connected (a friend of John Henry Newman) and zealous convert to Catholicism. As an Anglican he had been enthusiastically Tractarian and it is said that his conversion to Rome was precipitated by the appointment of a low-church bishop to the Anglican see of Hereford.

Wegg-Prosser built a Catholic school, chapel and an almshouse as a thank-offering for his conversion. The young Edward Pugin designed them and the church on which work began in 1854. It was built with no particular idea as to who would run it, but the Benedictines seized the chance to acquire a much-needed monastery for their monks and novices. More buildings were added and the church was extended, more than once, eastwards to make a choir and sanctuary. The High Altar was shifted three times. A northern transept was added in 1880. The firm of Pugin and Pugin finished the tower in 1882 and added a battlemented parapet. Wegg-Prosser asked Newman to preach at the consecration but he declined, pleading that the journey by train from Birmingham would be too arduous.

The resulting complex of buildings, with the abbey church dominant, is an eloquent testimony to Benedictine beliefs and style that still stir the Catholic faithful who come here from all over the country – especially for a celebrated processional day. They enter a nave where a dim, devotional light is cast by traceried windows, dormers and clerestory. The nave is the earliest part of the church and it seems inspired by the work of A W N Pugin, following the style of his Ramsgate church (see page 78). The capitals are carved with great complexity and sophistication. Above them are carvings of human and animal heads and angels. The tower is

Angelic orchestra: Belmont's reredos of 1866, the lower part of which was reordered in 1978.

supported by four columns with narrowly pointed arches that frame the view of the sanctuary and the much-moved east window. This is by Hardman & Co and was designed by J H Powell in 1860. It features the abbey's patron St Michael, slaying the dragon and attended by choirs of angels. Below is an extraordinarily dense and lively reredos by R L Boulton (1866) with carved white angels in attitudes of swooning adoration; their wings and musical instruments are painted gold, as is the crown they hold out reverently above the tabernacle. The original altar, more or less contemporary with the reredos, was destroyed in the 1970s re-ordering.

The chapel of St Joseph similarly has a vividly coloured reredos showing a number of saints. Behind the wall are the graves of the Wegg-Prosser family.

There is a chapel dedicated to St Benedict. The reredos shows scenes from the life of the saint – his hermit cave in Subiaco and his death at Monte Cassino – and various English saints. On the wall, behind the fine enamel doors of a reliquary, is a fragment of the True Cross. The west window (Hardman and Powell again) is a stirring tribute to saints with a Hereford connection. St Thomas Cantelupe (1218–82), who was Bishop of Hereford, stands in the middle. (His shrine is preserved at nearby Hereford Cathedral.) To his right, King Ethelbert (murdered near Hereford in 794) holds a model of Belmont.

Downside Abbey Church of St Gregory the Great, Stratton-on-the-Fosse, near Bath, Somerset (1872–1938)

Like Ushaw, Downside has roots that date back to well before the Reformation and to exile in France. An English Benedictine abbey was founded at Douai in 1607. It became a missionary centre and a school for Catholic English boys. The French Revolution drove the Douai Benedictines back to a now more tolerant England and the community eventually settled in Somerset. They built a monastery with a school and a chapel, all of which still survive. A W N Pugin drew up plans which, though they came to nothing, are of considerable interest to the Pugin *cognoscenti*. In 1872 the Newcastle firm of Archibald Dunn and Edward

St Gregory the Great: a detail from the frontal on the altar dedicated to St Oliver Plunkett.

Hansom (an old boy of Downside) drew up plans for new buildings on a scale to match the ambitious vision of the prior. They included a great new Gothic church. Work began on the church in 1878 and, with different architects taking over at different periods, building went on till the tower was completed in 1938. The Benedictine church of St Gregory the Great is still unfinished. Its rough-cast west end is, officially at any rate, temporary. Financial constraints have always slowed progress. Consequently, the various sections of the church, designed by different hands over many years, have led to a building that does have some of the layered unpredictability and complexity of a genuinely medieval church.

Hansom resigned in 1895 and the choir (1902–5) was built by Thomas Garner. The sacristy (1915) was the work of F A Walters. The nave (1922–5) was designed by Sir Giles Gilbert Scott. His initial plans were turned down but he completed the interior which is one of the great, largely unsung triumphs of 20th-century British architecture. It is of cathedral-like proportions, different from, but a perfectly mannered compliment to, the work of his predecessors, with light stone columns, a triforium and clerestory leading up to a tall arched vault. Scott eventually completed the 165-foot tower, which he based on the traditional church towers of Somerset, in 1938.

Downside Abbey Church is a collective achievement and its decoration and furnishings are no less splendid than the architecture. The transept by Dunn and Hansom was the first part to be completed. Huge screens blocked off work on the nave and choir as, for a time, it served as the church. Its large and elaborate altar owes its size to its previous status as High Altar. Above it are windows showing events in the life of Benedictine saints. To the right is a strikingly designed shrine to St Oliver Plunkett. A monumental carved and gilded oak casket standing on four stone columns contains the relics of the saint. There are more relics in the chapel of St Lawrence, which has an altar designed by F A Walters. The chapel of St Sebastian has a reredos designed by the High-Church Anglican Sir Ninian Comper. It is extraordinarily and delicately carved and coloured. The martyred saint is carved from alabaster and leans languidly out from a pinnacled niche in the centre.

Opposite: 'Pugin's dream come true': the south aisle of Downside, the largest Neo-Gothic church built in Britain since the Reformation.

In the north aisle there is the tomb of Bishop Baines, a convinced if unavailing champion of Classical architecture, rather poignantly placed here amidst the Gothic splendour. Thomas Garner, a convert, was the architect of this part of the church and he is buried under a panel of the Crucifixion – designed by his old colleague and partner, another Anglican, G F Bodley. The powerful carving in relief of the Crucifixion in the chapel of St Sylvia, mother of St Gregory, is by Dom Hubert van Zeller. On the north wall is a painting of

St John the Baptist by a rare 15th-century Italian master, Lazzaro Bastiani – a pupil of Mantegna. Comper designed the bewitching reredos in the Lady Chapel. It is in gilt alabaster and shows the Christ Child with Mary and St Ann. It is flanked by panels showing His childhood and Resurrection and the composition is framed by a Tree of Jesse with writhing, intertwined foliage. There are four arks above the screen: one contains the skull of St Thomas Cantelupe of Hereford and the others have relics of other English saints. Comper also designed the tester – gold and red – which hangs climactically above the altar and the vividly coloured (and mildly controversial – Scott thought they spoiled the view from the nave) stained-glass windows here and in the east end of the choir. Much more austere is a memorial to Edmund Bishop, a liturgical scholar, in lettering carved by Eric Gill. The choir-stalls were modelled on those at Chester Cathedral and carved by Ferdinand Stuflesser's studio. In the south aisle there is an unusual and moving carving in wood of the Virgin and Child from the Rhine, dated about 1465.

Pevsner, generally no enthusiast for buildings in period imitation, said the chapel was 'the most splendid demonstration of the renaissance of Roman Catholicism in England'. It was Pugin's dream come true.

Carthusian gravitas: the choir and altar at St Hugh's. The stone screen prevents visitors from seeing the monks at prayer.

St Hugh's Charterhouse, Parkminster, Cowfold, West Sussex (1877–83)

'The buildings are conceived in function of a spiritual ideal. They provide the setting in which a group of people can live the gospel message of Christ in a radical way according to a tradition handed down from the first centuries of Christendom'. (*The Spirit of Place*, 1998)

Before the Reformation there were nine charterhouses – monasteries of the Carthusian order – in Britain. All were dissolved: 18 of their monks were martyred and the rest were dispersed. In 1872 three monks from the mother house, the Grande Chartreuse in France, came over to Sussex to find land on which to re-establish the Order in England. (They were also looking for somewhere to provide a refuge if the Order was expelled from France, which it duly was.) They wanted a substantial amount of land in order to enable the monks to live at some distance from their neighbours and their brothers in the isolation and silence, contemplation and prayer, which are central to the Rule of the Order. Medieval charterhouses had often been in towns, so the rural site may have been a precaution against local hostility – East Sussex was famously unfriendly to Catholicism and the trio thought it wise to conceal their identities as monks from the vendor of just over 200 acres south of Cowfold.

A French architect from Calais was brought over. Clovis Normand had at his disposal an almost limitless budget. The order's finances were on a very good footing thanks to the huge popularity and sales of their own-brand liqueur, Chartreuse. Consequently the Charterhouse was built on a scale, and with a lavishness, that raised some disapproving eyebrows – including those of Cardinal Manning and Queen Victoria. Local quarries supplied most of the stone. Seven hundred workmen were employed. Sixty thousand bricks were made every fortnight in on-site kilns. The result looks, unsurprisingly, French in the early Gothic style and the whole epic achievement is topped off by a spire of 203 feet. Pevsner wrote: the 'plan is magnificent and can only be properly seen from the air'. As visits are only allowed with written permission, which is rarely given, this is practical, as well as aesthetic advice.

St Hugh's is a collection of buildings designed for every aspect of the Carthusian monastic life. There is a gatehouse leading into a cloister on the other side of which stands the church. The church is the heart of a central complex from which various spaces with different functions radiate. These include the famous library with its collection of rare books and illu-minated volumes, a lofty refectory and kitchen, the prior's chapel and ante-room, a lay brothers' chapel, the chapter house (with chilling paintings of martyrdoms of the monks' predecessors), as

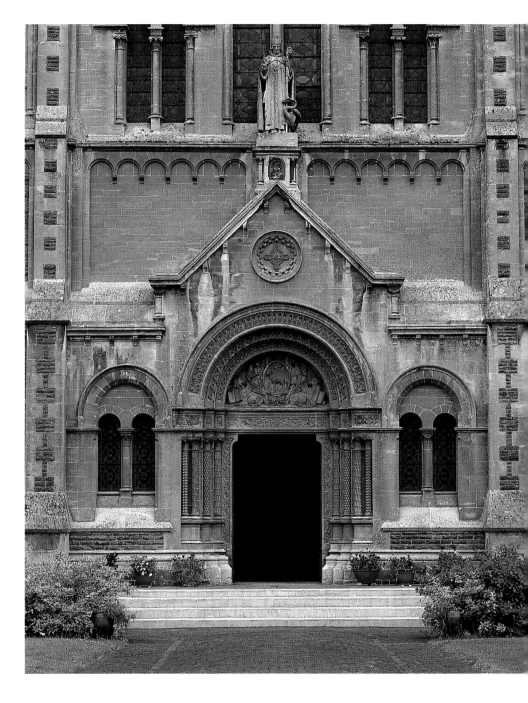

St Hugh's Charterhouse: the severity of the design of the chapel's west front reflects the austerity of the order.

well as workshops and garages. In the Relics Chapel are the stole of St Hugh, founder of the Carthusians, a hair of the Virgin Mary and the skeleton of St Boniface. Beyond the church is the Great Cloister, one of the biggest in the world. It encircles four acres of orchard and the cemetery where the bodies of monks lie beneath unidentified wooden crosses. The length of the Great Cloister, unwound so to speak, is more than a kilometre.

Leading off from the Great Cloister are 34 cells for the Fathers, simple but by no means grim. Circling the west end of the complex, they add an unexpected note of almost garden suburb cheerfulness to the high seriousness of the monastery. Each cell has two rooms, workshops, an ambulatory and a walled garden. In these silent spaces, the monks pursue the life of 'constructive solitude'. Once a month they all take a walk together through the Sussex countryside. Otherwise their routine is normally only broken by communal Sunday lunch and attendance, at regular hours, at Divine Office in the church.

For four to five hours a day the tall, unaisled church resonates to the sound of Gregorian chant which the Carthusians have sung since their foundation in the late 11th century. As would be expected, this is a sombre, meditative place with the choir-stalls formally opposite each other in the collegiate style. They are of fine carved wood with reliefs showing the Vision of Ezekiel and Christ giving the keys to Peter. The screen was painted by A Sublet, a 19th-century artist from Lyons.

The High Altar was the gift of nuns from a nearby convent and weighs 1 ton. It took eight men to carry it into position. The walls are panelled with carved wood, above which clear glass windows and grey stone columns rise up to the shadowy stone vault. An elaborate bronze sanctuary lamp hangs down in counterpoint to the general absence of flamboyance. The choir is separated from an ante-chapel by a carved stone screen and rood. This screen effectively prevents visitors in the gallery, who are allowed (by permission) to attend the service, from seeing the monks at prayer though they are able to hear the monks chanting. The atmosphere is solemn but not gloomy. The most sceptical visitor will be moved and is likely to leave in a reflective mood.

Visitors need permission before coming to see the buildings. Women, though most cordially welcomed, must remain in the gate house.

Byzantine style in Devon: painted by monks, Christ the Lord and the Saints fill the lantern ceiling at Buckfast Abbey.

Buckfast Abbey, Buckfastleigh, Devon (1907–32)

While the Carthusian monks at Cowfold allow no visitors without prior appointment, the Benedictine abbey church at Buckfastleigh is one of the most popular tourist attractions in south-west England. The cathedral-sized church stands, faced in yellowish and grey stone, steeped in the romance of its own story and its location next to the river Dart. It is also, remarked *The Builder* in 1933, 'unique as the only rebuilding of any ancient English abbey… one of the most important ecclesiastical buildings of modern times'.

In 1882 Benedictine monks came to Buckfast from France, discovered and excavated the foundations of the once great medieval Cistercian Abbey founded there in 1018, and built a temporary church. A committee, including Manning, Newman, Norfolk and a local peer, Lord Clifford, was formed to set the rebuilding of the monastery in motion. Frederick Walters (1848–1931), who worked for the Benedictines at Downside (see page 156), was

appointed architect. Abbot Anscar Vonier undertook the rebuilding of the abbey church as his first project. There was no money and the monks had to build it themselves. Vonier laid the foundation stone in 1907. Four, sometimes six, monks began work at the east end, cutting and dressing the stones themselves and raising them into position with manual hoists and block and tackle. Walters took all this voluntary labour in his stride and work never stopped. Thirty-three years later the church was finished; Abbot Vonier died just three weeks later.

Buckfast Abbey is a marvellous repository of the arts and crafts of the revived German Romanesque period. Many of the early monks were German and looked back to that time as a high water mark of their culture. Most of the furnishings are by Bernhard Witte of Aachen, date from 1928–32 and were inspired by medieval masterpieces of German metalwork. Behind the High Altar is a glorious copy of the 12th-century reredos in Koblenz, an artistic masterpiece so famous that Napoleon once made it his business to get hold of the original. It shows Christ in Glory and the tongues of fire descending to the Apostles at Pentecost. It took twelve craftsmen two years to make it in Witte's studio: the figures are in silver; the background is copper gilt; there is filigree work; and the columns are enamelled. The Aachen studios also made the *corona lucis* that is suspended above the altar.

Steeped in the romance of its own story, Buckfast Abbey was built by returning monks in the hills of south Devon.

High above, filling the lantern ceiling under the tower, is a wonderful painting of a stern Christ the Lord of Hosts surrounded by the faces of prophets and saints. It was largely the work of the Buckfast monk, Dom Charles Norris, assisted by E W Tristram and was painted (*c.* 1939) in egg tempera with gold lettering in the Byzantine style.

The floor of the sanctuary is one of the great decorative achievements of 20th-century England. The pavement was designed in the 1930s and 40s by Edward Hutton and based on the great floor at San Giovanni in Laterano in Rome. He used white Istrian marble, purple and green porphyry, verde antico, cipollino and Egyptian onyx in a breathtaking mosaic of circles and diamonds. Because of the war, porphyry was hard to come by and the porphyry that he did get hold of had been salvaged by Lord Elgin from a column in the ancient temple of Diana in Ephesus. The Lady Chapel has a similarly magnificent pavement.

The sanctuary has a bronze memorial to Abbot Vonier by Benno Elkan. The figure of Death taps at his shoulders, but he is seen witnessing the completion of the church. The baptismal font by Bernhard Witte, a replica cast in bronze of the famous original at Hildesheim, is sensational. It is huge and shows in relief, among much else, the Parting of the Red Sea and the Baptism of Christ. Huge kneeling figures, symbolising the great rivers of Paradise, support it. Witte also designed the Stations of the Cross.

At the far east end is the Blessed Sacrament Chapel designed by Paul Pearn. This was dedicated in 1966 and was built in a modern idiom and in fearless contrast with the medieval style of the rest of the church. The window was also designed by Dom Charles Norris (see also Harlow, page 199). It shows a large and challenging figure of Christ and fills the whole wall.

The choir at Quarr: its architect thought only Christians could design Christian buildings.

Quarr Abbey of Our Lady, Ryde, Isle of Wight (1908–10)

Seen across the Solent from the Isle of Wight ferry, the dark silhouette of the monastery outlined above the cliffs, promises something remarkable. Built in an austere, idiosyncratic style, entirely of red brick, it is like no other ecclesiastical building in Britain. It was designed by a Benedictine monk, Dom Paul Bellot (1876–1944) for his own community, which had pulled out of Solesmes because of the growing pressures of French anti-monasticism in the early years of the 20th century. Ironically, they came to an England which was by then happy to welcome them. The site they found was near the ruins of a medieval Cistercian monastery founded in 1131 and dissolved in 1537.

Dom Bellot was not just a monk turning his hand to architecture. He was the son of an architect and, before entering the mother house at Solesmes in 1904, he had studied at the École des Beaux Arts in Paris. He took architecture very seriously indeed and

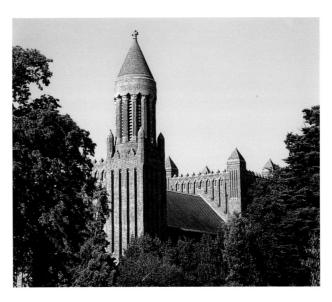

Far left: 'Moorish' design on the Isle of Wight: parabolas of brick arch up to the crossing.

The exterior of Quarr Abbey: Christian avant-garde architecture of 1911; unadorned brick in uncompromising and experimental form.

drew his ideas and inspiration from Plato, St Augustine and St Thomas Aquinas. He firmly believed that only Christians could design Christian buildings and built many churches in Europe and Canada, where he died, trapped there by the Second World War. Unlike Buckfast the work at Quarr was not carried out by monks. Three hundred local builders, more used to putting up seaside villas, worked under the supervision of Dom Bellot and experimented with unusual sorts of brick to an experimental design. The collaboration was a great success and the church was consecrated in 1912.

The abbey is approached from a lane which passes through fields and enclosures of sheep and chickens. The church stands somewhat back and apart from this setting and immediately makes clear its striking differences from conventional church building. There is no decoration or stone dressing. The west front has an oddly stepped gable over the broad entrance, flanked with squat, square towers. Over the choir is a much larger, conical tower, and over the sanctuary another massive, but lower, square tower. These are the components of that arresting view from the Solent.

The brickwork is thought to be influenced by Moorish designs in the Spanish south, and there are affinities with Antonio Gaudi's early work in Catalonia. The effect is still Gothic of a sort, but observers, like Pevsner, who admired it have put Quarr as firmly pointing towards the Modern Movement in architecture. Bryan Little thought it was 'more significant than any antiquarian copy'. Dom Bellot himself, however, had no time for Modernists and thought Le Corbusier was a destroyer of tradition and art.

The dimly lit but stirring interior of the church is severely functional. There is a broad short nave from which the laity can observe the monks performing the liturgy. This concession was allowed only after some debate and the monks in the choir, facing each other in four rows of carved stalls, are at a higher level than their visitors in the nave. Above and around them are walls of unadorned brick from which capital-less columns arch up to a shadowy pointed roof. The dizzying, diagonal parabolas of brick that support the tower, arch above arch, are a structural and aesthetic triumph. From the middle of the great and sombre space that they define hangs a rood, and above the High Altar, suspended on silver chains, is a round, glinting and mysteriously inscribed pyx.

Abbey Church of St Laurence, Ampleforth, York (1925–61)

The Rule of St Benedict was the foundation of much of western European civilisation. It set out the way of life for future centuries of monasticism, but did not ask for the impossible. The Rule was strict but could be lived by unexceptional men of faith. Sir Giles Gilbert Scott's church for the Benedictines in the pastures below the wild North Yorkshire moors perfectly captures the spirit of the founder's intentions. It is austere but far from heavy or oppressive. Its three saucer domes over nave, altar and choir suggest the inspiration of the Romanesque churches of south-western France. The structure looks simple; the impact it makes is memorable.

The monks came here from Lorraine in 1793, driven out by the events of the French revolution. The chapel and its furnishings (1855-7), designed by the Hansom brothers, Charles and Joseph, was replaced by a bigger one which in turn became too small. When Scott came on the scene (grandly declaring that the Ball Place where squash was played 'is your best building'), he found a site constricted by the surrounding school buildings and monastery. The domes were a good way of constructing a wide rather than a long building (as Scott was going to build for the Benedictines at Downside in cathedral-like Gothic grandeur).

Outside, the church shows Scott's trademarks of simplicity and beautifully proportioned mass. Inside the choir end was the first to be completed and the calm, meditative space is shaped from local stone as well as beautiful blue Hornton stone from Banbury. The nave end, completed when Benedictine austerity was reinforced by post-war shortages, used more concrete and was roughly plastered.

The extraordinary Arts and Crafts Gothic arch in the crossing under the tower fills the sanctuary and divides the monks in the choir from worshipping pupils and visitors. Its deeply incised crenellations and carvings are in potent contrast to the plainness of the church itself. Most of the lancet windows in the nave have plain glass. The Lady Chapel windows to the left of the sanctuary were deliberately intended to bring a

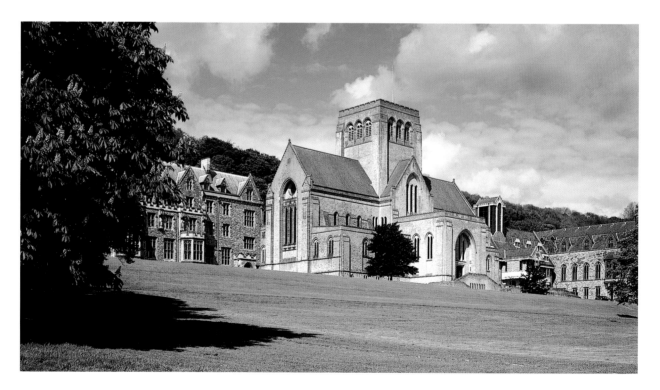

Giles Gilbert Scott's perfectly proportioned abbey church for the Benedictines at Ampleforth matched the spirit of the order.

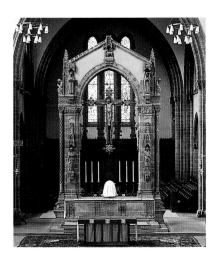

The huge Arts and Crafts arch separates the monks from pupils and visitors.

The Death of Our Lady by Reyntiens – a father-and-son collaboration for the Lady Chapel at Ampleforth, an area of contemplation and prayer.

burst of colour to the interior. *The Annunciation* is by Patrick Reyntiens, an old boy of Ampleforth. Reyntiens contributed other glass designs to the church, working with his son Richard. The glass they worked on in the south transept has an abstract representation of the apocalypse inspired by pre-Reformation medieval glass. The Lady Statue in the Lady Chapel was carved in the early 14th century and came from the Rhineland.

The choir is dominated by a splendid three-light window by Herbert Hendrie of Edinburgh. Hendrie trained Joseph Nuttgens, who also contributed glass to the church. The choir-stalls are outstanding; by Robert Thompson of nearby Kilburn. Scott himself designed the stone and wood reredos in the Memorial Chapel, dedicated to the old boys who died in the First World War. There is a 13th-century book cover from Limoges set into the tabernacle. The glass is by Hendrie and Nuttgens. St Benedict is remembered in St Benet's (Benedict's) Chapel in a fine oak reredos showing the saint at Monte Cassino. The altar stone below it was once at the great medieval abbey of Byland nearby. It was found in a farmyard.

In the crypt are twenty-five chapels which, until Vatican II, the priests used for private celebration of the Mass. Old boys of the Second World War are comemmorated in the largest chapel of St John Fisher and St Thomas More. There are four national chapels, for England, Wales, Ireland and Scotland. The Chapel of St Alban Roe (a martyred member of the community) has Stations carved from Welsh slate by Jonah Jones. There are more chapels in what is called the 'Old Crypt' (1925). There is blue Hornton stone, more woodcarving from Thompson, stained glass by Geoffrey Webb and a stirring memorial to the English Benedictines martyred by Henry VIII. There is a large, bronze statue of St Benedict (1997) in front of the church. The saint is gesturing encouragingly towards the school.

8 The Architecture of Change:
Arts and Crafts and a Return to Byzantium

The apse and stained glass at Ashton-in-Makerfield.

By the first half of the 20th century the Catholic revival could be taken for granted – and not just in terms of numbers of worshippers. The ideas and the preoccupations of Catholics were no longer a strange and foreign element in British life. They had been brought to a general public that still thought of itself largely as Protestant through writers like Hilaire Belloc and G K Chesterton and then, later, Evelyn Waugh and Graham Greene. Intellectual and imaginative life was enriched by writers who were not just Catholic; they wrote for a general public about subjects that might seem to concern only Catholics – the importance of confession, the sacraments, the validity of the one faith.

During the years around 1900, the mainstream of British architectural life too benefited from Catholic practitioners of the first rank. The convert John Francis Bentley was, in his last years, working on Westminster Cathedral. Both Leonard Stokes and Giles Gilbert Scott (later Sir) were the sons of converts and, while both had successful careers designing secular buildings, their churches were at the centre of their work. Stokes's first masterpiece, St Clare's, Sefton Park, Liverpool, took Bentley's Gothic elegance into the Arts and Crafts era. If Leonard Stokes would transform Gothic, others followed Bentley in looking back to styles still older, to Byzantium and the earliest days of Christianity itself.

Architects throughout the 1900s and 1920s were much influenced by Westminster Cathedral, and churches such as St Alphege, Bath, took the influence further in creating basilica plans which brought congregations and worshippers close together in the manner of the first recorded communions. Giles Gilbert Scott developed and took the tall, simple brick structure and the arcade mouldings of his father, George Gilbert junior, firmly into the 20th century.

Opposite: Our Lady of Peace (1938), Newbridge, Gwent, placed a new emphasis on clarity and simplicity.

The transition to this outpouring of talent had been slow but detectable. The meticulous copying of medieval detail was abandoned as architects, Anglican as well as Catholic, found new ways of expressing the Gothic ideal that was, by the early 20th century, subject to a much freer interpretation and lightness of touch.

Station of the Cross at St Alphege, Bath.

Much of the old power of the Gothic was penetrated and changed by the thinking of the Arts and Crafts movement. Like Pugin, William Morris exalted the craftsman and the builder, believing there was more to a building than aesthetics. He wrote: 'There should be no feature of a building which is not necessary for convenience and constructional propriety…all ornament should consist of the enrichment of the essential construction of the building.'

St Peter's, Gorleston, was designed by Eric Gill just before the Second World War. He believed that if things were made as fundamental and simple as could be, they would be beautiful. He said 'Look after goodness and truth and beauty will look after itself'. The Arts and Crafts may have been a minority movement that was swept away by the technological and social developments of the 20th century, but it nevertheless had a powerful effect on European design and influenced the forebears of the architectural philosophy that would eventually triumph – the Modern Movement.

Gold, marble and exquisite craftsmanship at St Andrew's Chapel, Westminster Cathedral.

The presbytery and church of St Clare form an intriguing L-shape.

St Clare, Arundel Avenue, Sefton Park, Liverpool (1888–90)

At first glance this red brick, late Victorian church with a minute spire in a staid suburb of Liverpool looks conventionally late Gothic. In fact it was innovatory, one of the first Catholic churches to reinterpret radically the Gothic style. It exploited the new sense of freedom and inventiveness that were the basis of the Arts and Crafts movement. When it was opened it received international attention. For many architects St Clare's is a seminal masterpiece, combining power, beauty and elegance.

The architect was Leonard Aloysius Stokes (1858–1925). He became President of the Royal Institute of British Architects (RIBA) in 1912. Although remembered chiefly for his many churches, he also designed houses, offices, public buildings and twenty telephone exchanges. Stokes was the godson of one of the cotton broker brothers (Francis Reynolds) who put up the money for St Clare's church.

Stokes designed a tall, light-filled interior which continued a now growing tradition, going back to the mid-19th century, of expressing Counter-Reformation planning in Gothic form. It gave unrestricted sight lines to the High Altar; it was pointless, he thought, to put seats behind columns. The aisles have no seats but just serve as passageways through the thick internal buttresses. (St Clare's is one of many English brick churches to be influenced by the internal buttresses of Albi Cathedral in south-west France.) Each aisle opens on to a much broader chapel at the east end. The semicircular arches of the arcades support galleries on both sides of the nave. Very tall, clear glass fills traceried windows which lead up to an elegant wagon roof. The white, undecorated interior is Gothic but far from suggestive of medieval mystery. This is a bright parish church, looking towards the 20th century.

Amid all the white purity of the interior, the 1930s marble High Altar, set against a flat east end with a tabernacle and grand candlesticks, is the more dramatic. It has a painted and carved triptych reredos above it by Robert Anning Bell and George Frampton from the 1890s which reaches halfway up the east wall. The church may be looking architecturally forward but the artists here were going back to the Renaissance for inspiration – in particular to the 15th-century Italian artist Pesellino for their central panel of the Trinity. The east window above the triptych commemorates the generous Reynolds brothers.

The pulpit that Stokes designed has open panels and sides that slope strangely outwards towards the base. His font, behind a low iron screen, is in bulging Arts and Crafts Gothic. It is carved out of alabaster and has a copper cover. Behind it, inset into the wall, is the chrysmatory. It echoes the stern, carved stone framework of the confessionals. There is a small shrine to St Clare, who was chosen as patron of the parish by the Reynolds brothers because both their wives were called Clare.

The brick presbytery attached to the north-east end forms an unusual L-shaped composition with St Clare's.

Arts and Crafts stone detail around the confessional at St Clare's.

Westminster Cathedral of the Most Precious Blood, Victoria Street, London SW1 (1895–1903)

A hundred years after Catholics were given legal freedom to have their own places of worship, Catholicism in England was buoyant and expanding and Cardinal Manning wanted a cathedral in the nation's capital. To match the confident spirit of the times, the cathedral would have to be of appropriate splendour. Manning

'A new kind of exterior': the west front of Westminster Cathedral. Portland stone, red brick, domes and a mosaic tympanum showing Christ with Mary and the Saints.

acquired a site near Victoria Station but rejected a design in extravagant Gothic by Henry Clutton. Manning then purchased another site nearby. Sir Tatton Sykes, a wealthy Protestant who proposed to convert to Catholicism, offered to pay for a new cathedral. Neither his proposal nor his conversion came to anything. When Manning died in 1892 Cardinal Vaughan succeeded him and pushed ahead with the scheme for a cathedral. He, too, rejected Gothic. He was then sixty and wanted a structure that could be completed quickly and where the decoration could follow later – a building that he could use in his own lifetime. Gothic also meant unwelcome comparisons with the truly medieval Westminster Abbey just down the road. He appointed John Francis Bentley as architect in 1894. Bentley had no liking for the Classical – and besides, that would have drawn comparisons with Brompton Oratory. He was similarly opposed to the Early Christian style that Vaughan favoured. They settled on Byzantine.

Bentley had worked with Byzantine-like mosaics before and, though he had designed a Byzantine church that was never built, he had never designed one that was. No one in England had. So he read and travelled for five months in Italy, studying the appropriate sites in Ravenna, Florence, Assisi, Venice and Rome. An outbreak of cholera stopped him going to Istanbul, but the design which he swiftly drew up on return seems to owe as much to Hagia Sofia – about which he had read in W R Lethaby and Swainson's learned book on the subject – as the places he had visited. Work started as soon as he got back. Vaughan, who trusted Bentley, said: 'He wished to build two campaniles; I said one would be enough for me. For the rest he had a free hand'.

The structure was completed in 1902. A year before consecration, the first London performance of Sir Edward Elgar's and Cardinal Newman's *Dream of Gerontius* was performed in the cathedral. The first great religious ceremony to be held there was the Requiem Mass for Cardinal Vaughan, who died in 1903. He had lived just long enough to see his cathedral completed. Bentley himself had died a year earlier at the age of 63.

The cathedral was all too much for outraged Gothic contemporaries at the time and later on it would still draw condescending dismissal. Over the years this has given way to almost universal admiration. Those who have participated in, or witnessed, great Catholic ceremonies taking place beneath the mysterious darkness of the huge cathedral's shallow domes acknowledge the power and the glory of Bentley's masterpiece.

It is an astonishing achievement. Not only had Bentley mastered a new and exotic style, he had more or less invented a new kind of exterior. The cathedral is still startling – particularly now that it is much more visible since the buildings in front of the west entrance were cleared to allow an open piazza. The façade is of red brick patterned with ingeniously layered Portland stone. The small domes around the roof are dwarfed by a slender 284-foot campanile with an octagonal lantern, itself domed. It was, until the 1950s, one of the few 'skyscrapers' on the London skyline. From ground level it is

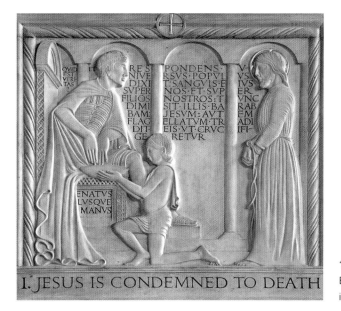

'Christ before Pilate': one of Eric Gill's Stations of the Cross inside the cathedral.

difficult to see the outlines of the three vast saucer domes that cover the nave and sanctuary, but they were cast in concrete *in situ* with an admixture of broken red brick.

The cathedral is 360 feet long and 156 feet wide. It will hold 2,000 worshippers. 'The interior is without a doubt one of the most moving of any churches in London', wrote Pevsner. But Bentley's vision is incomplete. He intended an interior space that would eventually glow with mosaic and marble. A hundred years on and the mosaics are only partly installed. The marble is magnificent. The eight massive piers in the very broad nave are sheathed in verde antico from Thessaly, the same marble that was used for Hagia Sofia. Beautiful but smaller marble columns across the transepts carry the gallery. The cathedral's upper walls and domes, however, are as dark and shadowy as at their beginning. The expense of the mosaic project brought it to a halt. This is not unwelcome to those who fear that a space of total, blazing polychromy would destroy the cathedral's sombre magnificence.

The nave, with eight columns of green marble, is the widest in Europe. The circular electric light fittings suspended over the nave look perfectly at home in their Byzantine setting and were probably designed by Bentley. The raised sanctuary is very long and leads up to the choir. The sanctuary was the most important part of the cathedral for Bentley, but he did not live to see his own designs for it completed. (H Farmer and W Brindley started work on it in 1905.) Bentley designed the colossal baldacchino of solid white marble that stands memorably above the High Altar. The eight columns that support the canopy are monoliths of yellow Veronese marble and are 14 feet high. All the columns in the cathedral are monoliths, shaped from a single block. The altar is a single block of unpolished Cornish marble which weighs 12 tons. Bentley designed the rood. The mosaics of Christ in Majesty on the arch behind date from 1934.

All around there are chapels of different character and of varying degrees of splendour and quality. Something of what Bentley had in mind for the whole cathedral can be seen in one of its best chapels, the Holy Souls; the elements were either designed or approved by him. The reredos of Christ the Redeemer Enthroned in Majesty was designed by W C Symons, a friend of Bentley's, in 1902–4. The walls are of black-and-white marble and the silvery mosaics by Symons glimmer with the artist's vision of the Risen Christ and the purification of the souls awaiting redemption in purgatory.

Lighter in tone, next to the sanctuary, is the chapel of the Blessed Sacrament – the most sacred part of the cathedral. It was covered in astonishing pink mosaics by Boris Anrep, an artist from St Petersburg who was commissioned in 1953 by Cardinal Griffin. Anrep covered every surface with bright mosaics portraying, among many other biblical figures, Abraham, Melchisedech, Noah, Elijah and, in the apse, the Miracles of Jesus. The chapel of St George has an altarpiece of Christ on the Cross by Eric Gill. Cardinal Basil Hume is buried in the chapel of St Gregory and St Augustine.

The chapel of St Andrew and the Saints of Scotland is a masterpiece of the Arts and Crafts movement. The altar is made of Scottish stone and the Scottish saints are appropriately represented. The 4th Marquess of Bute

The canopy above the High Altar. The sanctuary was, for Bentley, the most important part of the cathedral.

Opposite: 'The power and the glory': Westminster's nave will hold 2,000 worshippers.

Bentley wanted two campaniles – Cardinal Vaughan said: 'one would be enough for me. For the rest he had a free hand'.

commissioned Robert Weir Schultz, a Byzantine scholar, to carry out the mosaic decoration of the chapel. It was an inspired choice. St Andrew, the brother of St Peter, is shown in a powerful mosaic on the west wall dressed in traditional blue and white colours. Next to him is the diagonal cross on which he was crucified. St Andrew is patron saint of Greece as well as Scotland, and the Orthodox connection is commemorated in a mosaic showing Hagia Sofia in Istanbul and five other cities with which the saint is associated. The furniture of the chapel is of ebony and ivory and was designed by a master of the Arts and Crafts, Ernest Gimson.

In the Lady Chapel, the mosaics on the altar are particularly rich and are by Robert Anning Bell. The mosaics which cover the walls and vaulting are no less gorgeous and are by Gilbert Pownall (1932). Through the Lady Chapel there is an entrance to the crypt. Here, below the sanctuary, lie the tombs of Cardinal Archbishops of Westminster. Cardinal Wiseman has a Gothic monument by E W Pugin and there is a monument to Cardinal Manning, the cathedral's founder, designed by Bentley.

The font in the baptistery is enormous with marble and verde antico mirrored by the inlaid white squares of marble on the floor. It was made in Rome to Bentley's design.

The Stations of the Cross (1913–18) on the piers are by Eric Gill. It was a bold commission, as Gill was very young at the time and had only just converted. In striking contrast to the colour and glitter of the walls, they were carved from stone in low relief. They are beautifully lettered, formal, dignified and moving; comparable to the paintings of Masaccio and equal to their superb surroundings. There is a simplicity about them that matches the basic structure of Bentley's timeless interior. As architectural historian Denis Evinson says, both 'were to exert their influence upon the Modern Movement'. Westminster Cathedral may look back to Justinian, but it 'laid the foundation of 20th-century thinking on simplicity and design'.

St Anne's Cathedral, Cookridge Street, Leeds, Yorkshire (1901–4)

Leeds Cathedral is a big building in the heart of the city centre and it attracts a large city congregation. In the 1780s there were only ten Catholic families in Leeds. By 1838 the city had a large, busy Catholic church which was upgraded to cathedral status in 1878 when the diocese of Leeds was created. Twenty years later Leeds Corporation compulsorily purchased St Anne's to make space for a road-widening scheme, offering a new site not many yards from the old one in return. Construction of the present cathedral was completed in 1904. The stone cross that used to crown the spire of the old St Anne's is mounted outside the west window of the new one.

The architect, academic, critic and for many years a local, Patrick Nuttgens, called the cathedral 'wholly original and utterly distinctive… an outstanding example of the architecture which gave the country a special reputation at the turn of the century'. The architects were John Henry Eastwood (1843–1913) and Sydney Kiffin Greenslade (1866–1955). There is some debate as to who was the greater genius of the two architects: Eastwood was a Catholic, born in Leeds, who had a successful career in London; Greenslade was a more 'artistic' architect who had won many awards. Their church was Gothic Revival, designed in the spirit of the newly emerging Arts and Crafts style.

There were many difficulties. Eastwood spoke of the cathedral as 'a great and arduous task', and money was short. Canon Croskell, the administrator, remarked that 'there never yet was an architect who built a church without exceeding, if he had the chance, the amount allowed him'. Nonetheless, when finished, the cathedral was an immediate success.

The plan is almost square. Of necessity, Eastwood designed a broad but relatively short nave to fit the difficult site. The interior feels spacious and the tall columns rise up to the flattish roof to maximise the sense of space. It all seems quite simple, but the simplicity is counterpointed by the Arts and Crafts decoration.

Below the reredos of 1903 is the new main altar where the bones of Saints Tranquiltarius and Victor, brought from the catacombs of Rome, were placed in 1963.

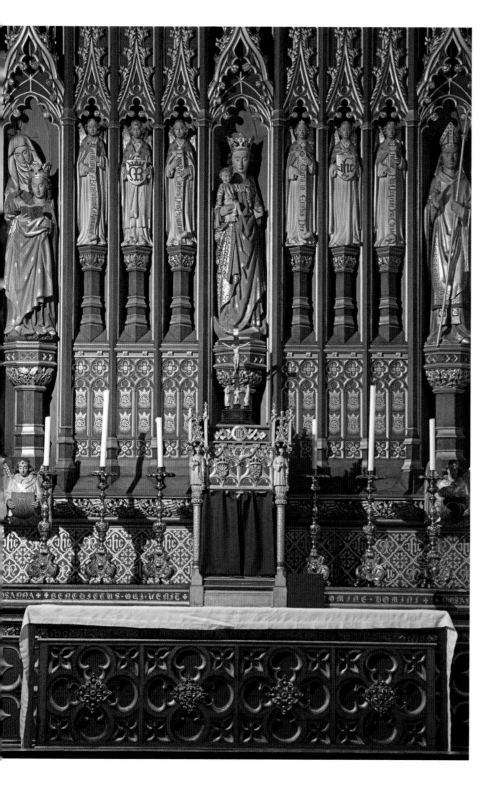

A W N Pugin's stunning reredos and altarpiece in the Lady Chapel, designed in 1842 and once at the centre of Leeds old cathedral.

The carved niches with sculpted panels at the entrance to the sanctuary were put there in the 1930s as a response to a general feeling that St Anne's needed to be 'beautified'. Fine as the architecture was, the whole effect was thought to be rather severe and more colour and decoration were needed. Cesare Formilli, who had taken over at Brompton Oratory (see page 127), was brought in. Much of what he (and others) did before the Second World War has since been removed, but his Stations of the Cross (1912) still survive in the nave and so too does Greenslade's mighty reredos in the sanctuary. It is a glowing red and gold relief of the Coronation of Our Lady, made from pine with dazzlingly carved niches. The reredos survived the re-ordering of 1963. On either side are mosaics (1928) designed by Formilli and made in Venice, but his paintings which used to surround the sanctuary deteriorated and were removed. The sanctuary walls are once again fashionably bare of decoration.

There are remarkable chapels all round the church. Eastwood designed the stone altar and reredos of St Joseph, and Greenslade the altar of the Sacred Heart and a reliquary for the bones of St Urban. Formilli designed the war memorial.

The pulpit, beautiful designed by J F Bentley, stands by the south transept with alabaster panels carved in relief. The front panel shows Christ appearing after the Resurrection to St Peter and the other disciples by the Sea of Galilee: 'Feed my Sheep'. Also from the old church must be the cathedral's single greatest *tour de force*: the altar and reredos in the Lady Chapel. They were designed by A W N Pugin in 1842 and depict St Anne amongst other statues of saints in gilded niches, shimmering angels, crockets, a shining tabernacle and a glorious statue of Mary with the Christ Child: a masterpiece.

The cathedral was re-ordered in 1963 by Messrs Weightman and Bullen of Liverpool and is now undergoing another re-ordering.

CHVRCH of the ANNVNCIATION.
BOVRNEMOVTH.

The Annunciation, Charminster Road, Bournemouth, Dorset (1906–7)

This was the first parish church to be designed by the young Giles Gilbert Scott, later Sir (1880–1960). He had already won the competition for Liverpool's Anglican Cathedral and, in time, he would design not just churches but, along with much else, Waterloo Bridge, Battersea Power Station and the old, red post office telephone kiosk.

His church, built for the Jesuits in a northern suburb of Bournemouth, is of no great size and looks undistinguished, even industrial. But in its way it was revolutionary. John Betjeman called it 'a brilliantly original design in brick'. The church has copies of correspondence with the architect, who had some decided views about the proposed church and his clients: 'The artistic taste of the Catholic Priests is appalling and I am most anxious to have a church in which everything is genuine and good, and not tawdry or ostentatious.'

Ostentatious it is not. The red brick profile – extended lately at the west end – makes little impact on the surrounding streets of semi-detached houses. The bell-cote stands out:

G G Scott's design for the reredos that was never executed is kept in the church at Bournemouth.

'cyclopean', according to Pevsner. The roof of the nave, which is flat, wide and supported by emphatic and darkly painted beams, makes the interior seem slightly oppressive, but look toward the east and there is a magical diffusion of light around the bare walled sanctuary and altar. This was Scott's master stroke – the unprecedented raising of the crossing, transept and sanctuary to the height of a tower, with plain walls and minimal decoration. Above, the bell-cote on the roof is serviced from a small gallery for the bell-ringer halfway up inside the tower (although apparently no bells were ever installed). There are galleries on the north and south sides of the sanctuary connected to each other by an unusual bridge with an elegantly wrought iron balustrade surmounted by a golden crown. Above it hangs a simple wooden crucifix. Below the bridge on the east wall is a gilt-framed copy of a painting by Guido Reni of the Annunciation. Scott's original design for a large reredos was never executed, but the church keeps his painting of what might have been.

The north gallery gives access to an odd feature. Until the presbytery was built in 1954 there was no accommodation for the priest, apart from a small room halfway up the tower. It was far from luxurious. Access was by ladder from a trapdoor in the floor. From another trapdoor in the room itself a rope ladder dangled down to the sacristy.

Master of space and light;
G G Scott's sanctuary at
Bournemouth. The painting,
a copy of one by Guido Reni,
hangs in place of the
unexecuted reredos by Scott.

Scott had very strong views on furnishings. He spent some time beating off unsuitable, though well intentioned, gifts for the church: 'Bad and trumpery articles will absolutely ruin the church…the fittings play an important part in the architectural effect…if tawdry things are put in, as Father Hornyold seems to wish, the church assumes a poverty-stricken air.' This was avoided. The communion rails, the font and the Arts-and-Crafts-style altar fit into Scott's church perfectly. In the north transept there is a touchingly beautiful low relief in gold and green of the Virgin and Child.

St Joseph, Potter Hill, Pickering, Yorkshire (1907–11, 1916)

An almost legendary and much revered figure still feels very present in this church. Early in 1901, Father Bryan, a former Anglican priest from Tasmania – who had become a Catholic priest – came to Pickering. There were very few Catholics in what was still a small, isolated town, but he set about building first a school and then a church. While the church was being built he lived very simply in a single room in the tower, the first part of the church to be completed. Bearded and eccentric-looking Father Bryan may have been, but he was by no means cut off from the affairs of the world. He commissioned Leonard Stokes (1858–1925), archi-

tect of the internationally known St Clare's in Liverpool (see page169). Stokes was a famous and successful all-round architect who would become President of the RIBA. Father Bryan caught him in a gap between designing a telephone exchange at Reading and an office block in London. St Joseph's was Stokes's last church in England.

The church stands back from the road in stone Perpendicular Gothic. It is approached through a forecourt next to the considerable church hall, also by Stokes, which has a large Perpendicular window facing south. You enter the church through a door at the bottom of the tower. Stokes designed a broad, light interior with a nave and one side aisle leading to a chapel. The style may be a spare Tudor Gothic, but the spirit and ethos are Arts and Crafts. The plastered walls of the broad nave are plain and undecorated and there is a high and quite small Perpendicular window on the east wall. The original altar and reredos were removed in the re-ordering and there is even less now in the way of detailing or decoration.

Father Bryan wanted Eric Gill to carve the font. From 1913, Gill was working on the Stations of the Cross at Westminster Cathedral but he found the time to carve the font, which arrived in sections by train, in 1916. Four sides of the octagonal stone are carved with reliefs of foliage. The other four show the Crucifixion, St Joseph and the Christ Child, the Baptism of Christ and St Nicholas. They are in the formal, hieratic style that marks Gill's work. Gill also carved a simple cross on the altar of the Lady Chapel. Outside, by the south wall, there is a statue of St Joseph thought to be by P P Pugin.

St Joseph holding the Christ Child: one of Eric Gill's carved reliefs for the font at St Joseph's.

St Joseph, Cromer Road, Sheringham, Norfolk (1908–36)

Until the railway came Sheringham was 'an insignificant fishing village with a few hundred souls on the beach… Not yet had Our Lord come to make his home in Sheringham', according to a local convert in 1912. The railway brought visitors, some of them Catholics. What had been a village grew into a town. The Deterding family moved in. He was Managing Director of Royal Dutch Shell. Mrs Deterding was a Catholic

Cliffs of red brick, G G Scott's trademark at St Joseph's.

who found the journey to the nearest Catholic church in Cromer trying. She persuaded her husband to provide the means to build a more convenient place of worship. Mrs Deterding and Father Carter, the priest, chose Giles Gilbert Scott to be the architect.

St Joseph's was built in stages over many years until the cliff-like walls of red brick – a Scott trademark – enclosed a finished church. Mrs Deterding is buried outside the walls, near the brick bell-cote, under an ornate headstone. 'Patience, patience, the world is nothing,' she commands, 'Children, do not neglect God' (her last words).

St Joseph's is a small but tall church of 1908–10, which was extended to the ritual west in 1934–6. Large traceried windows penetrate the sheer walls and the roof is all but invisible behind a high parapet. Inside, the sanctuary is the same height and width as the tall and narrow nave. The columns have no capitals. The undecorated walls run smoothly up past the clear glass of the large windows to a darkly enveloping king-post roof. There is, as at Scott's church at Bournemouth (see page 177), a wonderful sense of space and light. A great rood (made by the Stuflesser workshop of Ortesei and Tosi of London) hovers over the entrance to the sanctuary.

The tall and remarkable reredos (by Ratcliffe of London) fills the space between the altar and a high, round window. It has six panels that were copied from a medieval screen in a church on the Norfolk Broads. Represented in medieval style are a number of saints, and Mary with angels attending. Another, more recent panel shows St Joseph who had hitherto been left out. A blazing tabernacle stands at the heart of all this with a background of golden stars. The window above features a pelican – symbol of Christ feeding his people with his body and blood.

The large, graphic and vivid Stations of the Cross came from Ortesei. They took some time to arrive as they were impounded by the German authorities for the duration of the First World War while en route to Sheringham from Genoa. F Stuflesser's grandson carved the statue of St Joseph.

The expressive and elongated west window shows through a Jesse Tree the ancestry of Christ. It was made by Dunstan Powell of Hardman & Co and given as a thank-offering by the (non-Catholic) mother of the local convert. The Lady Chapel has the original High Altar that was moved there during the 1992 re-ordering. St Joseph's is prized as an important example of 20th-century architecture and the re-ordering was closely scrutinised and criticised by what the church guidebook calls 'the scurrilous press'. The front of the altar has an affecting relief carving, attributed to Eric Gill, of the Annunciation. The pulpit was carved in a Gothic style by a local man, Mr Palmer. Its panels show the Evangelists.

The side chapel (the first part of the church, completed 1908) has a lively reredos with large statues of St Joseph between two saints not often featured in English country churches – St Cyril and St Methodius, bringers of Christianity to the Slav peoples. St Cyril was the inventor of the Cyrillic alphabet.

Far left: Hovering above the entrance to the sanctuary at St Joseph's is the elaborately carved and coloured rood from the Stuflesser workshop in Italy.

Left: The medieval-style reredos and tabernacle at St Joseph's were inspired by a church on the Norfolk Broads.

Lithuanian Church of St Casimir, The Oval, Hackney Road, London E2 (1911–12)

St Casimir's was built for Lithuanian sailors working in the Baltic timber trade in the port of London. It is thought to be the only Lithuanian church in western Europe outside Rome. The first priest was Father Casimir G Matulaitis. The architect was Father Benedict Williamson, who designed the church and said Mass at the opening in 1912. He went on to design many churches around London, demonstrating a taste for the exotic which was also expressed in his writings on such subjects as hagiography and mysticism. Father Williamson employed Egyptian motifs in a number of his churches, of which this is an early example.

For the Lithuanians, Williamson designed a building of London stock brick whose walls are somewhat eccentrically punctuated by large round windows. It looks a bit lost set in its very urban, East End

The Coronation of Our Lady; exuberant Tyrolean craftsmanship in London's East End.

Hagia Sofia in Rochdale: the Byzantine dome of St John the Baptist.

surroundings. Inside it is a different story. The interior is dominated by the huge, cheerful, brightly painted altarpiece depicting the Coronation of Our Lady carved in wood. It is said, though it is much disputed, that it was shown at the Great Exhibition of 1851 as an example of Tyrolean craftsmanship and was, at one time, destined for Westminster Cathedral. Eventually it came out of storage and found an appreciative home in the East End. Indeed, the church was designed around it.

Our Lady is attended by angels in various attitudes of piety and prayer. A golden, winged crown hovers above her head. The seated figures of Christ and God the Father look on from above and behind Her. The Holy Spirit in the form of a dove sheds rays of light out towards cherubim who are half concealed in the clouds that form the background of the whole tableau. There are more angels painted on the wall above the altarpiece and in the niches. These are framed by columns with dull gold capitals in the 'Egyptian' style that Father Williamson favoured throughout the church and which can be seen in the round-headed arches.

Father Williamson's taste is less evident in other parts of the church. The statue in St Casimir's shrine (1951, by James Dagys), to the right of the altar, has the robust quality of Lithuanian folk art – as do most of the statues, the ornately framed paintings of the Stations of the Cross and the general decoration of the church.

The presbytery has a parish room with evocative photographs of old, neighbourhood football teams and parish functions. The original community has long since dispersed, but there is still a lively local Lithuanian congregation as well as those who come back on Sundays, as the church leaflet puts it, to 'say their prayers in Lithuanian, to see into the depths of their souls'.

St John the Baptist, Dowling Street, Rochdale, Lancashire (1924)

Canon Chipp was the parish priest from 1897 to 1936. Inspired by the example of Westminster Cathedral, he wanted a new church in the Byzantine style of Istanbul's Hagia Sofia to be built in Rochdale. Fortunately, given rising costs, plans were well developed before the First World War and St John the Baptist was opened in 1925. Cardinal Bourne opened the church which he likened to the most notable churches in the country and, more guardedly, 'not unworthy to rank with the great architectural achievements that already distinguished the town'.

The architects were E Bower Norris and Oswald Hill of Manchester. A campanile was planned but never built. The builders were R & T Howarth who had built the neighbouring fire station. This does have a considerable tower and it nicely complements the church's great dome.

The dome is 95 feet high – about half the height of Justinian's great church (the church's guidebook notes without comment that the first dome of Hagia Sofia collapsed). It is made from a single concrete structure which is only five inches thick, supported on concrete stanchions and faced outside with brick. As at Hagia

The devil prepares the fires of hell for the damned and St Peter is poised to welcome the saved: details from Eric Newton's gigantic 1933 wall of mosaic at St John the Baptist.

Sofia, the base of the dome is encircled by small, recessed clerestory windows. These and the other windows illuminate a memorable interior space.

Most striking is the apsed sanctuary. It was entirely covered in gloriously patterned mosaic in 1933. The designer was Eric Newton (1893–1965). Newton was best known as art critic of the *Manchester Guardian* and as a broadcaster on *The Critics*. But his father was a Manchester mosaic designer and Eric worked in stained glass and mosaics for the earlier part of his professional life.

Newton worked with Italian craftsmen. They took a year to put the mosaics in place and at the centre of their great achievement, high in the apse, is the figure of Christ the King. He looks challengingly towards the congregation. To his right, the devil rakes the fires of hell. To the left, St Peter prepares for the reception of the saved in heaven: 'Take for your heritage the kingdom prepared for you.' At Christ's feet, eleven grazing sheep represent the Apostles (an idea Newton took from Torcello). All around, in glowing tesserae, are scenes from the Bible. St John baptises Christ then awaits his own beheading. There are mosaics of Noah's Ark, the Ark of the Covenant, the Temple of Jerusalem and the Holy City of Jerusalem as well as the symbols of the four Evangelists, various saints, the Venerable Bede and Pope Pius XI – who was Pope at the time the church was being built. Art Nouveauish peacocks, ancient symbols of everlasting life, stand in profile on a Greek capital below a great, golden XP – the first two letters of Christ in Greek. The whole east end is an astonishing display of intricate, hierarchical design and colour.

Flanking the sanctuary, the curved walls have large transepts leading to circular chapels at the corners. They have been converted; one for accommodation and one for parish meetings. The font dates from 1830 and the pulpit from 1898. Both come from the old church that St John the Baptist replaced.

St Alphege, Oldfield Park, Bath (1925–9)

Sir Giles Gilbert Scott was so fond of what he called 'this little gem' of a church that he designed the presbytery in the 1950s for free. This was partly an act of generosity, but also partly for fear that someone else would get their hands on it. 'The church was my first essay in the Romanesque style of architecture. It has always been one of my favourite works', he wrote. It was based on the Roman basilica of Sta Maria in Cosmedin in Rome (*c.* 780).

G G Scott's west end and door to the sacristy. He said of St Alphege, 'though simple [it] gives no impression of cheapness'.

The church stands romantically backed by green fields and woods and has a Roman tile roof, a three-bay loggia porch and a short tower. Scott always regretted that the campanile he planned was never built. It was found that the ground beneath the church was incapable of carrying so large a structure.

Scott used rough Bath stone with coarse pointing – a marked contrast to most of the smoothly faced buildings in Bath. 'Bath stone…is usually used in an uninteresting way', he wrote. 'I have used stone that came out of the quarry in rough shapes and which needed little more treatment than knocking off the greater projections. Wide joints are not only necessary with this type of rough stone but add to the beauty of the walling.'

Scott continued, 'The design though simple gives no impression of cheapness and this is largely due to the fact that the walls are of stone both inside and out, and the craftsmanship is of fine quality'. The plan resembles that of Sta Maria in Cosmedin in having nave and sanctuary within a single space.

At the end of the nave, a stately baldacchino is symmetrically poised over the High Altar, its angular pyramidal roof striking up to, and in contrast with, the roundness of the semicircular arch above it. The arches are round and there are superbly carved capitals on polished columns. The floor looks, at a glance, like a mosaic pavement of the 12th century but is, in fact, made of linoleum. Scott used 'small pieces of linoleum in the same manner as marble is used to give a tessellated floor rich in colour and pattern. It follows the traditional effect given by the marble floors in some of the old basilicas in Italy'. The look of venerability has been enhanced over the years by the impact of many pairs of high-heeled shoes.

'My first essay in the Romanesque style…one of my favourite works.' Scott wrote of St Alphege. Above, the church's nave and a pyramid-roofed baldacchino from the Dolomites.

The tessellated floor: inspired by Rome, executed in linoleum.

The overall effect is severe but the sand colour of the stone walls makes the church feel warm. A new lighting system was installed in 1986 but it retains Scott's original hanging lamp holders of a cross in relief on cheerful, sunflower-like golden disks.

The baldacchino of gilded oak is attributed to the Ars Sacra workshop in the Dolomites and decorated by John Watts of London. The Stations are austere and moving. There is a fine carving of the Virgin in the Lady Chapel by Theodore Kearn, another Austrian artist. Scott described the capitals as having merely 'informative motifs'. In fact they bear comparison with the carvings on the capitals in the great Romanesque churches and cloisters of Europe. They tell the story of the life of Our Lady and of St Alphege. There is a capital naming Dom Leander Ramsay, Abbot of Downside and Dom Anselm Rutherford, Prior to St John's, Bath, who commissioned the church. A shield carved on the north side capital commemorates 'Giles, architect' and another the tools and initials of the man who did the carving, D W Gough (1928). The builders were Jacob Long and Co of Bath.

Arches inspired by Perigueux support the organ gallery at Ashton-in-Makerfield.

St Oswald and St Edmund Arrowsmith, Liverpool Road, Ashton-in-Makerfield, Lancashire (1930)

Lancashire is famously a county with a strong Catholic tradition and with some of the finest Catholic churches in the country. This tradition continued into the 20th century and the small town of Ashton-in-Makerfield has one of the most original churches of its date. Cardinal Bourne was said to have thought it the most beautiful Catholic church in England. It was built in the Romanesque idiom. It owes its origins to the Gerard family, an ancient recusant family who had seen out penal times fortified by their expanding coal mining revenues as well as their faith. With the coming of more tolerant times, the Gerards built a chapel and later put their money into building this church. A member of the family was St Edmund Arrowsmith who was hanged, drawn and quartered in 1628. When he was canonised in 1970, his name was added to the church, already dedicated to St Oswald, patron saint of the Gerards. St Edmund's 'Holy Hand', which was miraculously preserved and returned to the family, is kept and venerated here.

The church does not derive all its character from its aristocratic foundation. It was immediately seen as a communal project – belonging to the parish. Coal miners, who were on strike at the time, volunteered to dig out the footings and help the masons.

The architect was John Sydney Brocklesby. His original brief was to design the church in a conventionally Gothic style. On a visit to France, however, Brocklesby was so impressed by what he saw of the great Romanesque cathedrals of the 11th century that he persuaded Canon O'Meara to change the brief – even though the foundations had already been dug out for the Gothic church. He then designed a much heavier structure which needed much bigger foundations on a site already vulnerable to mining subsidence.

The church has a spectacular stone exterior with a formidable square tower, a turret and a giant arch over the entrance. Just above the entrance is a tympanum with the Coronation of the Virgin and nearby, a statue of St Oswald. The interior looks not just Romanesque but almost Byzantine. Two immense saucer domes, framed and supported by great arches, cover the nave. Thick grey columns, in clusters of shafts, stretch up to the high clerestory.

The altar is raised and forms, with candlesticks and cross, an impressive centre to a dignified and solemn curved apse. Behind are the round-arched columns of the ambulatory. The dark curve of the apse is pierced by high, narrow windows which are a glory of the church. They are exquisitely drawn and coloured (1930–7) and create a subtle and slightly eerie back light to the altar. Each window shows a different saint, not all widely known or recognisable – St Ita, St Paschal Baylon, St Juliana Falconieri and St Tarcisius, patron saint of those deeply attached to the Blessed Sacrament. They are all extraordinarily compelling and are by Harry Clarke of Dublin. The windows are usually described as 'Expressionistic' but their almost sensuous design and gorgeous deep colours suggest Art Nouveau as well.

There is a very powerful window of Christ in Glory over the organ on the west wall. The glass panels in the Lady Chapel show an other-worldly, almost Buddha-like, St Edmund Arrowsmith. All round the interior of the church the heavy architecture and the tenebrous light is pierced by the deep-coloured gleam of windows commemorating the lives and deaths of saints and martyrs.

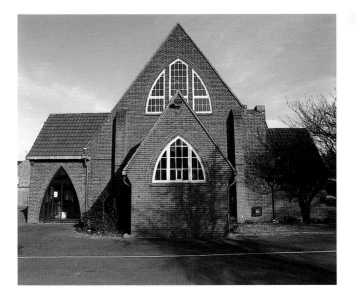

St Peter, Lowestoft Road, Gorleston, Norfolk (1938–9)

The tower looks odd and the windows are an unusual shape but, superficially, red brick St Peter's looks rustic and ordinary. It was in reality radical and revolutionary: the one architectural commission of the famous Catholic sculptor, engraver, type-face designer and polemicist Eric Gill (1882–1940). Father Thomas Walker, the parish priest of this isolated seaside town had previously served at High Wycombe, close to Gill's home and workshop at Pigotts Hill. He offered Gill the job of designing this church. Gill seized the chance to put into practice his strongly felt ideas about art and architecture, religion and churches. Prophetic of what

Left: Eric Gill's red-brick church at Gorleston has a radical cross-shaped interior space.

was to come, he wrote to Father Walker: 'There is a need…to design churches in such a way that the altar again becomes the central thing.'

And so St Peter's has one of the first altars in Britain to stand in the middle of the congregation, which sits in a cross-shaped space with the altar under the crossing tower. This was years before Vatican II. Gill had some training as an architect, having worked in the office of W D Caröe from 1899–1903, and had little time for religious rituals glimpsed in a faraway east end: 'The altar must be brought back to the middle of our churches…the vestments and the stained glass windows, the paintings and the statues, are all so much frippery compared with the altar.'

There are few fripperies in the church: 'It will be just a plain building done by bricklayers and carpenters.' Everything is painted white. There are no conventional columns: instead there are tapering arches. They have no capitals or bases and seem to lean towards each other under the scissor-braced roof. Above, at the top of the crossing, the arches intersect in satisfying geometry. The whiteness is occasionally relieved. On the spandrel of the east arch is a painting, to Gill's design, of Christ's Entry to Jerusalem. It was painted by Gill's son-in-law, David Tegetmeier. A rood hangs above the altar which Gill also designed, as he did the piscina, font and holy water stoups.

One addition Gill might have contested is the large, eye-arresting stained-glass window at the far east end. He had wanted clear glass throughout the church but this deeply coloured window was installed in 1963, paid for by the proceeds of parish bingo. It is a powerful work by Joseph Nuttgens. Nuttgens had introduced Gill to Father Walker but felt he never quite received due credit for this. When he got the job, Nuttgens joked: 'At last, my revenge!' The glass panels have a slightly Byzantine formality to them and show an enthroned and resplendent Christ the King who looks questioningly towards the altar and the congregation beyond and around it. St Peter is at his right.

Gill's decision to start from the altar and work outwards meant, as he said, that from that point outward he more or less trusted to luck as to how it would all turn out. The final result he said, with unusual modesty, was 'gawky and amateurish'. It was his one church. He died of cancer two years after St Peter's was finished.

Our Lady of Mount Carmel, Pontfein Road, Lampeter, Ceredigion (1939–40)

The church stands on a rise overlooking a green. The outside is simple, white-washed rough cast with an emphatic grey-green slate roof, closely linked to a large presbytery set at right angles to it. It looks like Eric Gill's woodcut of an unexecuted hillside chapel for the Community of St Joseph and St Dominic at Ditchling. Stone and wood carving, ironwork and paintings at Lampeter have been attributed to members of the Guild of Catholic Artists and Craftsmen that Gill founded there. If the inspiration was Arts and Crafts, the design was sophisticated and complex. The architect

Opposite: 'It will be a plain building…': Eric Gill's unadorned arches at St Peter's have no capitals or bases. He believed that if things were made as simple as could be they would be beautiful.

Different coloured bricks help to define a movingly serene sanctuary at Lampeter.

was T H B Scott (1872–1945), surveyor to the London and Brentwood dioceses, a prolific London specialist in churches and schools, and co-founder of the Guild of Catholic Artists and Craftsmen. Having designed the Belgian War Memorial in Kensal Green Cemetery, Scott was made a chevalier of the Order of Leopold II. Glyn Davies was the builder.

Our Lady of Mount Carmel was built at the inspiration of Father Malachy Lynch, despite the fact that there were only three Catholic families in Lampeter at the time. Soon there were many more, as the Second World War bombing drove Catholics out from Liverpool to safety as evacuees in Cardiganshire. The carved wooden Stations of the Cross commemorate those times. In the XIth Station, 'Christ is nailed to the Cross', the Roman soldier wielding the hammer is clearly based on Hitler.

Inside, the walls are made from sand-coloured brick. Where the walls open out to define the sanctuary in a semicircular arch, they are underpinned by a curve of blue-grey and dark grey bricks. The lunettes above too are defined by grey bricks. Invisible from the nave, high lunette windows light the sanctuary, the exposed roof timbers above and the reredos – a wonderfully serene and moving stone relief carving of the Mother and Child by P J Lindsey Clarke.

Around the nave there are paintings on canvas lunettes of Welsh saints by Mary Maltby with inscriptions in Welsh. Wooden statues of St Joseph and the Virgin are by members of the Guild of Catholic Artists and Craftsmen and there is a plaque commemorating the contribution that Polish workers made to the local community. Polish craftsmen contributed to the church's woodwork and it was a Polish craftsman who carved the Stations. There is a fine wrought-iron screen between the nave and the disused baptistery. Outside, enclosed in a porch, is a delightful blue-and-white plaque of the Virgin and Child in the style of Della Robbia.

Definitely not a chapel: P D Hepworth's grand basilica for Our Lady of Peace at Newbridge.

Our Lady of Peace, Ashfield Road, Newbridge, Gwent (1939–40)

There were some raised Baptist eyebrows when the tall white campanile of Our Lady of Peace was built high on the hillside overlooking the Ebbw Valley. The large iron cross on the foreign-looking tower and the huge cross outside the east wall proclaimed, if there was any doubt about it, that this was a church – not a chapel. This was in the very heart of Nonconformist Wales and the spectacular new church was seen by some as a symbol of late Catholic triumphalism. It was not long before the church authorities themselves were seeking to diminish the church's visual impact. During the Second World War, German bombers circling back from raids on Cardiff docks used it as a navigational aid and for occasional target practice. Our Lady of Peace was painted all over in war-like camouflage colours – traces can still just be seen today through the weathered whitewash on the walls.

It was paid for by Mrs Roche, a member of the Catholic family that lived at Llanarth (see page 37). She chose P D Hepworth, an architect who had done other work in south Wales. He had trained in Paris and Rome, which was why Our Lady of Peace was, uniquely for its time, measured out in metres rather than feet and yards. It also suggests why the church has an authentic Italian Romanesque look. It is a basilica, rendered in brick and painted white. It is joined to a presbytery built of the same materials.

The interior is a space of heart-stopping beauty. The white painted walls are lit from the south side by large, clear, round-headed windows and at night by the light from original, delightful, intricately designed wrought-iron light pendants. The High Altar has no window behind it. A wooden crucifix hangs above it on an indented but undecorated east wall. There are arches to the aisle on one side but no columns or capitals interrupt the flat sheerness of the walls. There is little decoration, but the tall ceiling and the beams are painted with abstract decoration.

The baptistery is separated from the nave by a screen that is lovingly shaped in thin metal bars and there is a simple stone font with a round wooden canopy. Levers and other items of 1930s gadgetry to open windows and raise the lights are set into the walls, and the sacristy has wooden cupboards, shelves and drawers in fine 1930s joinery. Heating a church this size has been a problem. The ceiling of the church is sadly disfigured by a hideous, suspended metal heating system.

At Newbridge, the unbroken symmetry of the walls is tempered by charmingly wrought original light fittings.

9 'Behold, I make all things new': Liturgical and Architectural Revolution

The dawn of the modern architectural day took some time to rise on Britain. Aesthetic conservatism and the general impoverishment of the times militated against the experimental Modernism that was taking root in Europe. Church architects in particular seemed unexcited by the possibilities offered by the new age. In England, the biggest ecclesiastical building project of the 1930s was Sir Edwin Lutyens's design for a new Catholic cathedral at Liverpool; an amalgam – on a Babylonian scale – of the styles of the past drawn from all over the world, described by John Summerson as '… the latest and supreme attempt to embrace Rome, Byzantium, the Romanesque and the Renaissance in one triumphal and triumphant synthesis'. To an advocate of modernism like Sir James Richards, writing in 1940, this sort of thing was comparable with 'Petrol stations that look like medieval barns and department stores that look like the palaces of Renaissance bishops …fancy costume borrowed from the past'.

The designs of Catholic churches by architects such as F X Velarde gave some sense that times were changing. Original – even slightly odd – they were subversive of the norm but evolutionary rather than revolutionary. Only after the Second World War did most patrons and architects begin to grasp the opportunities offered them by the new materials, new technologies and the new thinking of continental architects to whom Modernism was a faith and a crusade. The Festival of Britain in 1951 provided a showcase of adventurous new buildings. Ralph Tubbs, the designer of the Dome of Discovery wrote, 'we have seen the birth of a new architecture… not since the Renaissance has the land seen such a bursting forth of a new living architecture'.

The 'new living architecture' still failed to grip the imagination of church architects. But thanks to better photography in architectural magazines, a growth in book publishing and greater opportunities for travel, it was possible to see what was happening elsewhere. Edward Maufe's *Modern Church Architecture* (1948) looked to North European models. By 1955 Edward Mills (*The Modern Church*), was illustrating in colour Fernand Leger's stained glass in the church at Audincourt in France, to which

Liverpool's Cathedral of Christ the King. Sir Frederick Gibberd's design reflected the new thinking that was sweeping through the Catholic world.

193

Carving from St. Monica's,
Bootle.

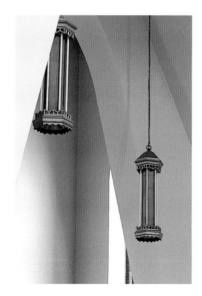

Lights from Sts Mary and
Joseph, Lansbury.

Gerard Goalen made a pilgrimage in 1958. Goalen had studied at Liverpool before working for Frederick Gibberd. At post-war Harlow he would be one of the first architects to put the new thinking into practice.

Liverpool was to have a more direct experience of Modernism when, in 1944–5, a Polish School of Architecture was established there for refugees and ex-servicemen. Jerzy Faczynski, later design architect at the Weightman and Bullen practice, was one of its most successful students. From the very late 1950s, the work of Le Corbusier at Ronchamp and Oscar Niemayer on Brasilia began to be seized upon, just as clients like the then Archbishop Heenan began to commission more advanced briefs.

It was not just the technology and the new architecture that drove the revolution. Social changes were at work too. Churches in the inner cities began to empty and new ones were built in the growing suburbs. Catholics accustomed to emphasising their apartness from other Christians were asked to join them in ecumenical prayer. Changing ideas on the liturgy seemed to be endorsed by the Second Vatican Council which, in the 1960s, formalised growing changes in the relationship between congregation, priest and altar. Of paramount importance was putting the drama of the Mass at the centre of the church – which was to be visible to all in the congregation who were invited to take a much more active part in the now English liturgy.

Functional efficiency did not always seem enough to fill the gap left when church furnishings and fittings, with all their associations, were removed. Many churchgoers felt that something priceless was being lost in the heady atmosphere of change. The vigorous re-orderings of the 1960s and 1970s provoked a reaction that is still in progress. The dawn of Modernism was followed by a more sceptical noon.

It was a symbolic moment when Bishop Thomas McMahon commissioned arch-Classicist Quinlan Terry to design the new cathedral for Brentwood in 1989. Here again were traditional materials, the Classical orders, and a conviction that architecture should serve and derive its essence from God, not 'style'. Friezes, the orders, entablatures and pediments were back. Le Corbusier, as well as Pugin, must have turned in his grave.

Our Lady Star of the Sea, Bull Bay Road, Amlwch, Isle of Anglesey (1933–7)

Amlwch was once the port through which copper mined in the nearby mountain was exported round the world. In the 1930s the Catholics of Amlwch boldly embraced a singular and unusual form of architectural Modernism that echoed the town's industrial and nautical past. Their church is a prominent landmark: a high, round-arched, concrete building that looks like the hull of an upturned boat or a small airship hanger. There is nothing else remotely like it in Wales or England.

The architect was Giuseppe Rinvolucri (1894–1963) who had settled in North Wales in about 1930. He designed the Catholic churches at Porthmadog and Abergele. As a European, Rinvolucri was perhaps more alert to what was going on among the architectural avant-garde than were his British contemporaries.

The Amlwch church was built in large part by workers recruited from the local labour exchange who were grateful for a job in a time of high unemployment. 'The construction of the building was no simple matter', remembered the foremen Percy Iball, 'but we were all young and strong. The unusual shape and the difficulty of erecting the framework was a challenge to us'. They made what is now a very weathered concrete structure on a white, rough-cast masonry plinth. The windows are shaped like portholes, and six clearly visible parabolic, stressed-concrete ribs arch into a roof. The entrance front has a dressed stone façade (a later addition) and, high on top, a 6-ft stone cross. Two flights of flanking stone steps lead up to the pointed doorway, above which is a star-shaped window surrounded by mosaic.

The interior is extraordinary, with concrete ribbing punctuated by blue-and-white

Modernism comes to Wales; concrete arches punctuated by blue-and-white glass at Amlwch.

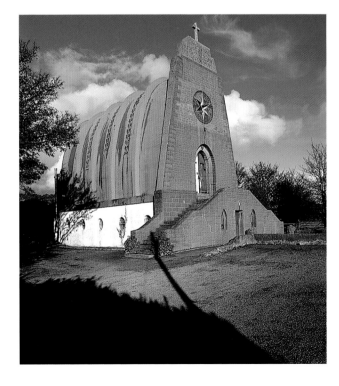

Rinvolucri's concrete ribs shape the church like a boat or an airship hangar.

patterned lights (claimed locally to be made from Milk of Magnesia bottles) and five smaller, star-shaped windows above the pointed curve of the sanctuary. Tradition reasserts itself, however, with statues of saints, marble panels, old-style Stations and painted scenes from the Bible. At the east end is a painting of the Crucifixion added in 1963 by Gordon Wallace of Colwyn Bay. Under the church is the large parish hall, like an ocean liner lounge, with large round, porthole-like windows.

The early and experimental use of concrete has caused problems. Sea gales have punished the structure and, for the moment, this remarkable church is closed and has an uncertain future.

'Many unusual features of design and decoration'; gold painted angels on the east wall of St Monica's.

St Monica, Fernhill Road, Bootle, Lancashire (1936)

Bootle spreads back from the Mersey docklands into pleasant suburbia. The new church that priest Father Foley and his parishioners worked together to build was both suburban and daringly continental in character. It was designed by Francis Xavier Velarde (1897–1960) and his plans indicated that a whole new approach to Catholic church architecture had arrived. At the opening, the local paper called St Monica's 'a striking example of modern architecture' adding, more doubtfully, that it 'embodies many unusual features, in design and decoration'. Quite deliberately so. The tower is constructed of square cliffs of brick with almost unmoulded windows. It could be a 1930s telephone exchange or government office. But three white, elongated reliefs of saints above the windows indicate the sacred purpose of the building.

Velarde was a Liverpool man who had travelled widely. He studied and admired the Romanesque in Spain and the Beaux Arts in France. He liked the North German tradition of building in brick, and all his buildings are very strong on exposed and unadorned brickwork. The rethinking of church design, with square brick towers over the narthex or sanctuary, the removal of the choir to a gallery over the west end or to the sides, and the use of modern sculpture, had all been adopted by the Anglican church in the early 1930s, but this was the first Roman Catholic church to do so.

The interior must have given the parishioners a shock at the time. It is a basilica; a large, rather sombre space with dark and unrelieved brick walls and arches. By contrast, the ceiling is flat and relatively light. The arcades are round and the aisles are punched through thick internal brick buttresses. All the glass is clear. A large west window above the narthex, large aisle windows and smaller lights in the clerestory prevent the church from being gloomy. There is only the slightest division between the sanctuary and nave, although the altar was traditionally placed against the windowless east wall. It was moved to a raised position centre-stage in a 1984 re-ordering.

The focal point is the east wall itself which has six relief angels painted gold, by Liverpool artist W L Stevenson, placed at intervals on the indented and patterned wall above the tabernacle. They are framed by pilasters and a rather stumpy, high baldacchino. In 1936 the closeness of the congregation to the altar was thought remarkable. The general austerity of the interior is softened by the Stations of the Cross – low relief on a green background in the style of Eric Gill – and the chrome and convoluted altar rails.

The west front of St Monica's: Modernism tempered by symbols of angels.

English Martyrs, St George's Road, Wallasey, Wirral (1952–3)

After the Second World War, church-building was limited by financial constraints and restrictions on building materials. But architect F X Velarde's post-war churches do not reflect this national impoverishment and this, his first Wirral church, is expansive, confident and substantial. He used his preferred medium of brick to dramatic effect, creating a large church with a slender, semi-detached square tower. The octagonal stone lantern above is topped by a pointed copper roof and cross, which hovers rather startlingly above the houses of Wallasey village. Towards the base of his tower there is a splendidly carved stone pieta. On the north side, under five round brick arches, are statues of the English Martyrs. This distinctive and personal design could be by no other architect.

The inside of the church is Romanesque, Velarde's favourite style. He used his favourite device of sheer brick walls and hunched, round-headed windows to create a space of real authority, deliberately using small windows to reinforce the sense of massiveness. The interior could have been oppressively dark, but any sense of religious gloom is lifted by Verlade's decorative touches – the unexpected diagonal silver bands on the plain columns, and the silver decoration on the capitals. The flat centre of the wooden roof is made up of decorated striped panels with exuberant zigzags down the sides.

A simple but massive brick arch separates nave from sanctuary. This is echoed by an inner arch around a plain brick east wall, against which hangs a poignant, large silver rood. Below is a reredos where the silver-painted heads of the apostles, in relief, rise in a flat, ethereal pyramid above and around the altar. From the right, high windows cast light on the stone altar and marble steps. To the left is an upper organ loft (not at

English Martyrs at Wallasey: against a flat brick wall a silvery rood and reredos with the heads of the apostles in relief.

the moment used) with coloured diagonal decorations on the ceiling. The tiles on the floor are reminiscent of the Festival of Britain era in which the church was designed.

The baptistery, now put to new uses, is remarkable. The extraordinary stone font has a marble base, a decorated stem and a square top with carved, silver-painted angels. The cover has a peculiar fish-scale motif supporting a cross.

Adrian Gilbert Scott's beautiful and functional interior for Lansbury. Scott also designed the lights and the fittings.

Saints Mary and Joseph, Upper North Street, Lansbury, London E14 (1952–4)

The old Victorian East End church of Saints Mary and Joseph was bombed during the war. After the war, the Catholic authorities wanted to build a big new church. Though the old community had been dispersed by the bombing and was being dispersed again by the post-war planners, they wanted the new church to provide for the needs of a much wider area. The authorities commissioned Adrian Gilbert Scott (brother of Sir Giles, son of George Gilbert junior), who produced designs for a very large church indeed. It dismayed the London County Council officers who had wanted something much smaller.

Eventually a compromise was reached. Scott provided seats for 850, though when it opened the average congregation was more than a thousand. The designs were exhibited as part of the Live Architecture Exhibition at Lansbury, which was part of the Festival of Britain of 1951. Initially it was not well received. When it opened, architectural writer Ian Nairn thought it '…both aggressive and flaccid, vulgar and genteel, pretentious and timid'. It was described as 'Jazz-Modern Byzantine' as well as 'Egyptian' and, more learnedly, as deriving its style from the Palace at Ctesiphon in ancient Persia. There again, it was said to owe much to St Alban's, Golders Green (by Sir Giles Gilbert Scott). Today the critical dust has settled and it is generally regarded as one of the most powerful churches of its time; its architect's finest achievement.

The builders were John Mowlem & Company, who had worked with the Scott brothers on the restoration of the House of Commons. Outlined against the East End sky, the church looks bulky among its more modestly sized neighbours. Rising from a large octagonal tower is a smaller lantern, topped by a stubby, reinforced-concrete spire. The windows narrow as they approach their round-headed tops. At the entrance, a large brick arch tapers giddyingly up to enclose a stone sculpted cross with two heraldic angels.

Scott's interior is a bright and expansive masterpiece. The site was square and a Greek cross plan was adopted, which enabled the parish to accommodate with ease the liturgical changes that were to come. A wooden forward altar at the centre of the crossing is now visible from all parts of the church. In 1981 architect Lionel (Lord) Esher, one of the Modern Movement's grand old men, conceded that what had seemed 'old fashioned' had actually proved very functional.

The success of the building lies not just in its architecture but in its art. Scott kept an eye on everything; the furnishings, the materials and the workmanship – he even designed the hymn boards. The Classical High Altar and marble baldacchino echo those of Westminster Cathedral and the pulpit is in a dominating position at an angle to the crossing, designed in greenish carved marble. The almost oval windows are of clear glass with coloured figures of the saints at their centre by William Wilson of Edinburgh. Running around the walls of the church is a blue stone dado, 8 feet high. At its top are Stations of the Cross in stone relief by Peter Watts. Above, great parabolic arches sweep up to support the tower. On the ceiling is painted an emblem of the Holy Spirit against the octagonal, red roof.

Our Lady of Fatima, Howard Way, Harlow, Essex (1958–60)

The needle-like, plywood and copper spire of this influential church contrasts sharply with the generally low-rise architecture of Harlow. The architect was Gerard Goalen, a former student at Liverpool University where he had briefly worked for F X Velarde. Goalen had toured the continent to see what avant-garde architects were building and what artists were doing with glass. He was *au fait* with the latest Modernist thinking.

The walls at Harlow are brick and the entrances unpromising, but inside are huge rectangular cliffs of stained glass that burn with colour. They were the work of a monk – Dom Charles Norris OSB of Buckfast Abbey. It was his first commission and, no sequestered hermit, he bravely exploited the possibilities offered by modern techniques of fused glass set in concrete. The resulting windows depict vivid, representational scenes of Our Lady of Fatima, the Fifteen Mysteries of the Rosary and the Tree of Jesse. The much smaller rose windows are more abstract. The heavily coloured windows tend to glow rather than

A vast stained-glass window by Dom Charles Norris at Harlow.

The elongated spire of Gerard Goalen's revolutionary church at Harlow pierces the sky above the new town.

Byzantium yields to sixties Modernism: Gerard Goalen's church and spire at Woodthorpe.

cast much light, and this is not a bright church. There are Stations of the Cross in stone (by Mrs Ford-Kelsey) which are reminiscent of Eric Gill's Stations in Westminster Cathedral. Goalen designed the tabernacle, the altar candlesticks and cross. There are monuments, memorials and a mosaic of Christ the King. The founders wanted a church that would seat about 500; a people's church in which the altar should be forward from the wall, in the midst of and clearly visible to, the congregation. The altar stands on a large, raised sanctuary that fills the crossing. Had the building followed harder upon its design and planning in 1953, it would have been among the first churches in England to anticipate the liturgical changes that would be introduced after Vatican II.

The windows were unlike anything that had been seen in Britain before and the design of the church was likewise revolutionary. This was Goalen's first church and it made his name; he went on to design Catholic churches across the country. But his vision was ahead of its time and, like so many buildings of that period, the church developed problems. The massive concrete beams that support the walls of glass weighed too heavily on the structure beneath them, and water penetrated areas of the church. It was closed for 18 months, but happily now it has been restored and reopened for worship.

The Good Shepherd, Thackeray's Road, Woodthorpe, Nottingham (1961–3)

Catholics in this northern suburb of Nottingham used to worship in the ball-room on the first floor of the Co-op building. In 1929 they built the parish's first church. The Byzantine mini-tower of that church is still the first thing you see as you approach the Modernist Good Shepherd. But the church was already too small when Father Bernard Mooney, the parish priest, visited Harlow, admired the church there and invited its architect, Gerard Goalen, to submit plans for an entirely new church.

A helicopter had to be used to mount the cross which crowns the church's elongated spire. This is in contrast to the bulk of the building which is low and semi-circular – with vertical concrete beams supporting a curving concrete roof. Goalen later said that he '…tried to produce a building in which a large number of parishioners can participate in something of the intimacy of the Last Supper as well as the awe and wonder of the events that followed it'.

Inside, Goalen's vision becomes apparent. Father Mooney could not afford whole walls of stained glass like those at Goalen's church at Harlow (see page 199). Instead he commissioned Patrick Reyntiens, a Catholic and one of the foremost stained-glass artists of the day, to design windows with louvered concrete mullions through which sunlight is deflected, creating the subtle shadings of light that give the church much of its character. The sanctuary is built with the altar at its centre so that the priest can celebrate Mass '…with his back to the congregation, as is at present customary, or he may face the people'. The seating is raked and semi-circular so that everyone gets a good view of the altar.

Three of Nicholas Mynheer's Stations of the Cross for Woodthorpe.

The window behind is especially muted lest it put the altar into silhouette. Though abstract, the windows do have a theme – trees – and represent, among others, the Tree of Life, the Tree of the Cross, the Tree of Jesse and the Burning Bush. As Goalen had hoped, '…the light of the building is not constant. It changes with the movement of the sun and the clouds'.

Fragile-looking hexagonal columns taper up to a broadly vaulted roof. There are excellent, understated, enigmatic Stations in stone carved by Nicholas Mynheer.

As at other churches, the use of new technology left the Good Shepherd a difficult legacy. Parish records report leaks, cracked mullions and condensation damage. The web of concrete holding Reyntiens's glass was crumbling. But huge sums of money were raised by the parish and now, with added help from the Lottery, the Good Shepherd is in better shape.

Patrick Reyntiens' glass enfolds the sanctuary at Woodthorpe. 'The light changes with the sun and the clouds.'

St Mary, Broadfield Walk, Leyland, Lancashire (1962–4)

In the early 1960s Leyland's Catholic community, like the town itself, was expanding, and a new church was needed for about 1,200 worshippers. The priest, Father Edmund FitzSimons, travelled Europe to see what progressive church architects were doing and when he came back he built a balsa-wood model of an octagonal church with a central altar based on what he had seen. The project was put in the hands of Polish architect Jerzy Faczynski of Weightman and Bullen, already known as a versatile exponent of modern building theory and practice.

St Mary's is a big, circular church of brick and reinforced concrete, with copper-covered roofs that fold down into a sort of zigzag at their outer ends. A spiky bell-tower, oddly detached from the church, rises on concrete shafts. The church is approached up steps from a great piazza and above the entrance looms a huge, ceramic tympanum of the Last Judgement by Polish artist Adam Kossowski, from which a stern Christ scrutinises approaching worshippers.

The interior is an in-the-round space that is largely top-lit from the zigzag of windows above the brick walls where the concrete roof begins. A more subtle light glows from windows in the ambulatory and the benches rake downwards. Beyond the raised, central marble altar, the Blessed Sacrament Chapel is clearly

New town, new church: Jerzy Faczynski's innovative exterior for Leyland with the tympanum below the curved canopy visible beyond the shafts of the detached bell-tower.

Patrick Reyntiens' wall of glass encircles the ambulatory at St Mary's

visible. Above the altar hangs a *corona lucis* and a hanging ceramic rood of Christ the King, also made by Adam Kossowski.

Art and architecture rarely come together in a late 20th-century church as successfully as they do here. When Arthur Dooley's bronze Stations of the Cross along the inner side of the ambulatory were first revealed, they were thought controversial; Liverpool's left-wing Catholic sculptor had incorporated Roman soldiers wearing swastikas, Liverpool housewives watching Christ's sufferings, Oxfam babies to jolt the conscience and a British workman helping to carry the cross. Furthermore, Dooley had provided a 15th Station showing the Resurrection: he thought the conventional 14th and last Station of the Entombment was too depressing (it is now in the All Souls' Chapel).

Sculptor Arthur Dooley's bronze Stations of the Cross line the other side of the ambulatory.

On the outer side of the ambulatory is a great circular wall of glass. In the aisle walls are 36 panels of abstract *dalles-de-verre* stained glass by Patrick Reyntiens. Representing the First Day of Creation, the windows are composed of thick chunks of glass, mostly in muted blues and greens, inspired by Fernand Leger's glass at Audincourt in France.

The Chapel of the Blessed Sacrament has a much-admired tapestry of the Holy Trinity designed by Faczynski. Robin McGhie designed the tabernacle. Elsewhere in the church are a font cover and a plaque of Christ receiving souls by David John, a copper statue of Mary by Ian Stuart, some wonderful carved lettering by George Thompson and statues by Charles and Mary Blakeman. With these elements and such a design, the church vividly expresses the spirit of Catholic confidence and patronage of the early 1960s.

Metropolitan Cathedral of Christ the King, Mount Pleasant, Liverpool (1962–7)

Two great cathedrals dominate the Liverpool skyline: the Anglican cathedral, with its great tower and Gothic silhouette, and the Roman Catholic cathedral with its concrete cone surmounted by a pinnacled crown. They complement rather than rival each other, but it might have been otherwise. Liverpool has the largest Catholic population of any city in England and yet was the last to have its own cathedral. In 1932 Sir Edwin Lutyens drew up plans for a vast cathedral in an ambitious mixture of styles – so colossal was its dome that it would have dwarfed the tower of the Anglican cathedral. Lutyens's cavernous crypt was built, but work was interrupted by the Second World War. Though half-hearted attempts were made to revive the scheme, his design proved unaffordable and too grandiose for the austere realities of post-war Britain.

Not until 1960 was the competition for the most important Catholic commission of the century announced by Archbishop Heenan. There were nearly 300 entries and the winner was Sir Frederick Gibberd

Gibberd's design for the Catholic cathedral was chosen because 'it powerfully expresses the kingship of Christ, because the whole building is conceived as a crown'.

(1908–84). Gibberd was a well-established figure, a designer of low-cost housing who had devised the 'live' architecture show of the Festival of Britain. He had designed buildings at Heathrow Airport and Harlow New Town in the late 1940s and later the Regent's Park mosque. His cathedral, too, reflected its times. Concrete beams shaped like boomerangs thrust up to support the conical, crowned roof, symbolic of the cathedral's dedication. The exterior buttresses give the cathedral famously something of the appearance of a great tent. The exterior is almost undecorated, though there are some mosaics and the free-standing bell tower has carvings by William Mitchell – a deeply incised geometrical arrangement of the three crosses.

The crypt remains as a tantalising (and much treasured) reminder of Lutyens's vision. Great, brick-lined, vaulted chambers run under what is now an open-air piazza. The subterranean gloom is enlivened by tapering columns, idiosyncratic arches and a rolling stone door. But Gibberd's brief was very different. His cathedral was not there to draw attention to its own beauty; it was there to shelter the High Altar which was to be the main point of focus for congregations of up to 3,000. Heenan had said, 'The attention of all who enter should be arrested and held by the altar', and Gibberd's plan achieved that.

Most cathedrals reveal themselves slowly, but Liverpool makes a powerful impact as soon as you enter. Gibberd staked almost everything on this first throw of the dice, a terrific *coup de théâtre* – a numinous, dark-ceilinged auditorium of great height and breadth. Deep colours are infused into it from the glass in the corona above and from great slits of glass between the walls of concrete at the sides. The eyes focus, as Heenan wished, on the High Altar – a single block of white marble, quarried in Skopje, Macedonia. In the midst of this vast and sombre space is the shining bronze crucifix on the altar by Elizabeth Frink. Gibberd's spiky baldacchino suspended above casts light down on to the altar, but it is the glass, designed by John Piper and made by Patrick

Deep colours cast by the lantern above the altar infuse a numinous light on to the shafts, walls and floor of the cathedral.

Right: Concrete flying buttresses support the cone-shaped roof.

Reyntiens, that gives the cathedral its luminous quality. The glass in the lantern – representing the Holy Trinity in an abstract progress of blues, golds and white – glows during the day above the centre of the cathedral and at night, lit from within, shines high above the city.

Thirteen chapels leading off the great central space show works of art commissioned after the church's completion. Liverpool artist Sean Rice made the burnished gold Stations of the Cross. He also cast and welded the dramatic statue of an angular Abraham in the Lady Chapel where there is also a terracotta statue of the Virgin and Child by Robert Brumby. Best of all is the Blessed Sacrament Chapel, with reredos and stained glass by Ceri Richards, who also designed the doors of the tabernacle. Arthur Dooley's small statue of the Risen Christ was added in 1986.

Gibberd's design was not to every taste and the severity of his great concrete panels has since been softened by large wall hangings designed by Sister Anthony Wilson. Some aspects of Gibberd's design were in advance of the materials and technology of the day and there were leaks and problems with the mosaic cladding. These have now been controlled and there is improved access, a new exhibition space and a café that cheerfully compliment the gravitas of Gibberd's epic building.

Right: John Piper and Patrick Reyntiens' glowing lantern tower.

Opposite: The monumental 80-foot-high Portland stone bell tower for which William Mitchell carved the three incised crosses. The central cross of Christ is flanked by those of the thieves; they are linked together by crowns.

Church of Our Lady Help of Christians, Worth Abbey, Turners Hill, Crawley, West Sussex (1964–89)

Worth Abbey was founded in 1930 as a daughter house to the Benedictine Abbey of Downside and its church is the biggest and most important structure in a complex of monastic buildings. It was designed by Catholic architect Francis Pollen (1926–87) and it changed and evolved over the many years of its construction. Pollen's career had also evolved over the years; he went from Classicism to Brutalism and back again, and consequently his achievements were underestimated in an age focused almost entirely on the avant-garde. Pollen fought against the 'physical shallowness' of much modern architecture and once wrote: 'I believe that churches must feel as if they had just happened as a result of the divine laws of geometry, mechanics and proportion, timeless laws'. His church at Worth synthesises the two worlds of progress and tradition; a work of modern architecture that looks at home in its rural setting, on a ridge looking towards the South Downs. 'You have produced single-handed a style that has reference to the past and gives hope for the future', wrote stained-glass artist Patrick Reyntiens to Pollen.

Progress in harmony with tradition: Worth Abbey is comfortably at home in the Sussex countryside. Architect Francis Pollen was said to have admired *Close Encounters of the Third Kind*.

Indubitably modern: the great circular interior of Worth's church of Our Lady.

At the church of Worth Abbey, Pollen's roof of pre-cast beams supports the lantern.

The narthex has a feeling of the Sussex vernacular, but in the great, round interior space, the materials, the design and the manipulation of light are indubitably modern. It is a large, bravely conceived building with a circular roof resting on a square base – always a technical challenge. The design responded to the liturgical thinking of the time with a central altar under a circular lantern (though local contractors were reluctant to quote a price for the difficult, curved brickwork, so the school's carpentry teacher supervised the work using direct labour).

The cone-shaped roof is made of pre-cast beams supported by two ring beams. The beams bear down on tapered, brick-encased, concrete columns. Light floods down from the lantern, which is braced by strong cross-beams. Pollen's design provides extraordinary perspectives from the sanctuary or the chapels up to the powerful geometry of the cone.

The Lady Chapel has a statue of the Virgin and Child designed by a monk of Downside. Pollen's father, Arthur, carved the other Virgin and Child set in a niche to the side and designed the stark crucifix that hangs high above the central raised altar, which is a single, uncarved stone. There is a memorial stone to the architect of this brilliant synthesis of modernity and tradition.

At Our Lady Help of Christians modern glass and concrete achieve 'a kind of poetry'.

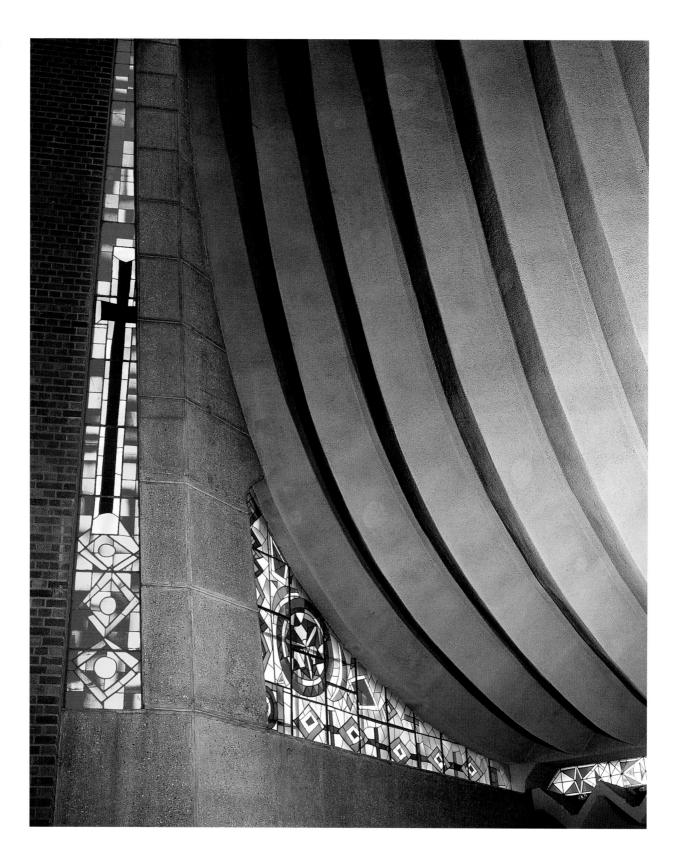

Our Lady Help of Christians, East Meadway, Kitts Green, Birmingham (1966–7)

Richard Gilbert Scott's astonishing church roof curves above a suburban Birmingham cityscape.

While Archbishop Dwyer was carrying out his vigorous re-ordering of St Chad's Cathedral in Birmingham he also wanted to build a ring of new churches to serve the city's expanding suburbs. This church is the most remarkable of them. It was designed by another member of the great Scott dynasty – Richard Gilbert Scott – who had joined his father, Sir Giles, as a partner in 1953. His brief was to design a church which accommodated the new liturgical thinking. His response was no dry, clinical solution to a technical problem – it was astonishing. He came up with a bravura design that demanded new materials and state-of-the-art technology, as well as a bold approach to the art of stained glass. Scott said he wanted to imbue the church with the Gothic inspiration of his father's churches but mobilising all the possibilities of the modern idiom.

The copper-covered, concrete wings of the church's roof soar exuberantly above the flat streets of Kitts Green. They enfold the interior, swooping above the heads of the congregation in great curves. The sail-like

The celebrant stands in a theatrical space framed by brick walls and crescents of glass and concrete.

Inside the church at Kitts Green John Chrestien glass commemorates the Christian victory at the Battle of Lepanto in 1571.

Unflinchingly modern:
St Margaret's, Twickenham,
stands back from the car park.

shape of the church roof reflects an ancient victory at sea. Pope Pius V established the Feast of Our Lady Help of Christians, in thanksgiving after the naval battle of Lepanto – the epoch-defining victory of the Christian forces over the Muslim Turks in 1571.

From his central position in a T-shaped space the celebrant can look across the congregation to mesmerising, glowing bands of blue-and-white glass in front of him. Between the concrete roof and the brick walls are stained-glass windows in a variety of shapes, that not only light the interior but are themselves hypnotic points of focus. They are the work of a friend of Scott's, John Chrestien, who had studied in Paris and lived in India, which perhaps gave him a taste for the exotic. His windows blaze between the grey ribs of the building, their largely abstract design perhaps reflecting acknowledgement of the non-figurative Islamic tradition of design.

The church's dedication is dramatically marked by more magnificent figurative glass in the Lady Chapel. The defeated Turks are symbolised by the crescent moon, vanquished by a ferocious, grimacing Lion of St Mark's, Venice – the port from which the victorious fleet sailed. The baptistery has more splendid, symbolic glass. The octagonal font is bathed in the reflected glory of the glass. The church has been described as 'the ultimate in pop architecture' and as '... achieving a kind of poetry' by Elain Harwood. It might be added that this is 1960s Modernism in extravagant mood; far from formal or brutal but going for, and achieving, good old-fashioned beauty

St Margaret, St Margaret's Road, Twickenham, Middlesex (1968–9)

'Almost before the ink was dry on Vatican II...' so parish records relate, Twickenham's energetic Father Sidney Dommersen had set in motion plans for a new church to replace a prefabricated hut that was affectionately known as 'the cardboard cathedral' and which had served the mission for more than 30 years. 'It was more important to build a community than a church', Father Dommersen said. In response, architect Austin Winkley designed an unflinchingly modern building. 'Forticrete block walls, with steel trusses supporting flat roofs' is how the DCMS listing (Grade II) describes its uncompromisingly utilitarian exterior.

St Margaret's is set back from a busy main road behind its own car park. There is an unobtrusive cross on the roof but the exterior of the Complex – the founders resisted even the word 'church' – gives little indication of its function. Inside it is indeed a Complex, with interlinked spaces for meetings and social functions, a reading room, a basement, boiler room and sunken vestry. There are two areas for worship: the Mass Room and the Weekday Chapel which has Stations of the Cross and a white stone statue of Mary by Lindsey Clarke, a gift to Father Dommersen.

The Mass Room itself is a large, square space, raked down towards the altar and lit by large, plain clerestory windows. The back of the space is bare and sliding doors give access, when required, to the large meeting room that adjoins the Mass Room. The floor is carpeted, the walls are bare. The stern edicts of architectural Modernism (within which Adolf Loos asserted 'Ornament is Crime') have been somewhat tempered by children's art stuck to the concrete walls. The free-standing altar is a wooden table pierced by a consecrated stone which matches the ambo. Above the altar hangs a gilded cross by Stephen Sykes, showing Christ as Priest-King, which was given by the parishioners in memory of Father Dommersen (who survived the completion of the church by only a few days). The sight-lines to the font are excellent and beside the font is a stained-glass representation of St Margaret of Scotland that used to be in the 'cardboard cathedral'. High up, behind the altar, is a fine abstract stained-glass panel by Patrick Reyntiens, inspired by the Triumph of Christ.

Cathedral of St Peter and St Paul, Clifton Park, Bristol (1969–73)

'A sermon in concrete' was one phrase used to describe this building – a neat enough way of summing up a cathedral that exploits all the technical possibilities of the late 20th century while never losing sight of the deep-rooted religious needs that such a building traditionally enshrines. Its architects were members of one of the biggest post-war practices in the country, the Cardiff-based Percy Thomas Partnership.

Concrete arches and granite panels contribute a notable silhouette to Clifton's skyline.

At St peter and St Paul the sanctuary looks towards a fan-shaped auditorium where 900 worshippers can be close to the High Altar.

Cyclopean roof beams at Clifton.

The design team – Frederick Jennett, Ronald Weeks and Antoni Perembo – were inspired, they said, by the eternal geometry of the Greek temple, which they would interpret with modern materials and technology, coupled with advanced acoustics and sophisticated heating systems. Computer experiments, for instance, showed that electric under-floor heating would be the most efficient means of keeping the huge space warm, provided the whole cathedral was sealed like a sort of thermal storage unit, with substantial and highly insulated walls.

Their main task though was to design a vast space that would accommodate around a thousand worshippers, who should feel that this was indeed a place of prayer. Vatican II had indicated the desirability of a central altar, but the architects knew that a round building with the altar at the centre presented problems. Their solution was a spacious hexagonal sanctuary on the edge of the plan, from which the congregation ranges out in an expanding fan-shape into the great space of the nave. No one is more than 50 feet from the High Altar. The sanctuary, with its altar and sheer, unadorned east wall, is

The narthex at Clifton; glass by
Henry Haig, font by Simon Verity.

bathed in diffused daylight washing through rooflights and reflected off the ring-beam walls. The architects
used white concrete for the outer walls to enhance reflection but exposed concrete inside to avoid glare.
Above, cyclopean concrete beams support a gallery and great beams of boarded concrete, which in turn
support a conical, multi-levelled roof.

Amid all the modern technology, the traditional arts play a big part in the impact made by the cathedral's
immense interior. Great walls of stained glass set in epoxy resin line the narthex. They represent Pentecost and
Jubilation in abstract patterns of colour, in strong contrast to the subdued, matt concrete, and were designed by
Henry Haig. The monumental font in the baptistery was carved from Portland and Purbeck stone by Simon
Verity; fishes, the ancient symbol of Christianity, are carved into the bowl. On the massive, square, Portland
stone altar are candlesticks designed by architect Ronald Weeks who also designed the free-standing lectern.
The lectern was made by William Mitchell, who also created the uncompromisingly expressive concrete
Stations of the Cross which line the walls of the ambulatory. Mitchell designed the main doors of the cathedral
which are finished in fibreglass and metallic filler. Brother Patrick, a monk from Prinknash, made the screen
that separates the Blessed Sacrament Chapel from the nave, to the designs of Weeks. In the chapel itself, the
tabernacle was the work of John Alder. The cathedral has avoided the technical problems that bedevilled its
predecessor at Liverpool.

Cathedral of St Mary and St Helen, Ingrave Road, Brentwood, Essex (1989–91)

The last Catholic cathedral to be built in Britain is revolutionary, but in quite a different way from those at Liverpool and Clifton. Bishop Thomas McMahon, an architecture enthusiast, quite deliberately turned away from the supposed benefits of modern design and materials promoted by architects since the war. He wanted a cathedral in the Classical style. The architect he chose was the controversial Quinlan Terry, for whom Classical is not a 'style' at all but the God-given form of architecture which goes back long before the Greeks – to the Old Testament. Terry is not a Catholic but a committed Christian whose religious beliefs were shaped as a boy at the evangelical Westminster Chapel. He has designed country houses, university buildings and a big, traditional-looking mixed-office complex overlooking the Thames at Richmond.

The shock of the old at Brentwood. Architect Quinlan Terry was inspired by the early Italian Renaissance.

Brentwood Cathedral may come from an architecturally radical-conservative agenda but it is a restrained, impeccably mannered building – Baroque in the style of Christopher Wren and Bernini. It fits into the Essex town's conservation area as if had been there for years. The north walls are built of natural Kentish ragstone divided by Doric pilasters in Portland stone. In the centre is a giant portico that bulges out in a huge semicircle. Around and above the portico the frieze has carved metopes between the triglyphs (these are words not often used in describing modern buildings). The clerestory of hand-made bricks supports a gently sloping slate roof crowned by an octagonal lantern.

Inside, clear light from leaded windows of hand-made glass floods into a rational, opulent space that might have been designed during the Age of Enlightenment. It is harmonious, ordered and unmysterious. There is little colour: the walls and the Portland stone floor are largely white. All the Classical orders are here: giant Doric pilasters; an arcade of Tuscan arches; and Ionic pilasters on the Palladian windows. In the spandrels below the frieze there are terracotta roundels of the Stations of the Cross which were modelled by Raphael Maklouf – sculptor of the Queen's head as it appeared on earlier coins. The beautifully constructed lantern above illuminates the altar directly below it: a white stone table resting on eight Tuscan columns. The stone came from Pisa. Paradoxically, for a building looking so determinedly backward, it conforms with the liturgical expectations of Vatican II, with three aisles of chairs for the congregation all facing the altar.

All the liturgical furnishings are white. There is a substantial octagonal font, standing on a round base. The ambo is of octagonal, panelled stone with a gilded eagle as lectern and is the same height as the altar. Behind the bishop's chair – again made from stone from Pisa – the Blessed Sacrament Chapel was created from the old Victorian church that existed before the new building. This unusual juxtaposition of Classical and Gothic gives a sense of continuity of worship to the cathedral. There is no altar, but one's attention is struck by a carved Classical tabernacle of great beauty standing on a pedestal. Above it is a tall Gothic east window. Terry designed the white Corinthian organ case that sheaths the old Hunter organ of 1881.

The money for the cathedral was given anonymously or, as the bishop puts it in his introductory booklet, by 'the intervention of Divine Providence'. Cardinal Hume, preaching at the cathedral's dedication, said: 'I have looked and thank God for what has been created here…'.

Civilized and urbane; the Neo-Classical interior of the cathedral at Brentwood. Behind the bishop's chair the Blessed Sacrament Chapel was created from the old Victorian church.

Further reading

Aslet, Clive 1986 *Quinlan Terry: the revival of architecture*. Harmondsworth: Viking

Carthusian, A 1998 *The Spirit of Place: Carthusian reflections*. Parkminster: Darton Longman Todd

Champ, Judith 2002 *A Temple of Living Stones*. Oscott: St Mary's College Oscott

Clifton-Taylor, Alec *et al* 1975 *Spirit of the Age*. London: BBC

Curl, J S 1995 *English Heritage Book of Victorian Churches*. London: B T Batsford/English Heritage

Dixon, Roger and Muthesius, Stefan 1978 *Victorian Architecture*. London: Thames & Hudson

Duffy, Eamon 1992 *The Stripping of the Altars: traditional religion in England c1400–c1580*. New Haven: Yale University Press

Evinson, Denis 1998 *Catholic Churches of London 1623–1916*. Sheffield: Sheffield Academic Press

Finnigan, Robert 1988 *The Cathedral Church of St Anne Leeds, a history and guide*. London: The Universe

Girouard, Mark 1971 *The Victorian Country House*. Oxford: Clarendon Press

Harwood, Elain 2000 *England – a guide to post-war listed buildings*. London: English Heritage

Hodgetts, Michael 1990 *Midlands Catholic Buildings*. Birmingham: Archdiocese of Birmingham Historical Commission

Hodgetts, Michael 1990 *St Chad's Cathedral Birmingham*. Birmingham: Archdiocese of Birmingham Historical Commission

Horner, Libby and Hunter, Gill 2000 *A Flint Seaside Church*. Ramsgate: The Pugin Society

Howell, Peter and Sutton, Ian (eds) 1988 *Faber Guide to Victorian Churches*. London: Faber

Little, Bryan 1966 *Catholic Churches since 1623*. London: Robert Hale

O'Donnell, Roderick 2002 *The Pugins and the Catholic Midlands*. Leominster: Gracewing

Pevsner, N *The Buildings of England series*. Harmondsworth: Penguin

Powers, Alan 1999 *Francis Pollen: architect, 1926–1987*. Oxford: Robert Dugdale

Pugin, A W N 2003 *The True Principals of Pointed or Christian Architecture*, with an introduction by R O'Donnell. Leominster: Gracewing

Pugin, A W N 2004 *The Present State of Ecclesiastical Architecture in England*, with an introduction by R O'Donnell. Leominster: Gracewing

Rogers, Nicholas (ed) *2003 Catholics in Cambridge*. Leominster: Gracewing

Rowlands, Marie 1989 *Those Who Have Gone Before Us*. Birmingham: Archdiocese of Birmingham Historical Commission

Sharples, Joseph 2004 *Pevsner Architectural Guides: Liverpool*. New Haven & London: Yale University Press

Stamp, Gavin 2002 *'An Architect of Promise': George Gilbert Scott Junior (1839–1897) and the late Gothic revival*. Donington: Shaun Tyas

Willis, Peter 1996 *Dom Paul Bellot: architect and monk*. Newcastle upon Tyne: Elysium Press

Index

Illustrations are denoted by page numbers in italics.